A Vexing Gadfly

Princeton Theological Monograph Series

K. C. Hanson, Charles M. Collier, and D. Christopher Spinks,
Series Editors

Recent volumes in the series:

Oscar Garcia-Johnson
*The Mestizo/a Community of the Spirit:
A Postmodern Latino/a Ecclesiology*

Samuel A. Paul
*The Ubuntu God: Deconstructing a South African Narrative
of Oppression*

Ryan A. Neal
*Theology as Hope: On the Ground and Implications
of Jürgen Moltmann's Doctrine of Hope*

Scott A. Ellington
Risking Truth: Reshaping the World through Prayers of Lament

Jeanne M. Hoeft
*Agency, Culture, and Human Personhood: Pastoral Thelogy
and Intimate Partner Violence*

Jerry Root
*C. S. Lewis and a Problem of Evil: An Investigation
of a Pervasive Theme*

Lisa E. Dahill
*Reading from the Underside of Selfhood:
Bonhoeffer and Spiritual Formation*

A Vexing Gadfly

The Late Kierkegaard on Economic Matters

ELISEO PÉREZ-ÁLVAREZ

With a Foreword by Enrique Dussel

⌒PICKWICK *Publications* · Eugene, Oregon

A VEXING GADFLY
The Late Kierkegaard on Economic Matters

Princeton Theological Monograph Series 112

Copyright © 2009 Eliseo Pérez-Álvarez. All rights reserved. Except for brief
quotations in critical publications or reviews, no part of this book may be
reproduced in any manner without prior written permission from the publisher.
Write: Permissions, Wipf and Stock Publishers, 199 W. 8th Ave., Suite 3, Eugene,
OR 97401.

Pickwick Publications
A Division of Wipf and Stock Publishers
199 W. 8th Ave., Suite 3
Eugene, OR 97401

www.wipfandstock.com

ISBN 13: 978-1-55635-960-6

Cataloging-in-Publication data:

Pérez-Álvarez, Eliseo.

   A vexing gadfly : the late Kierkegaard on economic matters / Eliseo Pérez-Álvarez.
   Foreword by Enrique Dussell.

   xxii + 214 p. ; 23 cm. — Includes bibliographical references.

   Princeton Theological Monograph Series 112

   ISBN 13: 978-1-55635-960-6

   1. Kierkegaard, Søren, 1813–1855—Criticism and interpretation. I. Dussell,
Enrique. II. Title. III. Series.

B4377 .P470 2009

Manufactured in the U.S.A.

To

My Regina

Contents

Foreword

ONLY A *HISPANIC* THEOLOGIAN COULD HAVE UNCOVERED PREVIOUSLY unknown aspects of Søren Kierkegaard. I recall speaking with Eliseo on the subject more than ten years ago, when I was teaching a semester at Loyola University and at the Lutheran School of Theology in Chicago. Since then, I have looked forward to the conclusion of his doctoral dissertation in order to find out about the interesting research on the economic problem in the anguished *Zeitgeist*[1] of Copenhagen, during the Golden Age of the Danish Empire. Kierkegaard was the vexing gadfly of this happy Denmark—in the eyes of the dominant classes of the bourgeoisie, of the state, of the Lutheran Church, and the conservative intelligentsia. The Kierkegaardian critique against the monarchic state, the traditional church, and its intellectual accomplices was well known whereas his critique of capitalism and the bourgeois class is less well known. Herein lies the uniqueness of this excellent work, which opens a new path in Hispanic liberation theology (if the author allows me to recognize his original discourse as such).

As a matter of fact, Søren Kierkegaard (1813–1855), the scholar of humble upbringing, of imperfect and sickly body (which would send him to his grave at the young age of forty-two) had a prophetic spirit and never measured the consequences of his criticism of the institutions that he would, like the prophets of Israel, pronounce against—"the most honorable" personages embodying the structures of domination of his native land in its Golden Age.

His doctorate in Copenhagen, and above all his stay in Germany during the period immediately following Hegel's death, allowed him, thanks to Schelling, to use a "positive" and "material" dialectical theological narrative of unexpectedly fertile soil. His methodology disconcerted those who felt under attack by that "vexing gadfly," like the

---

1. "Spirit of the age."

Athenian Socrates,[2] apparently skeptical of all assertions. Kierkegaard, deep down, departed from a critical, creative source well rooted in an innovative reinterpretation of the Christian sacred writings. This was a true foretaste of the liberation theology of the twentieth century, and more so thanks to Eliseo Pérez-Álvarez's groundbreaking exposition in this work.

In fact, the great critic (at that time still conservative) has inspired many philosophers of the twentieth century, from Martin Heidegger to Carl Schmitt. The Kierkegaard of 1846 (barely thirty-three years old) was impelled by European social events of the decade in a Europe that was already suffering the crisis of growing metropolitan capitalism— with colonies, as Kierkegaard was well aware due to his father's and other relatives' experience. As Marx wrote his famous *Manifesto* in 1848, Kierkegaard initiated a transitional period in his life that would last until 1952; from that year until his death (only three years later), we encounter Kierkegaard's most definitive thinking. In all this Eliseo Pérez-Álvarez corrects Kierkegaard's most distinguished biographer Walter Lowrie. These biographical periods will be covered in chapters 2 and 3 of this innovative work.

Kierkegaard's *Two Ages: the Age of Revolution and the Present Age* (1846) is the most political of his books. Kierkegaard feels committed to a republican and democratic society. But in *Christian Discourses* (1848) he delves fully into the criticism of money, which, like Marx, he identifies as the mammon of the New Testament. Money is exclusionary: "What I have, another cannot have," quotes the author of our book time and time again. A rich person results in many poor ones. Kierkegaard takes charge of the prophetic criticism of economic riches, without "romanticizing poverty."

The criticism of fetishist money runs alongside the criticism of political fetishist power, in the name of a "Christian state"—which Marx criticized at the time with almost the same terms.[3] Kierkegaard

---

2. Kierkegaard at the time did not distinguish between Socrates's Indo-European death (the Athenian "gadfly"), and the death of Joshua of Nazareth from the Semitic tradition. While one rejoiced with the return of the gods for the "immortality" of the soul, the other would suffer to the point of sweating blood when facing death, although he affirmed the "resurrection" from death. Two totally different anthropologies (see Dussel, *El dualismo en la antropología de la Cristiandad*). The concept of "Christianity" in this research was explicitly Kierkegaardian—as in all my works.

3. See my *Las metáforas teológicas de Marx*.

also targeted the Lutheran Church, represented by Mynster and identified with the state in "Christendom" as well as The *Philistine Bourgeois*, referring to the capitalists who exploited the farmers and the slaves in the colonies. Eliseo Pérez-Álvarez takes great care to clearly differentiate "Christendom" from "Christianity" throughout the text. This Kierkegaardian distinction was adopted by the Latin American liberation theology proposed since 1963 by the great Uruguayan theologian Juan Luis Segundo. Professors such as H. L. Martensen or artists such as J. L. Heiberg were not spared his criticism either. The paradigmatic example was a poor, humiliated Christ, and not a *Pantokraton* that identified with the triumphant and metropolitan, illustrated and bourgeois, healthy and beautiful state Christendom.

All this is retrieved from works such as *Works of Love, The Sickness unto Death, Training in Christianity, For Self Examination, Judge for Yourselves* or the *Instant*, and many others on which Pérez-Álvarez skillfully comments, forever extracting the themes referring to his research: the economic elements of his critical reflection.

Even the colonial matter is touched tangentially by our theologian, although one cannot say it was central in his critical discourse. The same applies to themes such as feminism or racism, distant from his progressive concerns.

Against what I myself had believed, and that which Pérez-Álvarez quotes explicitly, Kierkegaard deals with the "material" theme par excellence: if "matter" implies the *content* of human actions in regard to reproduction and the development of human life, such as eating, drinking, clothing oneself, or being hospitable to the homeless; such as affirming the culture of the oppressed, their gender, their race, their age (whatever it may be). All these "determinants" (in the Hegelian sense that Kierkegaard understood) illustrate the "positivity" of concrete Christianity, which is also expressed in the new economic realities of poverty, pain, colonialism, slavery, and the like. Kierkegaard did not forget these aspects, which are so relevant for a *Hispanic* theology, in solidarity with its people, where many are despised for being undocumented, many are economically exploited with low salaries, many are excluded from educational systems, etc. These essential "material" aspects are fundamental criteria of the Final Judgment expressed in Matthew 25, and thirty centuries before in the *Book of the Dead*, chapter 25, of the Egyptian Menfis by the great pyramids that Joshua of Nazareth already must have admired, in his exile in these territories. A *Hispanic* theology, I repeat, has the sensitivity of discovering, given that it is analogically in the position of the Danish theologian facing the poor in the Golden Age of the Danish Empire.

Therefore, the post-Hegelian similarity between Kierkegaard and Marx is not surprising. Both criticize the "Christian state" as non-Christian Christendom—the sublime Sunday Christianity (or Saturday of the Jews for Marx), forgetting the "god" of the whole week that is an idol, a fetish. Kierkegaard (and it could just as well be Marx) writes: "If one . . . prays, but prays in a false spirit . . . in truth to God though he worships an idol."[4] It is like Bartolomé de la Casas, who understood (reading Ben Sira 34:24) in Cuba in 1514 that it means "to kill the son in the presence of the father," to offer to God the goods robbed from the poor (the Indians). Idolatry covers modernity and colonialism. Bartolomé, Marx, and Kierkegaard belong to the same prophetic tradition.

Thus Kierkegaard was able to oppose the false "patriotism" of the great and powerful of his time and of his nation, as the prophet Nathan reminded David (the powerful) of his trampled duties. The perennial dialectic of the king and the prophet was highlighted innumerable times by professor Paul Ricoeur, the exiled evangelical French philosopher in Chicago, another contemporary Kierkegaard, my professor in La Sorbonne in the 1960s.

Enrique Dussel
Department of Philosophy
Universidad Autónoma Metropolitana
Unidad Iztapalapa, Mexico
May 7, 2008

---

4. *Concluding Unscientific Postscript*, 179–80.

Acknowledgments

We live in a perichoretic, or totally related, society and cosmos; therefore it would be unfair to mention only a few names to which I am in debt throughout my graduate studies, because I am aware that the people who have accompanied me in this journey are legion. On the other hand, it would be sinful to universalize my gratitude without particularizing at least the closer people who shared my dreams. Therefore, in a telegraphic style, allow me to pay tribute to a small group of the wide loving community of sisters and brothers that surround me:

To Mark Thomsen for his unstinting help, valuable criticism and for the resonance I found in his Danish roots. To Cynthia Lund, whose efficient and kindly support in bibliographical research have been extremely helpful, for her hospitality during diverse events hosted in the Kierkegaard Library of St. Olaf College, Northfield, Minnesota. To José David Rodríguez Hernández, whose accompaniment made my life and studies lighter and much more bearable. To Irene Connor for her warm and gracious encouragement at all times. To Bruce Kirmmse with deep appreciation for his hospitality and the vast generosity of his wisdom and time. For his intercession in prolonging my stay in Denmark from one semester to two. And to Hans Raun Iversen, a sharp theologian, a sensitive pastor, a trusting friend who, through a scholarship of the Danish Research Academy, hosted my wife and me for one wonderful year in Copenhagen.

I would be remiss if I do not acknowledge my thanksgiving to Catherine González and her husband Justo L. González for their mentoring and solidarity in publishing my book *Introducción a Kierkegaard; del cristianismo entretenedor al del Tenedor.* In the same vein I also recognize the valuable support of my editor Charlie Collier and his very professional team of Diane Farley, Jeremy Funk, and Patrick Harrison.

Abbreviations

AN   *Armed Neutrality: and An Open Letter* (1848–1849, 1851).

AUC   *"Attack Upon Christendom"* (Lowrie translation).

AUCb   *"The Moment" and Late Writings* (Hong translation).

CD   *Christian Discourses; and The Lilies of the Field and the Birds of the Air; and Three Discourses at the Communion on Fridays* (1849).

CUP   *Concluding Unscientific Postscript* (1846).

ED   *Edifying Discourses* (1843–1844).

E/O   *Either/Or* (1843).

EUD   *Eighteen Upbuilding Discourses* (1845).

FSE   *"For Self-Examination" and "Judge for Yourself"* (1851–1852).

FT   *Fear and Trembling (*with *Repetition)* (1843).

JP   *Søren Kierkegaard's Journals and Papers* (7 vols.).

LD   *Letters and Documents* (2 vols).

PA   *The Present Age and the Difference between a Genius and an Apostle.*

Pap.   *Søren Kierkegaards Papirer* (16 vols. in 25 books).

PC   *Practice in Christianity* (Hong and Hong translation) (1859).

PV   *The Point of View of my Work as an Author: A Report to History, and Related Writings* (1859).

SUD   *The Sickness unto Death* (1849). (Hong translation)

SUDb   *The Sickness unto Death* (1849). (Hanney translation)

TA   *Two Ages: The Age of Revolution and the Present Age: A Literary Review* (1846).

TC   *Training in Christianity* (Lowrie translation) (1859).

UDVS *Upbuilding Discourses in Various Spirits* (1847).

WL   *Works of Love: Some Christian Reflections in the Form of Discourses* (1847).

Introduction

We must see the need of having nonviolent gadflies to create the kind of tension in society that will help men to rise from the dark depths of prejudice and racism to the majestic heights of understanding and brotherhood.

—Martin Luther King Jr.[1]

[I was] consecrated and dedicated by the highest approval of Divine Governance to becoming a vexing "gadfly," a quickening whip on all this spiritlessness, which in secularized mediocrity has blabbered Christianity down into something meaningless, into being spiritless impotence, suffocated in illusion.

—Søren Kierkegaard[2]

Right now we look like a cricket. What is a cricket? King of the insects; a little, tiny animal. All the cricket can do is [say] "cricket, cricket, cricket." Just a noise, that's all. But you know, if that cricket gets in the ear of the lion and scratches inside, there is nothing the lion can do. There is nothing; there is no way the lion can use his claws and jaws to destroy the cricket. The more the lion scratches himself the deeper the cricket goes.

—Reies López Tijerina[3]

A ONE-DIMENSIONAL AND SOMETIMES UNSYMPATHETIC READING OF Søren Kierkegaard has prevailed. That approach has portrayed him as an asocial, acosmic "single individual,"[4] to use sociological terms; or as the father of existentialism, in philosophical jargon.[5] But listening more

---

1. King, *Testament of Hope*, 291.

2. Pap. XI, 3 B53 n.d., 1854, JP, 6943. In my citations of quoted journal entries, the first citation is from the Danish edition (*Søren Kierkegaards Papirer*) and the second from *Søren Kierkegaard's Journals and Papers* (hereafter JP).

3. Busto, *King Tiger*, 1.

4. Garff, *Søren Kierkegaard*, xxi.

5. This is definitely a caricature of existentialism. For a vigorous interpretation of

closely, one discovers that the misuse of his pseudonymous books, as well as the selective forgetfulness of his last writings, have been the cause of many misunderstandings. I am more in agreement with those scholars who clearly distinguish the early and late stages in Kierkegaard[6] and have been studying more carefully the late period. In order to substantiate my point, I would like to draw attention to his second authorship.[7] It is my contention that in such understudied writings, through the use of a simple and sometimes more direct style, Kierkegaard, while making his powerful critique of Danish Christendom, addresses economic issues in a very enlightening way.[8]

Therefore, the critical point of this study is to assert that within Søren Kierkegaard's larger attack upon Christendom, his critique of economic matters is a fertile field for exploration. This will do justice to his thought despite many misreadings and will, above all, illuminate our current socioeconomic and political situation from the theological

---

Kierkegaard and existentialism, see Miranda, *Being and the Messiah*, 1–26. See also Garaudy, *Marxism in the Twentieth Century*.

6. Kirmmse, *Kierkegaard in Golden Age Denmark*; Nordentoft, *Kierkegaard's Psychology*; Nordentoft, *Søren Kierkegaard. Bidrag til kritikken af den borgerlige selvoptagethed*; Plekon, "Introducing Christianity into Christendom," 327–52. Garff, *Søren Kierkegaard: A Biography*.

7 By "second authorship," I am referring to the works written after *Concluding Unscientific Postscript* until his death in 1855. Kierkegaard planned to close his cycle of books with *Concluding Unscientific Postscript*. An important shift is noted in this second period especially due to Kierkegaard's dispute with the media in 1846 and, above all, because of the political and social European revolutions of the late 1840s. Those events were the direct cause of the end of the Danish absolute monarchy in 1848–1849. Among the authors who make this distinction of the two Kierkegaards are Nordentoft, Kirmmse, Lindhardt, Bukdahl, Sløk, Deuser, and Plekon. This period includes the numerous entries in his diary, besides the following books and articles: *Two Ages: A Literary Review*, *The Book on Adler*, *Upbuilding Discourses in Various Spirits*, *Works of Love*, *Christian Discourses*, *A Crisis and the Crisis in the Life of an Actress*, *The Point of View for my Work as an Author*, *Armed Neutrality*, *Two Minor Ethico-Religious Treaties*, *The Sickness unto Death*, *Three Discourses at the Communion on Fridays*, *Training in Christianity*, *An Edifying Discourse*, *An Open Letter to Dr. Rudelbach*, *On my Work as an Author*, *Two Discourses at the Communion on Fridays*, *For Self-Examination*, *Judge for Yourselves*, some articles in *The Fatherland*, "This Must be Said, so Let It Now Be Said," *The Moment*, "Christ's Judgment on Official Christianity," and "The Unchangeableness of God."

8. The problem of interpreting Kierkegaard in conservative ways comes partly from Walter Lowrie, his biographer and first English-language translator, who was himself an aristocrat. Lowrie influenced interpretations of Kierkegaard. See Pérez-Álvarez, "Walter Lowrie," 204–5.

point of view. It is a commonplace misconception to view Kierkegaard as a well-to-do theologian who had nothing to say about social and economic issues.[9] In spite of that, it is my conviction that he is not only of interest but a very important interlocutor for our present time.[10]

A few scholars have introduced a new paradigm from which to read Kierkegaard (particularly his late writings), namely, from a social and political perspective. However, it is my claim that Kierkegaard's language about economics has not been fully appreciated. Furthermore, we can derive relevant contributions to the theological arena, such as Christianity's preference for the poor, the critique of dominant ideologies, the relinking of theory and practice, the denunciation of a competitive society, the illegitimacy of irresponsible wealth, the critique of the romanticization of poverty, and so forth. Consequently, this research is undertaken in order to demonstrate how the later Kierkegaard is worthy of our attention—in our case, specifically in relation to economic affairs.

The development of Kierkegaard's economic ideas should not be studied apart from his entire historical setting. Kierkegaard studies that have been undertaken from the biographic, hagiographic, and pseudopsychological approaches are legion. Therefore, I will refrain from utilizing those methods in this investigation. Instead, I will place Kierkegaard within his sociopolitical and economic context. At the same time, since I plan to deal with particular issues and concepts related to money and poverty, I will make use of the thematic method, developing it through a historical approach. In doing so, I will be quoting Kierkegaard extensively, in an attempt to counterbalance earlier misinterpretations with a general examination of the Dane's historical evolution.

It would not be right to interpret Kierkegaard without taking into consideration the specific socioeconomic, political, and cultural situation connected with his task of doing theology. His social critique starts with his concrete location, i.e., the Danish Golden Age (1800–1860). Denmark had been an absolute monarchy since the late seventeenth century. The crown as well as the families of the oligarchy shared the

---

9. González, *A History of Christian Thought*, 373. See also Best and Kellner, "Modernity, Mass Society and the Media," 36.

10 The relevance of Kierkegaard's thought for today is such that the idol of right doctrine is still alive in the Latin American context. Cf. Alves, *Protestantism and Repression*. For a blunt treatment, cf. Khan "Opposition within Affinity," 189–203.

rule of society. King Frederick VI substantially improved the conditions of peasants during his twenty-year rule until 1807. In spite of that, even in the late 1840s, 90 percent of Danes belonged to the menial agricultural working class.[11] It was not until 1848–1849 that, through a bloodless revolution, Denmark became a constitutional monarchy, pressured by economic, political, and nationalistic motives. From that followed the emergence of a new social class of emancipated peasants who, within the new representative government, were granted male suffrage. In addition to other changes, Kierkegaard passionately awaited the constitution of the new Danish folk church (*Folkekirke*), but it never materialized. The revolutionary events of 1848–1849 had prepared the ground for Kierkegaard's shifting of focus, but it was not until his last years (1852–1855) that this changing of paradigms was more obvious. That conversion did not happen in a political or social vacuum but rather in the midst of relevant historical events.

This research will be limited to Kierkegaard's "second authorship," that is, the books he wrote after his *Concluding Unscientific Postscript*, with which he supposedly had planned on ending his writing for good. Throughout this developmental approach, I am including both the Dane's published and unpublished writings. It is my contention that Kierkegaard's unpublished literature will shed much light on his published writings.

This study will focus on primary sources. Yet, critical secondary sources will be consulted as well, in order to better understand the way Kierkegaard's thought took shape. Special emphasis will be placed upon his treatment of economic ideas on both the structural and the individual level, within the historical matrix of Golden Age Denmark.

In order to reach the goal of this dissertation, I propose three chapters. The first is devoted to an in-depth analysis of the philosophical, economic, and social context of mid-nineteenth-century Denmark. This chapter focuses mainly on three areas: First, it provides a general historical overview of Kierkegaard's relationship with the academic world inside and outside his country and of his intellectual contacts with Hegel, Schelling, and the Young Hegelians. Here we find the irritating gadfly stinging his audience in the field of the ideas by questioning the idealistic rationalization of Christianity and the elitist and bour-

---

11. Kirmmse, "'Out with it!'" 16–17.

geois conception of the same. The second subdivision gives expression to Denmark's succinct economic history, particularly to the history of its colonies, which have been neglected in dealing with Kierkegaard. At this point, I will highlight revealing connections between the flourishing Golden Age Continental Denmark and its slavery and trade enterprises. We will perceive a different economic angle of Kierkegaard's family business and of notable Danish figures. Finally, I address the social-religious landscape in order to situate and appreciate Kierkegaard's contributions in the economic sphere. I explore the role clergy played in society as an instrument of social control, and I introduce the topic of the "ordinary person," namely, the poor peasantry and the urban proletariat with whom Kierkegaard sided.

The second chapter delves into Kierkegaard's economic language together with his important semantic differentiations of the concept of poverty and its correlation with wealth. In this segment I analyze Kierkegaard's views concerning his years of transition (from 1846 to 1852). The goal of this chapter is to fully grasp Kierkegaard's treatment of the interplay between wealth and poverty. The revolutionary gadfly manifests his concern with concreteness, actuality, specifically with economic matters, from the social, cultural, political, and religious dimensions. We delve into Kierkegaard's appraisal of social institutions such as the church, the theater, and the university alongside its top representative figures. Lastly, a word must be said about the well-disseminated portrait of Kierkegaard as a bourgeois. Consequently, I take issue with Kierkegaard's own fortune and his use of it, which will reveal the correspondence of his thought with his practice.

Central to the third chapter is Kierkegaard's radicalization of his judgments on economics. This is an important and neglected dimension of Kierkegaard's final, devastating critique of Christendom in Golden Age Denmark. This part is undertaken in order to demonstrate that economic issues are of major significance throughout Kierkegaard's final, prophetic years of 1852 to 1855. The first, socially conservative Kierkegaard planned to close his career as an author on February 1846 with his *Concluding Unscientific Postscript*. However, the effervescent years of the late 1840s played an important role in his thought. A month after he had finished writing *Concluding Unscientific Postscript*, he wrote his *Two Ages: The Age of Revolution and the Present Age*, followed by other works such as *Works of Love, The Sickness unto Death, Training in Christianity*, and *"For Self-Examination" and "Judge for Yourselves."* In these major books Kierkegaard shows his move to a radical social critique. The shift of 1848–1849 from an absolute Danish monarchy to a democratic government, within the general framework of other political European revolutions of the same time, announced relevant social transformations. Since these expected changes were delayed, at least in the ecclesiastical arena, by 1852 there is a clear shifting of paradigms in Kierkegaard's thought. During this period, he orchestrated his assault on the gospel of the prosperous, which consisted of the ideology of adaptation that privileged the rich to the detriment of the poor. He also denounced the hidden economic agendas of the religious and political rules of the state-church monism, better known as Christendom. I thus deal with the molesting gadfly's task of combating the oppressive, self-complacent and static world order, as it had been sanctioned by the academy and the clergy. Within this historical framework and as part of my task of linking Kierkegaard's thought with social and political events, I introduce three lesser time periods: the Voluntary Silence Stage (1852–December 18, 1854), the *Fatherland* Stage (December 18, 1854–May 1855), and the *Instant* Stage (May 26, 1855–October 1855). His treatment of economic themes (not in individualistic but in structural terms) will be more obvious in this segment of the research.

Finally, the fourth chapter summarizes and highlights the findings of the preceding pages by showing the relevance of the Dane's thoughts for today.

1

Golden Age Denmark

ALLOW ME TO START BY PROVIDING A BRIEF HISTORICAL, PHILOSOPHI-
cal, and geopolitical framework of Kierkegaard's Denmark. In doing
so, it is necessary take into consideration a broader context. Therefore,
I begin by highlighting the main consequences and contributions of
the French Revolution. Hegel's influence upon the Young Hegelians
and Kierkegaard is revisited in the philosophical map section. Last, I
close this chapter with an overview of mid-nineteenth-century Danish
geopolitics.

The French Revolution

This section addresses the general impact and the main contributions
of the French Revolution to the theme of this dissertation, rather than
a detailed report of its history.[1] Whether the French Revolution is the
revolution par excellence is questionable; however, from that does not
follow the denial of the role it has played in inspiring sociopolitical
transformations all over the world.

The Secularization and Mechanization of Nature

The French Revolution is inconceivable without the Industrial Revolution.
In fact, the beginning and closing of the French Enlightenment is com-
monly dated between these two events.[2] The French Enlightenment[3]

1. See Hobsbawn, *The Age of Revolution.*

2. Silva, "Del empirismo inglés a la ilustración francesa," 37.

3. For the relevance of these movements to our study, let us consider the case of the
Physiocrats' economic school of François Quesnay (1694–1774). Diderot's *Encyclopédie*
included Quesnay's *Tableau économique* (1758), where this enlightened French economist stated the main Physiocrat thesis: that the only real productive sector of the

itself is rooted in the English empiricism personified by its founders, John Locke, and by Isaac Newton, David Hume, George Berkeley, and Francis Bacon[4] among others.

English empiricism and the French enlightenment took their experimental method from Newton (1642–1727), switching the traditional *Weltanschauung*. Nature lost its enchantment. The world and the entire universe were interpreted through natural laws, particularly the gravitational one. Even though this great physicist never denied the existence of God, he set the foundations for the mechanistic view of reality ruled by natural laws and therefore subject to its manipulation through the knowledge of natural science and physics.[5]

---

economy is to be found in agriculture. Joseph Townsend introduced a new point of departure for political science by understanding humanity from the animal side and linking it with the laws of Nature: "Hunger will tame the fiercest animals, it will teach decency and civility, obedience and subjection, to the most perverse. In general it is only hunger which can spur and goad them [the poor] on to labor; yet our laws have said they shall never hunger. The laws, it must be confessed, have likewise said, they shall be compelled to work. But then legal constraint is attended with much trouble, violence and noise; creates ill will, and never can be productive of good and acceptable service: whereas hunger is not only peaceable, silent, unremitting pressure, but, as the most natural motive to industry and labor, it calls forth the most powerful exertions; and, when satisfied by the free bounty of another, lays lasting and sure foundations for good will and gratitude. The slave must be compelled to work but the free man should be left to his own judgment, and discretion; should be protected in the full enjoyment of his own, be it much or little; and punished when he invades his neighbor's property" (Townsend, *Dissertation on the Poor Laws*, Sect. IV).

4. Francis Bacon (1561–1626) shared with Descartes the central place they represent in the emergence of modern Europe. In his *Novum organum scientiarum* (1620), he ventured his famous watchword "knowledge itself is power," meaning that scientific knowledge can be derived exclusively by experience, advocating in this way the scientific method of induction. In his view, natural science provides humans power against *primitive* races of native people from Africa and America, against members of the same society, against women, and against nature. English Lord Chancellor Francis Bacon in fact was responsible for trials during the time he was in charge of the war against witches, extirpating them by torture methods. According to him, knowledge is power; it is useful in our dealing with nature and in exercising our dominion over Mother Earth. He literally recommended extracting the secrets from nature by torturing it, in the same way he extracted confessions from witches by torturing them (Duchrow, *Alternatives to Global Capitalism*, 54). See also Duchrow and Liedke, *Shalom: Biblical Perspectives on Creation, Justice and Peace*, 66.

5. "The invisible hand" of Adam Smith (1723–1790) found a fertile land in Newton's thought. Although in a naive and dogmatic way, Smith was of the opinion that the laws of the market economy eventually would bring order in society and a natural freedom. Therefore, the only role of the state was to protect private property and the social con-

John Locke (1632–1704) earned his money from the slave trade.[6] He was an investor in the Royal African Company and, as secretary to Lord Ashley, he transcribed the Fundamental Constitutions of Carolina: "every freeman of Carolina, shall have absolute power and authority over his Negro slaves."[7]

As a pioneer empiricist, Locke wrote in the *Essay Concerning Human Understanding* (1690), following Aristotle, that at birth the human mind is a tabula rasa, and that every one of our ideas come from the impressions of the senses. Reason then is not defined by eternal, innate ideas but by the way it works in reality; in fact, all true knowledge comes through the exercise of our senses, and all true knowledge is tested by the way it functions in reality. His *Two Treatises of Civil Government*

---

tracts, and not to block the path of the market economy. Smith reduced the state to the *laissez faire, laissez passer, le monde va de lui-même*. The invisible hand itself would keep the market working harmoniously. In his *The Wealth of Nations* (1776) Smith takes for granted that the competing market partners have the same decision-making power. Smith, the founder of economic liberalism and of the modern national economies as well, exalted the self-interests of entrepreneurs and confounded the common good with the well-being of the elite. This customs inspector's theory that the market regulates itself was of the idea that inequity is the main force of economic progress; that the base of society lies in the competitive spirit; and that the social crisis that requires "necessary sacrifices" will be temporary because of Smith's faith in the invisible hand of the market will redeem society. Since the market laws were inspired by Newton's physics, in Smith we can trace the modern conception of economics as a "hard science," although the mysterious and mystifying elements of the "invisible hand" are present (book 4, chapter 2).

From Smith's work, modern economists such as Hayek have articulated the idea of necessary human sacrifices for the sake of the market. The people who are well integrated into the market have reached equilibrium in their interests; therefore they don't have to die. Following the lead of Darwin's social determinism, Hayek states that the self-regulated systems of the market assure the surviving of the fittest: "A free society requires certain ethics that, in the last resort, are reduced to keeping the people alive: but not keeping alive all the people because chances are that individual lives would need to be sacrificed in order to preserve a bigger number of other lives. Therefore, the only valid ethic is the one that leads us to the 'calculation of lives', private property and social contracts" (Hayek, Interview in *El Mercurio*, quoted in Franz J. Hinkelammert, *La fe de Abraham y el Edipo occidental*, 89, n.5). It is not for nothing that Helmut Maucher, the managing director of Nestle Co. can rely on this authority: "Nobody can deny that the 'destructive creativeness' of the market creates extreme hardness . . . and with F. A. von Hayek I believe that the concept of 'justice' as a last resort, is irrelevant for the operation of the market mechanisms" (Hinkelammert, *Sacrificios humanos y sociedad occidental*, 165). See also Assmann, *Sobre los ídolos y sacrificios*.

6. Duchrow, *Alternatives to Global Capitalism*, 50.

7. Davis, *The Problem of Slavery in Western Culture*, 118.

(1690) were basic for Western liberal democracy.[8] He dismissed any intervention of the king in the laws of the market, because he held that human beings are property- and wealth-accumulating beings in competition with one another; therefore, property owners can exercise their power with all legitimacy over the propertyless, particularly the slaves.[9] Meeks has argued persuasively that the traditional concept of God as a self-sufficient being who does not have the need either of humans or of creation is really pointing to God's absolute freedom of choice. Now, this idea of God's freedom is akin with the absolute power of the disposal of property inherited from Roman law and rearticulated in our modern age by Locke and others:

> Freedom is sovereignty of owning. *Those who own are free to rule.* Freedom can only belong to the absolutely sovereign deity and to the sovereign *homo politicus.* The dominative character of many traditional Christian doctrines of God was that their logic of divine freedom was the ground for slavery, the patriarchal family, "skin privilege" and other forms of master-servant relationships.[10]

For Locke then, private property has to be understood "as" an institution of nature, in accordance: property rights are natural rights as

---

8. Let us recall that he together with Hobbes are considered the fathers of the economic theory which states that humans are property- and wealth-pilers, beings in competition with each other. See Duchrow, *Alternatives to Global Capitalism*, 52.

Thomas Hobbes (1588–1679) expressed his political theory in *Leviathan* (1651), where he argues that "man treats man like a wolf"; i.e., human beings are inherently selfish; thus it is the role of "Leviathan" or the State, to rule citizens with firmness and thus guarantee public order. His loyalist theory, nevertheless, was not very distant from Locke's defense of private property. If humans are by nature selfish, from that follows the idea of a society built on private property striving for the accumulation of more property. Or better yet, if humans are by nature selfish, from that we can infer that society is formed by mechanical systems competing to defeat one another. In short, by the "natural law" of "man treats man like a wolf," Hobbes is really taking "the condition of the emerging market society, determined by competition, and projects it backwards onto a supposedly natural state, re-applying it to society and then drawing political conclusions" (MacPherson, *The Political Theory of Possessive Individualism*, quoted in Duchrow, *Alternatives to Global Capitalism*, 52).

9. Ibid. See also Hinkelammert, "Sacrificios humanos y sociedad occidental," 172–73.

10. Meeks, *God the Economist*, 67 (italics original).

the ones of life and liberty, and it is the task of government to assure the preservation and inviolability of them all.[11]

Even though the French philosopher Jean Jacques Rousseau (1712–1778) argued, in the *Discourse on the Origin and Foundations of Inequality Amongst Man* (1754), in favor of the goodness of nature in general and of the human being's perfect nature in particular, the concept of nature that prevailed was the one set by the English empiricist: the awareness of the unlimited capacity to transform, manipulate, and have dominion with respect to nature. The trinity of empiricism, experimental sciences, and the Industrial Revolution is what stands behind the French Revolution: "The birth of the experimental sciences had already signaled the beginning of humanity's new dominion over nature, but this dominion reached consciousness and maturity only as scientific knowledge began to translate into technology-techniques for mastering the material world and satisfying his necessities of human life on a large scale."[12]

The Enslaving of Human Beings

The statement of the French Revolution, the Declaration of the Rights of Man and the Citizen (August 26, 1789), left out of the discussion the issue of economic oppression and focused its attention on the protection of the inviolable and untouchable right of private property.

The big words *liberté, egalité,* and *fraternité,* considered the great legacy of the French Revolution ideals for humankind, were not officially integrated into the French Constitution until 1848 and were also equivocal words. By *liberty* was meant freedom from the absolutist, feudal rule of the Bourbon kings and nobility. *Equality* kept in mind that everybody has the same rights before the law, or better yet: "the rule of law imposed on everyone, but the bourgeois would be able to make laws which favored themselves."[13] By *fraternity* the first revolutionaries understood the well-being of people who own property.

Both the Constituent Assembly that enacted the Declaration of the Rights of Man and the Citizen, as well as the Legislative Assembly that two years later (October, 1791) did the same, included in the category

11. Ibid., 108.

12. Gutiérrez, *The Power of the Poor in History,* 48.

13. Comblin, "The French Revolution: A Bourgeois Revolution," 64.

of citizens whites, mulattos, and free blacks. Both of these Assemblies excluded the slaves, who were supposed to remain slaves. The slaves from Santo Domingo (later Haiti), the favorite and most prosperous of the French colonies, revolted and in 1804 earned their freedom in spite of the rhetoric of the antislavery French Revolution program.

The Anti-Revolution Spirit of Christian Churches

Whether the French Revolution was betrayed by the Jacobin terror or by Napoleon's proclamation of French supremacy, I'm not going to address those topics. I must confine myself to the theological, economic, and social topics related to this dissertation.

Since the church sided with feudal monarchy and nobility circles, the French Revolution saw the church as part of the authoritarian triangle, unveiling her possessions of political power and material wealth. Furthermore, there were other intellectual movements that undermined church authority, such as Deism and rationalism.

The emergence of Deism at the end of the seventeenth and beginning of the eighteenth century received a significant impulse, although involuntary, from Locke's *Reasonableness of Christianity* (1695) and from Thomas Hobbes. In both cases, Locke and Hobbes underlined the most rational elements of religion. Voltaire and Rousseau were found within the followers of Deism.

Rationalism, the new cult of the Supreme Being of Reason, or Goddess Reason are other ways of referring to the enlightenment even though it is the inheritor of the work of Descartes and of the Renaissance among others. The natural sciences had already shown that nature possesses its own laws and therefore is a subject to be known and mastered. The rationalist philosophers then tried to construct a religion and an ethic based on their unmovable faith in reason and in their rejection of tradition.

Within this philosophical context it is not surprising to find Christian leaders with odd judgments against the French Revolution: the still pervasive influence of Abraham Kuyper (1837–1920) and his appraisal of the Revolution as the anti-Christ, to mention just one name. Kuyper was a Calvinistic theologian, political leader of the Dutch Anti-Revolutionary Party, and prime minister of the Netherlands (1900–1905). He reduced the French Revolution to the anarchist slogan:

"ni Dieu—ni maître" ("neither God nor master")." Kuyper considered the principle of popular sovereignty against divine authority in state and family. He praised Calvinism because within it "men and women humbly bow the knee before God, but raise their head proudly towards their fellow men."[14]

Blaming the French Revolution as the instrument of dechristianization nevertheless dissimulates an important fact. Prior to the Revolution, theology professors of the Sorbonne carried out a very fine and professional censorship that included the years of 1750 to 1780. Under the name "of our sacred dogmas" and "the healthy theology which is entirely within Holy Scripture and venerable tradition,"[15] Rousseau and others were anathematized. Writings such as Buffon's *Histoire naturelle* were condemned as well, in this case because his calculation of the age of the Earth did not correspond with the chronology of the book of Genesis. In any event, what is relevant to notice is that with regional differences, as early as 1750 people began to break with the church in a considerable way. Forty years before the Revolution, there was no such a thing as a unified Catholicism: "'public opinion' rose to become a real political power which neither clergy nor king could suppress: *vox populi, vox dei* became the slogan of the time."[16]

Vox populi, Vox Dei

Let me quickly affirm that the main contribution of the French Revolution for humankind has been the assertion that each and every human being has the right to participate in the shaping and building of society.

Regarding the French Revolution, Kant wrote in 1798; his watchword, *sapere aude!* ("dare to think!"), took form in the French fellows who, abandoning tutelage began using their own reason: "A phenomenon like this can never again be forgotten, because it reveals a disposition and a capacity in human nature for betterment, a capacity which no politician could have thought out for himself from the previous course

14. Moltmann, "Revolution, Religion and the Future," 47.

15. Quoted in Perronet, "Les censures de la Sorbonne au XVIII siècle," 27–35, 29, 32. Quoted in Eicher, "Revolution and Church Reform," 98.

16. Ibid.

of events."[17] Hegel's appraisal of the French Revolution went beyond Kant's: "Never as long as the sun had shone in the firmament and the planets had revolved round it, had it been perceived that man stands on his head, that his existence centers in his ideas, and that it is there that he forms reality. Anaxagoras was the first to say that the *nous* [the intellect] governs the world; but only now has man come to recognize that he should govern spiritual reality. And this was indeed a glorious sunrise."[18] Fichte equated his whole work with the French Revolution: "My system is freedom's first system. Just as that nation is striking off mankind's outward fetters, so my system strikes off the fetters of things in themselves, of outward influence, and as its first principle sets up man as an independent being."[19]

The year of 1789 was considered a turning point, that is, the setting of an age built on tradition, and the emergence of a new age of history based on popular sovereignty. The Industrial Revolution meant unimaginable possibilities for human beings to master nature and to re-create it according to their own wishes. The French Revolution had meant the great capacity of human beings to reshape or transform the social order in accordance with the Enlightenment's ideals: "*human rights* and human dignity, *democracy* as the constitution of liberty, *reason* as the means whereby to build a free and humane world."[20]

Granted, we can disagree whether or not the legal state is fiction, whether democracy is always completely democratic or not, whether human rights is merely an ideology that privileges exclusively the property owners or not, or whether reason is reason as it is conceived by the people in power or not.[21] What is undeniable is the truth that the legal state was emulated by nations all over the world: that the issue of democracy provided the masses with a protagonist role as popular sovereignty became the criteria of legitimacy for political power and equality before the law, that the topic of human rights provided a posi-

---

17. Kant, *Der Streit der Fakultäten*, 361. Quoted in Moltmann "Revolution, Religion and the Future," 44–45.

18. Hegel, *Vorlesungen über die Philosophie*, 557. Quoted in Moltmann, "Revolution, Religion and the Future," 45.

19. Fichte, *Briefwechsel*, 349–50. Quoted in Moltmann, "Revolution, Religion, and the Future," 45.

20. Ibid.(italics original).

21. See, e.g., Comblin, "French Revolution," 67ff.

tive and powerful image of human beings, and that encouraging the use of critical reason bestowed upon the crowds a sense of freedom in affirming themselves in society.

Yet more important, the French Revolution provided a new social imaginary—a new way of perceiving human beings, society, and social relations. The future was no longer mortgaged. The state is the result of popular sovereignty. Men and women are no longer objects but subjects of their own destiny, by having discovered their capacity to determine their plot or place in the cosmos. Indebted to the Industrial Revolution, the French Revolution inaugurated a new era: the age of popular sovereignty, which "put an end to a certain type of society and instilled in the popular masses the desire for an effective share in the exercise of political power—the desire for an active role in history; in a word, the desire for a truly democratic society."[22]

The Philosophical Map

> It was characteristic of all previous philosophy to deal with precisely that field of being which does not depend on our free will in order to be what it is. It is a being that *does not disturb us, that does not upset us* . . . Nietzsche, Marx and Kierkegaard rebelled against and broke with it. Of the three, Kierkegaard was the most conscious of the novelty of this method, which was to detect which fields of being can exist only if I make a decision.[23]

Under the heading of the French Revolution, I attempted briefly to provide the sociopolitical background within which Kierkegaard's work took place. We now enter the philosophical milieu. An overview of Hegel and the Young Hegelians is necessary in order to better contextualize the thought and prophetic commitment of the Nordic social philosopher.

In France, England, and Belgium, the years of 1830 to 1832 brought significant political changes. The poor working classes organized into a revolutionary force and "revealed the pervasive impact of the dynamic, transformative power of industrial capitalism."[24] Throughout Europe, Hegel's all-embracing (*Umgreifende*) thought dominated the philosoph-

22. Gutiérrez, *The Power of the Poor in History*, 49.

23. Miranda, *Being and the Messiah*, 23 (emphasis mine).

24. Toews, *Hegelianism*, 207ff.

ical and theological arena for at least three decades. This dominance occurred from 1818 to his death in 1831, while he was the brilliant professor in Berlin, and up until 1848 through his heirs such as Johan Ludvig Heiberg (1791–1860), Hans Lassen Martensen (1808–1884), and Kierkegaard's brother Peter Christian.

In Germany up until 1840, the political environment was more or less favorable for the idealist philosophy and theology. Karl Freiherr von Stein zum Altenstein (1757–1831), the minister of public worship, was a very important member of the Prussian administration and very sympathetic towards the German Enlightenment. Moreover, monarch Frederick William III (1770–1840), though a reactionary king, granted freedom to the intellectuals as long as they did not touch the state, that is, the Prussian state. The landscape completely changed in 1840. The influential leader of the conservative faction in the bureaucracy, Johann Albrecht Friedrich Eichhorn, occupied the post of the Prussian minister of public ministry.[25] To make matters worst, Frederick William IV replaced the tolerant politics of his father with an aggressive stance, interpreting religious criticism as an attack on the monarchy. Two years after these had assumed their positions, Eichhorn declared that the cultural orientation of the new regime was "not neutral, but partisan, totally partisan."[26] The ideology of the new king was "the Christian State," but from a conservative point of view. Thus, the new protégée of the authorities was the conservative *Evangelische Kirchenzeitung*, antagonist to all kinds of Hegelianism.[27]

George Wilhelm Friedrich Hegel (1770–1831)

The great German philosopher published the first edition of the *Encyclopedia of the Philosophical Sciences* in 1817, and the third edition in 1830. This magnum opus contains three parts: 1) the science of logic, 2) the philosophy of nature, and 3) the philosophy of the spirit. From then on, Hegel devoted all his teaching and researching to this colossal project, i.e., his "system."

25. In fact, twice Eichhorn unsuccessfully attempted to bribe Bauer with a research stipend and teaching post. Eichhorn ended up suspending Bauer's teaching license (ibid., 316, 318).

26. Ibid., 363.

27. Stepelevich, *The Young Hegelians: An Anthology*.

In *Philosophy of Right* (*Rechtsphilosophie* [1821]), Hegel dealt with the theory of bourgeois society or the *homme* as bourgeois, and the theory of state or *citoyen* as citizen, as it was inherited from the French Revolution. It was Marx, the intellectual, who highlighted the fact that in the social movement that emerged as a result of the French Revolution, the *droits de l'homme* are alluding exclusively to the member of the bourgeoisie; they are not universal human rights. This is opposed to the general individual who has been classified within the *droits du citoyen*.[28] Nonetheless, Kierkegaard also conceived of Hegel as a defender of the bourgeois style of life, showing the "town and country taste."[29] In effect, Hegel did not take into account the fact that French equality before the law avoided dealing with economic and social inequalities, that the law was elaborated by the ruling class in order to favor themselves, and that the legal state created by the French Revolution was in practice a mere fiction because the law only ruled the poor.[30]

Another issue relevant for our purposes is derived from the preface of the same work of Hegel and is related to his dictum: "whatever is rational is real; and whatever is real is rational." According to Engels, one of his disciples, this is not a reactionary but a revolutionary judgment, because reality is not what happens to exist; on the contrary, it is what is necessary and true.[31] Reality does not refer to facts or data. Reality is real-idealism: it has to do with the unity between essence and existence, what is real is what is necessary. Or to say the same, Hegel's realism is the current equivalent of idealism. However, Hegel's concept of reason is also problematic. The spirit is what makes human beings be humans; it is the essence of humans, logos or reason. The Absolute Spirit is not an anthropological category for Hegel but a theological one. His system was advocating a monism in which the Holy and the Truth, self-knowledge and knowledge of God, faith and knowledge, religion and metaphysics, were interchangeable. In short, he was proposing a gnostic soteriology. Hegel continued the long Christian-Greek tradition of thinkers such as

28. Löwith, *From Hegel to Nietzsche*, 246. "Curiously, the Rights of Man pass as the great innovation of the French Revolution. In reality, the bourgeoisie was able to make a propaganda machine out of this, a rationalization and justification of its power." Cf. Comblin, "The French Revolution," 63.

29. Mullen, *Kierkegaard's Philosophy*, 167 n. 1.

30. Comblin, "The French Revolution," 67ff.

31. Löwith, *From Hegel to Nietzsche*, 70.

Clement of Alexandria, Origen, Thomas Aquinas, Melanchton, and the rationalists, who identify the Holy with the Truth, namely, the acceptance of a set of truths or the construction of a system of knowledge as a means of salvation:[32] "salvation is through right thinking, and mankind is divided into a spiritual aristocracy of philosophers who can grasp abstract concepts and a spiritual proletariat who are capable only of knowing the truth in its interior garb as doctrine or mythology."[33] Faith in reason, even if many authors disagree, made of Hegel the father of demythologizing[34] since Christian dogmas were true but opaque. They are, he continues, a sign of human immaturity and a poetic intuition, in contrast to the scientific and abstract language of metaphysics. That is correct. Hegel called this Christian language *Vorstellung* or "representation": "religion is grasped by means of representational thought whereas philosophy is understood through rational comprehension."[35] In spite of that, in another place, Hegel uses the word "myth" in a univocal sense: "We find in the Bible a well-known myth [*Vorstellung*] abstractly termed *the fall*. This representation is very profound and is not just a contingent history but the eternal and necessary history of humanity—though it is indeed expressed here in an external and mythical mode."[36]

David Friedrich Strauss (1808–1874)

With his *Das Leben Jesu* (*Life of Jesus Critically Examined*), Strauss made apparent once and for all how Hegelianism in fact destroyed Christian orthodoxy. As Kierkegaard put it: "Myths fall under the guillotine when the modern critical allegorizing school declares without further ado that all Christianity is a myth" (Pap. IX 182). Of course, Strauss's reading of Hegel has been questioned. While Hegel attempted to harmonize philosophical knowledge with the Christian faith as it is expressed in symbolic or representational forms, Strauss polarized the two *Weltanschauunger*. In *Das Leben Jesu* and with his application of

---

32. Cf. Pelikan, *Fools for* Christ, 1–27.

33. Forrester, "The Attack on Christendom in Marx and Kierkegaard," 182.

34. Ibid., 181.

35. Hegel, *Lectures on the Philosophy of World History*, 113.

36. Hegel, *Lectures on the Philosophy of Religion*, 527.

the principle of immanence, Strauss divorced faith from experience and reason, traditional Christianity from modern consciousness.[37]

This instructor of Tübingen attempted to apply Hegel's method of criticism to biblical studies, and by doing so, Strauss directly addressed the issues of the historicity of Christianity and the history of myth in the New Testament. There is a contrast between form and content of truth. According to Strauss, Hegel's method of criticism allowed us to find the biblical truth that is wrapped up with myths. The mythological narratives in the New Testament writers' minds must be replaced by critical philosophy, which is by nature unorthodox: "The early Christian community formed its image of Christ just as the God of Plato formed the world looking at the ideas. Stimulated through the person and fate of Jesus, it framed the picture of its Christ, having in mind unconsciously the idea of humanity in its relationship to Divinity."[38]

Strauss started with theology; later on he moved to philosophy and by 1872 with his *Del alte und der neue Glaube* ended up embracing positivism and its faith in scientific progress: "How should we order our lives?—he raised this rhetorical question by our great poets and musicians."[39] Strauss's *Das Leben Jesu* was followed by other writings[40] in which he classified different groups of Hegelians according to philosophical discrepancies. The Hegelites (*Hegelitern*) or Old Hegelians preferred not to modify substantially the master's thought and included Marheineke, Goeschel, K. Fisher, K. Rosenkranz, Haym, Erdmann, George Andres Gabler (successor in Hegel's chair of philosophy), and Bruno Bauer. The Hegelists (*Hegelinge*) or Young Hegelians, including Strauss himself, took the radical left-wing from Hegel and were identified as Ruge, Feuerbach, Engels, Marx, the late Bruno Bauer, Stirner, and Kierkegaard among others. For our purposes it is immaterial to mention all of them; I am exclusively going to refer to those who in some way may help us to better understand our Danish philosopher.

37. Toews, *Hegelianism*, 255.

38. Stepelevich, *The Young Hegelians: An Anthology*, 50.

39. Löwith, *From Hegel to Nietzsche*, 334–35.

40. Strauss, *Stretschriften zur Verteidigung meiner Schrift Über das Leben Jesu*, 95ff. *Geschichte der letzen Systeme der Philosophie in Deutschland*, 654ff.

Bruno Bauer (1809–1882)

Bruno Bauer entered the University of Berlin in 1828 and by 1834 became a teacher. He was on very good terms with Marheineke and the Old Hegelians. Lorenz von Stein also favored Bauer to the extent of appointing him to the University of Bonn so as to infiltrate the conservative Hegelian philosophy. Nonetheless, in 1841 he was converted to the Young Hegelians. In his *Critique of the Evangelical History of the Synoptic Gospels* he began to use negative criticism in attacking the historicity of the gospels. In order to reach truth, it was indispensable to use negative criticism: "Criticism is the last act and only through negation was progress possible."[41] During the same year, under the new spell, in the introduction of his *The Trumpet of the Last Judgment*, he exalted the human self-consciousness and the apotheosis of self-reflection: "God is dead for philosophy and only the self as self-consciousness lives, creates, acts and is everything." In his judgment, Hegelianism in the version of the Young Hegelians, gets rid of masks and exposes the whole truth of humanism: "they [the Young Hegelians] have only torn away the thin veil which briefly concealed the thought of the master and have revealed—shamelessly enough! the system in its nakedness."[42] According to some authors,[43] Bauer reduced the absolute spirit to human self-consciousness. In this train of thought, and in his goal to supplant Christianity with humanism, in 1843 he wrote *Christianity Exposed*, but it was not published until 1927 due to censorship.

In his *The Jewish Question* published the same 1843, Bauer shows his anti-Semitism in opposition to the dualistic *Weltanschauung* promoted by the Jews. The idea of a transcended God, or the separation between church and state, was contrary to his concept of the human being. Bauer, whose father had wanted him to become a pastor, ended up embracing atheism, but a qualified atheism: "His atheism was that of all Young Hegelians: it did not deny God, it denied the possibility of a spiritual existence apart from man."[44]

41. Bauer, *Kritik der Evangelischen Geschichte*, 1:xxi.

42. Stepelevich, *The Young Hegelians: An Anthology*, 178 n. 2; 179.

43. Toews, *Hegelianism*, 288.

44. Brazill, *The Young Hegelians*, 197.

Ludwig Feuerbach (1804–1827)

Feuerbach ("fire stream") shared with Bauer and Max Stirner the privilege of listening to and meeting Hegel. After his studies in Heidelberg, he went to Berlin where for two years he studied with Hegel. He was also able to attend the lectures of Schleirmacher and Marheineke. In Berlin he joined the "Doctors' Club," later known as the "Free Ones" or the Young Hegelians. He also shared with the majority of the Young Hegelians the destiny of losing his post in the university because of his radical positions. In his *Das Wesen des Christentums* (1842), he sought to translate Hegelianism into tangible and concrete terms, and Kierkegaard, as his avid reader, bought his book in 1844, after having read it. The ultimate essence of the human being was, in Feuerbach's view, the corporeal and finite human being. In *Das Wesen des Christentums*, he emphasizes the love of human beings by their fellow human beings. He is proposing a "realistic humanism" (Marx), or a "monistic humanism."[45] Humans are both nature and spirit, and we need to end the alienation that fragments that unity. God and humans are also only one reality, because the divine is inherited in humans, and humans are in fact God. For Feuerbach, the philosophy of the absolute means a philosophical theology that departs from the corporeal and finite human being. In the same place, Feuerbach tried to harmonize the idea of God with humanity, and in his *Gedanken Über Tod und Unsterblickeit* (1832) he sought to unite the idea of heaven with the present earthly life. In his *Vorläufige Thesen zur Reformation der Philosophie* (*Provisional Theses for the Reformation of Philosophy*, [1843]) Feuerbach condensed his understanding of Hegelian theology:

> The secret of *theology* is *anthropology*, but the secret of *speculative philosophy* is *theology*, the *speculative* theology. Speculative theology distinguishes itself from *ordinary* theology by the fact that it transfers the divine essence into this world. That is, speculative theology *envisions*, *determines*, and *realizes* in this world the divine essence transported by ordinary theology out of fear and ignorance into another world.[46]

---

45. Ibid., 154.

46. Stepelevich, *The Young Hegelians: An Anthology*, 156 (italics original).

Feuerbach disagreed with Strauss and Bauer in his affirmation of Christianity.[47] In his opinion, philosophy was itself religion, and in his goal to humanize theology he wanted to preserve the essential part of anthropology. He promoted a "devout atheism" (Stirner), or a "religious atheism"[48] based on the apotheosis of humanity. Feuerbach's principle of sensuousness was far away from being a spiritless materialism (*geistlose Materialismus*). However, Marx was right in criticizing Feuerbach's concept of the human being as a bourgeois, private individual, as the latter stated very clearly: "God was my first, Reason my second, and Man my third and last thought."[49]

Arnold Ruge (1802–1880)

This philosopher included a review of Kierkegaard's dissertation in his the *Hallesche Jahrbücher für deutsche Wissenschaft und Kunst* (1838–1843). However, the Dane continued to be ignored in Germany. Ruge was forced to leave Prussia because the government forbade him to publish; thus, he settled in Saxony, where he renamed his publication *Deutsche Jahrbücher*, but due to the pressure of Prussia he had to leave Saxony in 1843. Eventually he had to seek shelter in Paris, Switzerland, and England. Ruge was born in Sweden. He studied in Halle and Jena, where he was imprisoned for five years because of his criticism of the holy alliance between church and state. Eventually he began teaching at Halle; however, he lost his teaching post due to his radical theological and social views.

According to Ruge's understanding of Hegel, Hegel's philosophy not only contains a religious criticism but also an invitation to political action in the sense of reforming social and political life. Ruge attempted to translate the liberating Hegelian philosophy into the world of reality. He advocated a political humanism and a political democracy, emulating the French development. Ruge's political agenda had the social-democratic state as its paradigm of the true political form of humanism. In that kind of society, human beings (even Negroes!) would be equal not only before God but before the law.[50] Ruge's social democratic state is

---

47. Löwith, *From Hegel to Nietzsche*, 339.

48. Lichtheim, *Marxism*, 16.

49. Marx and Engels, *Economic and Philosophic Manuscripts*.

50. Löwith, *The Young Hegelians: An Anthology*, 312.

contrary to Feuerbach's sentimental, private notion of Christianity, and it is far from Hegel's *Philosophy of Right* (§190), which grants humanity only to the bourgeois society. Ruge's political form of true humanity is color-proof: "Do you believe that Negroes are human beings? You in Germany probably believe it, for you do not have any Negroes, but there are plenty of men who deny it, namely, those who have Negroes."[51]

For Ruge, philosophy and revolution went hand in hand. To quote just one example, he together with the Young Hegelians was at odds with the "born-again" Schelling. In his "A Self-Critique of Liberalism," Ruge stamped his impressions: "The most frightening example of philosophical self-seeking, of self-praise, of bitterness about someone else's conclusions, and of total hollowness and depravity in egoistic attempts at brilliance is so famous that I would be superfluous in making a celebrity still more renowned."[52] Ruge and the Young Hegelians in general opposed the separation between church and state because, in their opinion, it encouraged escape from the world. Kierkegaard has been charged for his distinction between his otherworldly impulse and inner-worldly strain, but the core of the matter consisted in the fact that scholars fail to distinguish at least two Kierkegaards. The late one is clearly combating the absolutization of the state in detriment to religion, or the religion that has been taken in tow by the state: "What Christianity needs is not the suffocating protection of the State; no, it needs fresh air, it needs persecution, and it needs . . . God's protection" (AUC, 140). Before God, then, for Kierkegaard means that this relationship has a priority before any form of collective or institutionalized form which holds absolute claims. But from that does not follow the *fuga mundi*.

Max Stirner (1806–1856)

Much of what has been associated with Søren Kierkegaard's thought[53] is more accurately related with Johann Caspar Schmidt, whose *nom*

---

51. *Unser System*, III, 85–86; cited in ibid.

52. Stepelevich, *The Young Hegelians: An Anthology*, 255.

53. Kirmmse has persuasively argued that Hans Christian Andersen's bitter tale "The Snail and the Rosebush" ["Sneglen og Rosenhækken"] has contributed to this portrait of Kierkegaard. Here Kierkegaard is forced to assert: "The world does not concern me! What do I have to do with the world? I have enough with myself and enough in myself." Or still again: "I am retreating into myself, and there I will remain" Kirmmse, "A Rose with Thorns," 69–70).

de guerre (pseudonym) was Max Stirner, the promoter of a society of "isolated individuals": "the divine is God's concern; the human, man's. My concern is neither the divine nor the human, nor the true, good, just, free, etc., but solely what is *mine*, and it is not a general one, but is unique (*einzig*), as I am unique. Nothing is more to me than myself."[54] He heard Schelling in 1827 in Berlin. After that, he studied in Erlangen, Königsberg, and again in Berlin. In 1841 he became a member of the *Freien* (Young Hegelians). He lost his teaching job and ended up in a life of poverty, marginalized because of his radical ideas.

His name is associated with an anarchic subjectivity. His point of departure was the "naked I," i.e., himself. He asserts in *Kleine Schriften* (369) that the meaning of life has to be found in his own individual self. His chief categories are the private individual and private property. His solipsistic position, then, has also the distinctive note of a radical bourgeois perspective, as Brazill has highlighted: "What Stirner frees himself from is not real conditions of existence, but merely conditions of consciousness which he himself cannot see through because he is engrossed in private egoism as the principle of bourgeois society."[55] His rejection of any kind of social restraints was expressed in his *Der Einzige und sein Eigenthum* [*The Individual and His Rights* or *The Unique and His Property*] (1845):

> Because Christianity, incapable of letting the individual count as an ego, (*Einzige*), thought of him only as a dependent, and was properly nothing but a *social theory*—a doctrine of living together, and that of man with God as of man with man—therefore in it everything 'own' must fall into most woeful disrepute: selfishness, self-will, ownness, self-love, and the like.[56]

Karl Schmidt

If Johann Casper Schmidt was an extreme individualist, then Karl Schmidt was the only one who went beyond Johann Casper, as he showed in his enclosure in the cocoon, i.e., in his desert of egoism:

---

54. Stepelevich, *The Young Hegelians: An Anthology*, 337.

55. Brazill, *The Young Hegelians*, 248.

56. Stepelevich, *The Young Hegelians: An Anthology*, 348.

If someone has once heard of Hegel, he must proceed to Strauss, from Strauss to Feuerbach, from Feuerbach to Bruno Bauer. I accomplished the consequence of this thought in myself, but soon came to the further conclusion . . . that Stirner makes more sense than Bruno Bauer and that one must proceed beyond Stirner to arrive at the most abstract individualism.[57]

Schmidt was studying in Halle in 1841 when through his reading of *Das Leben Jesu*, he changed religion for humanism. In 1844 he joined the Young Hegelians in Berlin, and in 1846 he published his *Das Verstandestum und das Individuum*. However, by 1862, with his three volumes of *History of Pedagogy* he broke with the Young Hegelians.

Karl Marx (1818–1883)

Marx became a member of the "Doctors Club" in 1837. He was a student of Bruno Bauer. He had the same fate as his colleagues: he was not able to get a post at Bonn, and due to his unconventional thought he had to flee to Paris, Brussels, and London.[58]

By the year 1845 in his *Theses on Feuerbach*, specifically in thesis eleven, Marx conceived religious criticism as prior to all criticism of society. But for him, religion and its disease could not be removed by simple recognition; political action was needed. Therefore, he himself moved in that direction, and by 1867 he delivered his *Das Kapital*. In this work, he shows the nature of his "atheism," which fights against the "fetish-nature" of merchandise. He denounced it as one of the capitalist idols that reduces humans to mere things.[59] In his *Selected Works*, Marx branded the Young Hegelians as "sheep in wolves' clothing" because he perceived in their "atheism" the result of a bourgeois Christendom.

---

57. Ibid., 379.

58. At this point it is interesting to hear Toews's reading. He argues that in order to do justice to the left Hegelians, one needs to take into account the whole evolution of Hegelianism. His point consists in stating that the ideological discrepancies of both parties were related to the lower academic status of the Young Hegelians, which, in fact, was but an example of the social and political problems of the society at large. According to Toews, the young Hegelians as *privatdozenten* (unsalaried lecturers) or as expelled from the Academia radicalized their political, religious, educational views in front of the Old Hegelians who represented the establishment: "The failure to obtain secure academic positions was a significant factor in the transformation of some of the Younger Hegelians into radical cultural critics" (Toews, *Hegelianism*, 216).

59. Löwith, *From Hegel to Nietzsche*, 354.

As a Young Hegelian, Marx reacted against his master, Hegel, as well. In the introduction of *A Contribution to the Critique of Hegelian Philosophy of Right* (1842), he rejected the Hegelian melting of religion and society: "The wretchedness of religion is at once an expression of and a protest against real wretchedness. Religion is the sigh of the oppressed creature, the heart of a heartless world and the soul of soulless conditions. It is the opium of the people."[60] Marx "turned the criticism of heaven into a criticism of earth; the criticism of religion into a criticism of right and the criticism of theology into a criticism of politics."[61]

Marx took from Hegel and from the "Free Ones" (the Young Hegelians) the humanistic element: "The only practically possible emancipation of Germany is the emancipation based on the unique theory which holds that man is the supreme being for man."[62] Nevertheless, contrary to all of them, he added specific elements to the social critique: "Philosophy cannot be actualized without the abolition [*Aufhebung*] of the proletariat; the proletariat cannot be abolished without the actualization of philosophy."[63]

Friedrich Engels (1820–1895)

In Barmen, Engels's hometown, as well as in Manchester, Friedrich Engels became aware of the harsh circumstances of the industrial proletariat. He joined the Young Hegelian club in 1841. Through his reading of Strauss he arrived at Hegel. In 1841, under the strong influence of Feuerbach's *Wessen des Christentums,* he broke with the Christian church and with religion in general: "You should have experienced personally the liberating effect of this book in order to have a conception of it. The enthusiasm was universal: suddenly we all became Feuerbachians."[64]

He wrote three critical essays against Schelling and at the beginning endorsed a reform-minded economist position, as he published his *Umrisse zur einer Kritik der Nationalökonomie (Outlines of a Critique of the Political Economy)* (1843).

60. Stepelevich, *Young Hegelians: An Anthology,* 310.

61. Ibid., 311.

62. Ibid., 321–22.

63. Ibid., 322.

64. *Marx-Engels Werke* 21:272, 283–86.

In 1844 Engels had an encounter with Marx in Paris and established a permanent friendship. Between 1845 and 1846 both wrote *The German Ideology*, which signified their break with Bauer and their attempt to overcome Hegel's philosophy, by addressing the German ideology as it was interrelated with German reality more than with absolute knowledge and Hegel's Idea. In this respect, Engels made a significant contribution in defining German ideology (*ideo–legein* = I saw it, I say) as the bourgeois ideology, which tries to hide reality and ends up being alienated from reality. It is a "false conscience" that legitimizes social reality.

Engels collaborated with Ruge to write *Deutsche Jahrbücher* and with Marx's *Rheinischen Zeitung* and other works.

Friedrich Wilhelm Joseph von Schelling (1775–1854)

The old Schelling was hired by the new government with a huge salary of 4,000 thalers, as the person capable of "combating the dragon-seed of Hegelian pantheism."[65] This Senior Governmental Privy Councilor (*Geheimerat*) occupied Hegel's chair of philosophy from 1841 up until 1846. Among the audience were Engels, Feuerbach, Burckhardt, Bakunin, et al. [66] and on November 15, 1841, Marx and Kierkegaard shared the same crowded auditorium.[67]

One chief controversy that was at stake addressed the wide ugly ditch between whatness (*Was-sein*), what it is, and thatness (*Dass-Sein*), facticity. Starting with Descartes, the problem was solved with the unification of being through reason. Consequently, Hegel's negative philosophy sustained that it is only through reason that one can comprehend reality, and the act was possible only in the concept. Schelling combated the principle of the rationality of reality in German classical idealism. In accordance with such a principle, there is an idealistic identity between being and concept, or between the real and the logical. In Schelling's words, Hegel made a fool of himself in identifying the logical

65. Noack, *Philosophie)geschichliches Lexikon*, 782. Quoted in Heiss, *Hegel, Kierkegaard, and Marx*, 188.

66. Schelling's lectures of 1841 included two sections: "Philosophy of Mythology" and "Philosophy of Revelation." The former consisted of forty-one sessions. Kierkegaard listened to only the first 36, writing a careful synopsis of them (Bykhovskii, *Kierkegaard*, 2ff).

67. Garff, *Søren Kierkegaard: A Biography*, 209.

with the actual.[68] According to Schelling, "Pure being is in fact nothing, just as whiteness does not exist without a white object."[69] Hegel's mere potentiality for being, in contrast to reality, transforms the real into a "wasteland of being," "pure thinking" is "pure potentiality." Or in Kierkegaard's words, "a pure I is a mere tautology" (CUP 211–12). In his thirteenth lecture, Schelling criticizes speculative philosophy because of the main Hegelian mistake of pretending to be a Christian philosopher, or in Thulstrup's formulation: "Hegel's God as spirit comes about only when the whole development is completed, *post festum*. God is for Hegel, mistakenly, a conclusion, not a point of departure."[70]

Schelling's Berlin lectures marked the end of German classical idealism. Hegel's teaching about essence was counteracted by Schelling's philosophical teaching about being or existence (JP, 5536). However, at the same time as the speeches, the conquest of German classical idealism was indicated through the beginning of a new era: the anti-Schelling utterances of Feuerbach, Engels, Marx, and Kierkegaard.[71]

Denmark, Hegel, and Kierkegaard

Prior to 1835, Søren Kierkegaard started getting a secondhand knowledge about the great German philosopher.[72] Nevertheless, one must hasten to add that the Dane soon became acquainted with the primary sources, mastering them as one can see in his corpus.[73] Kierkegaard learned a great deal of his philosophical and technical terminology from his great, respected "Master Hegel." However, from the outset Kierkegaard raised strong criticism against "the System," and he never

68. Lecture 10, in ibid., 8.

69. Schelling *Werke*, Part I, Vol. 10, 212ff. Cited in Löwith, *From Hegel to Nietzsche*, 117.

70. Thulstrup, *Kierkegaard's Relation to Hegel*, 272.

71. Bykhovskii, *Søren Kierkegaard: A Biography*, 15.

72. Thulstrup, *Kierkegaard's Relation to Hegel*, 56–57.

73. "The many quotations and allusions, shows that he particularly, intensively and with never-slackening critical attention read in the seventeen whole volumes, in *Phenomenology of the Spirit*, in *The Science of Logic*, in both the little *Philosophische Propädeutik* and the large *Encyclopedia of the Philosophical Sciences*, in the *Philosophy of Right*, in the *Lectures on Fine Art*, on *Philosophy of Religion*, on the *Philosophy of History* and on the *History of Philosophy*. Only the section on the philosophy on nature in the *Encyclopedia* seems to have left no mark on Kierkegaard" (ibid., 380).

considered himself Hegel's disciple.[74] In fact, this highly gifted Dane has "the System" as his target throughout his work. He developed the literary genres of parable, fable, short story, anecdote, allegory, and fairy tale with that purpose in mind:[75] "The form of the Story is to be used as a weapon against the system" (Pap. IV, B 1).

Kierkegaard became familiar with Hegelianism during his years of studies at the University of Copenhagen. In 1834–1835, Kierkegaard started reading Hegel's most prestigious heir: Philipp Konrad Marheineke (1780–1846). Kierkegaard had some entries in his *Journals* related to the work *Grundlehren der christlichen Dogmatik als Wissenschaft.*[76] It is likely that Kierkegaard heard Marheineke for the first time in 1836 when the German visited the University of Copenhagen and took part in the celebration of the three-hundredth anniversary of the Reformation.[77] Furthermore, Marheineke's work *History of the Reformation* was the first book from which Kierkegaard elaborated a report as a student (Pap. I C i). In 1841 Kierkegaard attended Marheineke's lectures on dogmatic theology delivered in Berlin: *Einleitung in die Öffentlichen Vorlesungen über die Bedeutung der Hegelschen Philosophie in der christlichen Theologie.* And, in fairness to Marheineke, Kierkegaard's appreciation must be mentioned: "I have begun to attend lectures. I heard one by Marheineke with which I was quite pleased, for although it did not contain anything new, it was very nice to hear much of what one is accustomed to see in print."[78]

Kierkegaard heard and read the theologians and liberal politicians H. N. Clausen and M. H. Hohlenberg. Both were the editors of *Tidskrift for Udenlandsk Theologisk Litteratur* (*Journal of Foreign Theological Literature*). In 1836 they translated chief passages of Strauss's *Das Leben Jesu.* Kierkegaard also had a subscription to Bauer's *Zeitschrift*

---

74. "Already in the youthful entries he pours irony down upon Hegel and the Hegelians and the Hegelian cud-chewing process with the three stomachs." Brandt, *Den unge Søren Kierkegaard,* 353. Quoted in Thulstrup, *Kierkegaard's Relation to Hegel,* 113 n. 42.

75. See Bjerg, "Kierkegaard's Story-Telling," 111–25.

76. *Fundamental Doctrine of Christian Dogmatics as Science.* Cf. Thulstrup, *Kierkegaard's Relation to Hegel,* 49 (Pap. I C 25, 9; I A 273).

77. Thulstrup, *Kierkegaard's Relation to Hegel,* 50.

78. Letter to Emil Boesen, October 31, 1841, in Kierkegaard, *Letters and Documents,* 90.

fur Spekulative Theologie where Schaller raised many objections to *Das Leben Jesu* (Pap. III C 54ff. XIII 167–68).

As early as 1832, Kierkegaard paid private tutoring to Martensen, who introduced him to Schleiermacher's dogmatics. Later on, the ship captain's son established himself as the main Danish Hegelian Professor of "the System." Martensen studied for two years in different European universities; at his return to Denmark, he was Heiberg's and Mynster's protégé and a leading figure of Danish Hegelianism. In November of 1837, Kierkegaard registered in his course: "Forelæsninger over Indledning til den spekulative Dogmatik" (Lectures on Introduction to Speculative Dogmatics).[79] Nonetheless, it was not until 1849 that the aristocratic Martensen published his *Christian Dogmatics,* whose original title was *Speculative Dogmatics,* in which the future bishop of Denmark attacked the Young Hegelians and claimed to "go beyond Hegel."

In the same year, 1837, Kierkegaard heard the presentation of *The Speculative Logic* by the other renowned Danish Hegelian: Heiberg (Pap. II C 37) (JP, 193). Heiberg had already published his famous *On the Significance of Philosophy for the Present Time* (1833). And in June of 1837 he started publishing his *Perseus, Journal for den Speculative Idee,* to which Kierkegaard was a subscriber. Heiberg, who visited Hegel at his home in Berlin in 1824, introduced Hegel's philosophy in Denmark. He was a playwright, critic, translator, and the director and top figure of the Danish Royal Theater for half a century. He married Johanne Louise (1812–1890), the most famous actress in Denmark, and one to whom Kierkegaard dedicated his *The Crisis and a Crisis in the Life of an Actress.* Heiberg held a doctorate in Spanish Literature from the University of Copenhagen.[80]

Søren Kierkegaard's first study trip to Berlin took place from October 1841 to March 6, 1842. In December he attended Karl Werder's lectures on "Logic and Metaphysics." Kierkegaard did not write down many comments (Pap., III C 28, 29, 30) (JP, 5537, I 257) because he had

79. Thulstrup, *Kierkegaard's Relation to Hegel*, 196, 157, 133.

80. As a significant observation, Heiberg's review of Lope de Vega's *The King and the Peasant* was the occasion for his "classical and most articulated Golden Age defense of absolutism." Obviously, Heiberg ignored Lope de Vega's play *Fuenteovejuna* (*All Are One*) where he encourages solidarity to the whole population before the tyrant Don Fernández Gómez (González, *Mañana*, 28) Cf. Kirmmse, *Kierkegaard,* 160 and 165ff.

already taken a course on the same topic in Denmark. It was Frederick Christian Sibbern (1785–1872), his University of Copenhagen professor and walking companion, who delivered that course, based on his *Logik som Tænkelære* (*Logic as Doctrine of Thinking*).

Immediately after finishing his dissertation, Kierkegaard made a four-month trip to Berlin in order to listen to Schelling's lectures on positive philosophy. The Dane followed with interest Schelling's first lectures (III A 179 n.d., 1841) (JP, 5535) although later he stopped attending (JP, 5552). In the book he was writing in Berlin, Kierkegaard faulted Hegelianism with remaining too abstract:

> What the philosophers say about reality [*Virkelighed*] is often just as disappointing as it is when one reads on a sign in a secondhand shop: "Pressing Done Here." If a person were to bring his clothes to be pressed, he would be duped, for the sign is merely for sale. (EO/I, 32)

Faced with that reduction of the Christian faith by the professors, Kierkegaard raised his ironic voice:

> When Christianity came into the world there were no professors and *privatdocents* at all; then it was a paradox for everyone. In the present generation it may be assumed that one out of every ten is a *Privatdocent*; hence Christianity is a paradox for nine out of ten. And when finally the fullness of time arrives, that extraordinary future when an entire generation of male and female *Privatdocents* peoples the earth, then Christianity will have ceased to be a paradox. (CUP 198)

Kierkegaard's Social Philosophy

Kierkegaard did not seek to isolate the concrete self; rather he wanted to strengthen human beings in order to face the gigantic power of the leveling of the masses, which subsumes the individual.[81]

In 1847 Kierkegaard deliberately counteracted his supposedly asocial position, writing in his own name his *Works of Love*: "You should love your neighbor" (*WL* 79). There he is proposing an ethico-religious-dialogic love before God. In the relationship where God is the middle term, the neighbor is neither the first I nor the other I but the first you,

---

81. Cf. Weiss, "The Leveling Process as a Function of the Masses in the View of Kierkegaard and Ortega y Gasset," 7, 22–36.

or the first person you see (70). "To love those one sees" is in fact the title of his fourth chapter. God and the neighbor are two doors we must open simultaneously: "The matter is quite simple. The human being should begin by loving the invisible God, for hereby he himself shall learn what is to love. But the fact that he then really loves the invisible shall be indicated precisely by this that he loves the brother he sees" (158). On the other hand, Kierkegaard's individualism is neither compositional nor bourgeois but dialectical:[82] "The Dialectic of Community or Society is as follows. . . . The individual is primarily related to God and then to the community, but this primary relation is the highest, yet it does not neglect the second" (Pap. VII 1 A 20, n. d.,1846) (JP, 4110).

Kierkegaard shared with Hegel (via the Young Hegelians) the emphasis on humanism, based on commitment to human beings as opposed to a mere sentimental act of charity. Now, Kierkegaard's love is neither a platonic nor an idealized nor "natural but a paradoxical love"[83]; it is the result of a divine commandment: "You should love your neighbor"; it is "scandal for the Jews and . . . gentiles"; in short, it is Christian humanism.

Kierkegaard methodologically made the distinction between Christianity (Christendom) and Christendom (Christenhed).[84] Instead of fleeing from the world or legitimizing the status quo, Christianity has to play a prophetic role. Starting in 1843 and through his category of paradox, Kierkegaard articulated his critique of society. For him, "The paradox of faith is this, that the individual is higher than the universal, that the individual . . . determines his relation to the universal by his relation to the absolute, not his relation to the absolute by his relation to the universal" (FT 70). Kierkegaard opposed the glorification of the state, the society, or the universal by reminding the individual that God is the only Absolute.[85]

Our prophetic thinker, on the other hand, was also aware of the humanitarian emphasis of some left-wing Hegelians. Nonetheless, in contradistinction to them, he perceived how from the speculative dei-

---

82. Cf. Westphal, *Kierkegaard's Critique of Reason and Society*, 33.

83. Valls, "Amar o Belo—Amar o Feio—Amar o Pobre," 111.

84. Søren Kierkegaard used the German-Scandinavian word *Christenheit/ Christenhed* which means *orbis christianus* or *corpus christianum* when he referred to a Christian country (SV XIII 564, PV 22).

85. Cf. Westphal, *Kierkegaard's Critique*, 77ff.

fication of humans followed the apotheosis of the same. Furthermore, Kierkegaard warned us in a timely way of the dangers of the tyranny of humanity's fear (*Menneske frygtens tyrannie*). Kierkegaard was a sharp observer of the epoch-making events taking place in his country and in Europe. For instance, in 1849 (JP, 6307) he denounced how *vox populi* was equated with *vox dei* and then became a slippery slogan. In his opinion, the rebellion of the masses was justifying any crime committed in the name of the people. In 1853 (JP, 2046, 2047) Kierkegaard continued insisting that the motto *vox populi vox dei* was being used in order to disregard human responsibility into the manipulation of the masses.[86]

Decide to Decide

Søren Kierkegaard is so attractive, in effect, because as the first quotation of this subsection tells us, the Danish gadfly forces us to take sides and to act. He criticized the philosophical stream that assumed an aesthetic position of mere intellectual contemplation without the commitment to action. This was the attitude of people whose decision (*beslutning*) consisted of "choosing not to choose." He rejected the systems that divorce dogma from ethics, doctrine from discipleship, faith from action, and thought from existence. In effect, *Practice in Christianity*, *Works of Love*, his *Journals*, and his religious writings provide objective examples of Kierkegaard's positive constructive criticism of society.

Søren Kierkegaard's leap of faith displays the Dane's dialectical thought in which he understands knowing and doing in a dynamic way. Kierkegaard did not subscribe to the motto *prorsus credibile est, quia ineptum est* ("it is by all means to be believed, because it is absurd"). On the contrary, the leap is his term for decision or choice. The transition from thought to action is possible through the Dane's leap of faith or through Niebuhr's "Leap from the chair"[87] moving in the moment from

---

86. Currently we can realize the great relevance of Kierkegaard's warning in our idolatry of the market, which equates the voice of the market with God's voice: "the paradise previously expected to come by divine action mediated through the church, is now expected to come as a result of progress. In the capitalist world this redeeming progress is expected to come about through the market. That is why the market, the new foundation of society, claims for itself the characteristic of the sacred" (Sung, *Desire, Market, and Religion*, 43).

87. Niebuhr, *Christ and Culture*, 233.

insight to decision; or through Sobrino's "Leap of faith" as an experience of rupture from a historical statement to a doxological statement about God; or from the historical partisan Jesus to the eschatological poor human being Jesus.[88]

The jump of faith refers to the transition from one sphere to the other. By living in the aesthetic stage, the Hegelian philosophers, had chosen not to choose, and if they really wanted to become themselves, they needed to make the leap, i.e., the dialecticity between will and intellect.

> A thinker erects a huge building, a system, a system embracing the whole of existence, world history, etc., and if his personal life is considered, to our amazement the appalling and ludicrous discovery is made that he himself does not personally live in this huge, domed palace but in a shed alongside it, or in a dog-house, or at best in the janitor's quarters. (SUD, 43–44)

In contradistinction, we realize the correlation between Kierkegaard's thought and his life as it is reported in his *Journals*.

In Judge William, the prototype of the ethical sphere, the alienated self becomes a true self. However, in pursuing the religious sphere represented by Abraham, he has to recur to the leap of faith. Precisely because in reaching the religious sphere—with its categories of forgiveness and sin—one transcends the ethical sphere. Nevertheless, the ethical demands are not canceled; therefore that tension produces anguish and guilt. The leap of faith, then, tells us there is no continuity between thought and faith, between doctrine and faith, between moral actions and faith. The transition is not automatic; the leap with fear and trembling is the way.

Miranda's introductory citation of this subsection tells us about Kierkegaard's radical realism, which raises ironic objections against the realism built on changeless, static realms of objective reality. In Miranda's view: "the true God has no connection with ontology (the true God is not *a* being nor *the* being nor the *supreme* being); *rather* God is identified with the ethical imperative."[89] The Dane's existentialism searched to know reality but not from the serene Cartesian mathematical mind. Miranda argues quite the opposite: Kierkegaard approached reality with

88. Sobrino, *Christology at the Crossroads*, 324.

89. Miranda, *Being and the Messiah*, 28.

a guilty conscience, with concern, and with the moral imperative that forces us to make a decision.[90]

Life is not something to be avoided; as ethical beings and as beings of option, we have to decide, and in deciding we learn to decide: "decide, break, opt."[91]

Theory and Practice

Kierkegaard's dictum "Livet kan kun forståes baglæns—men det må leves forlæns" ("Life can only be understood backwards, but it must be lived forwards.") (Pap. IV A 164 n.d., 1843) (JP, 1030)[92] points toward his philosophy that begins from practice and no longer from the Cartesian *cogito ergo sum*. Kierkegaard aspired to elucidate reality by means of Schelling's positive theology, which started from existence, from immediate being to thought. This is compatible with the Latin dictum *Primum vivere, deinde philosophare* ("To live first, and to philosophize later") or the still more radical *Primum est edere, deinde philosophare* ("To eat first, and to philosophize later"), where there is a reciprocation between theory and practice.[93]

Similarly, in commenting on Kierkegaard's *Works of Love*, Álvaro L. M. Valls, a Kierkegaardian from Brazil, has rightly pointed out: "The never-ending problem of the Danish thinker was the one of '*Virklighed*,' (reality) which gives his work the conquering of a realistic dimension, or we could even say: materialistic."[94] Contrary to popular belief, according to this scholar, the Dane introduced a powerful, realistic, and even materialistic dimension, underlining an intentionally sensorial criterion: "to love means to commit oneself with this man that 'I see,' and it seems as though this formula is very well chosen when it says 'this man that I see', while simultaneously collaborating with the creation and salvation work."[95]

---

90. Ibid., 5, 16.

91. Cf. Freire, *Pedagogía de la autonomía*, 41, 69.

92. Alastair McKinnon helped me find this reference.

93. Following the formula of St. Anselm, *credo ut intelligam* (we believe in order that we may understand), Gutiérrez arrived at similar conclusions. The locus of reflection is a second stage of theological enterprise due to the fact that faith comes first and the discourse about God comes second (Gutiérrez, *A Theology of Liberation*, xxxiii).

94. Valls, "Amar o Belo ," 112–13.

95. Ibid.

In Enrique Dussel's opinion, Schelling lectured on the philosophy of revelation (i.e., the Christian Revelation); consequently, *der Herr des Seins* [the Lord of being] is God, as opposed to the being *to óv*: "beyond the dialectic ontology of being and thought there is the positivity of what is unthinkable."[96] With the negation of Hegelian ontology, Dussel continues, takes place a critique of the divinized European civilization, which, with its *"ergo cogito,"* "is located at the 'center' of an imperial world as *rational* domination of the 'colonies' (the periphery)."[97] The Other, Dussel adds, is prior to the very principle of the cosmos, the System. Dussel credited Kierkegaard with being the founder of the "prehistory of Latin American Philosophy and the immediate antecedent of our new Latin American thinking."[98] Since for the Dane the absurd is not something without reason or fundament [*Grundlos*] but the supreme rebinding to the Other and the acceptance of his exteriority to any speculation, then the metaphysical (transontological) overture to the Other has overcome the ontological horizon (the System): "Beyond the horizon of being as thinking or as universal ethical norm there is the reality of the Other who is able to discover what it is, not against reason but beyond its possibilities."[99]

The wide, ugly ditch between whatness and thatness, on the other hand, has a direct connection with the horrible gap between knowing and believing. In this respect, Kierkegaard's concept of absurdity acquires quite a different meaning. The wholly other is not beyond the present reality but in clear contradiction with it.[100] Now the Other has been mediated in those who have reality beyond the system of the totality: the poor, women in many cases, the poor countries, etc. Kierkegaard, in this sense, was an authentic critic of dominant European thought:

> But no, it is not necessary to say that he had this notion, it might even be possible that he was the "gadfly" which the established order had need of to keep it from falling asleep, or, what is still worse, from falling into self-deification. Every individual ought to live in fear and trembling, and so too there is no established order which can do without fear and trembling. (TC 89)

96. Dussel, *Método para una filosofía de la liberación*, 176.

97. Ibid., 131.

98. Ibid., 176.

99. Ibid., 154.

100. Cf. Sobrino, *Resurrección de la verdadera iglesia*, 43.

Economic, Religious, and Social Landscape

> Marry a rich girl, play the lottery, *travel to the colonies*, spend a
> few years scraping money together, insinuate yourself into the
> good graces of an old bachelor so that he will make you his heir.
> (EO/II, 278, italics mine)

Kierkegaard's Denmark of the mid-nineteenth century has to be addressed within the broader scope of the world organization; that is, in the geopolitical perspective of the slave trade. It is granted that the connection between Kierkegaard, the Danish colonies, and Denmark is a virgin field. However, from that does not follow that the peripheral territorial possessions did not play an important role in the economy of continental Denmark. In fact, the imperial nations have been intentional in hiding the ugly side of their imperialist enterprises.[101] However, my goal in this segment is more modest.[102] My aim consists merely of providing more historic, economic, and geographical data that will throw light on the relationship between economics, the West Indies, the slave trade, and Danish society. This will enhance our reading of Kierkegaard from the economic point of view and within the general subject of the attack upon Christendom.

La Belle Epoque

> "The State's general interests are more closely linked with the
> welfare of the company." —Schimmelmann[103]

Particularly in the years 1787–1807 the future king Frederick VI promoted significant agricultural reforms, and the peasants started achieving their independence from landowners. However, the situation changed due to the neutral policy of Denmark during the French

---

101. For a current geopolitical action in favor of the poor, see Vigil, *¿Qué es optar por los pobres?* 123: "[we] should not accept any longer to live disoriented, without geopolitical co-ordinates, but to orientate our own life, our work, our profession, our heart, our interests, our solidarity ... with an accurate compass that constantly points towards the South of the poor. That always points towards the concrete field of geopolitical co-ordinates, never towards the clouds of the abstract universality indifferent to the concrete historical space and time."

102. See Appendix A for a longer treatment of Denmark's geopolitics.

103. He means his company: Feldbaek, "Organization and Structure of the Danish East India, West India and Guinea Companies in the 17th and 18th Centuries," 135.

Revolutionary wars. The years between 1801 and 1807 marked the greatest flourishing of commercial business of Copenhagen with France in the Napoleonic Wars. But on August 16, 1807, since Denmark refused to join an alliance against France in the Gunboat War, England bombarded and burned a considerable part of Copenhagen. In October of the same year, the British closed the era of the Danish fleet. Ernst Schimmelman, the finance minister, put into circulation no backing banknotes. In 1812, Sweden, Russia, and England gave Denmark one more opportunity to join them against Napoleon, but the Danes refused. As a consequence of ill-oriented diplomacy, in 1813, the government of Denmark declared bankruptcy. That same year when Kierkegaard was born, the fake banknotes were worth only one-sixth of the value of genuine bank notes. In 1814 Denmark lost Norway at the Congress of Vienna. The next years saw the decline of the famous Danish shipping industry. The former progressive young prince Frederick, sympathetic with the peasants' cause, by between 1815 and 1830 became the conservative, aging, and autocratic king opposed to any kind of reforms and stubborn in his absolutist position. In spite of this, in the late 1820s due to the rise of the price of grain, the peasant movement achieved a new impact in its task of economic freedom. The 1830s saw the religious revival of the peasantry, the emergence of the Danish liberal movement, and the national issue of a separatist movement involving the German- and Danish-speaking populations of southern Jutland. These movements eventually exploded into the 1848 revolution, which in turn helped bring about the 1849 constitution.

The Golden Age refers to the development of the arts and culture of a very select group from the capital. In Copenhagen there existed a tremendous gap between the poor and the rich. At the same time, there was a gap between the city and the countryside, and also between metropolitan Denmark and the Danish West Indies.

The Atlantic slave trade was important for Golden Age Denmark. To mention just one case, Count Ernst Schimmelmann, the Danish finance minister, who was the owner of a large plantation and a slave trader, was known as the patron of poets such as the Danish romantic Adam Gottlob Oehlenschläger, the German Enlightenment scholar Friedrich Schiller,[104] and other figures such as Jens Baggesen, K. L. Rahbek, and

---

104. Green-Pedersen, "Economic Consideration behind the Danish Abolition of the Negro Slave Trade," 403 n. 2.

Friedrich Gottlieb Klopstock (JP, vol. 5 473, n. 116.). Oehlenschläger was in fact Denmark's prominent poet and founder of the golden age in literature. He was also the brother-in-law of A. S. Ørsted, who will be identified later, and brother-in-law to the wife of K. L. Rahbek, the doyen of Danish literary criticism of the end of the eighteenth century.

Henrich Carl von Schimmelmann bought the Royal plantations and slave holdings on the islands of St. Croix, St. Thomas, and St. John in April 1763. In 1782 Count Ernst von Schimmelmann (1747–1831) inherited all and continued the tradition of being a typical European absentee landlord but added to his possessions his sugar refineries in Copenhagen. Ernst von Schimmelmann became *Generalgouvernør* (governor general) of the Danish West Indies two years later and justified slavery by quoting the conventional idea that Africans were a stiff-necked race that could only be governed by the threat of severe punishment.[105] Nevertheless, the scientific acceptance of racial inferiority and the scientific blessing of slavery were already provided by the Swede, Carolus Linneaus. He described the four races accordingly: *Homo Americanus* as tenacious, contented, free, and ruled by custom; *Homo Eurpoaeus* as light, lively, inventive, and ruled by rites; *Homo Asiaticus* as stern, haughty, stingy, and ruled by opinion; and *Homo Afer* as cunning, slow, negligent, and ruled by caprice.[106]

Hong has blamed Henrich Ernst von Schimmelmann for being "culpable for the bankruptcy of the Danish government in 1813" (JP, *Vol. 5*, 473, n. 116). However we know that King Frederik VI bore the main responsibility for that.

There were many other persons linked with the Danish Enlightenment who had connections with the West Indies and the slave trade: merchant Christian D. Reventlow, and the very governor general of St. Croix, Ernst von Wanterstorff (1781–1796), who, after finishing his period in the West Indies, became the director of the *Kongelige Teater* (Royal Theater).[107]

105. *Rigsarkivet, Copenhaguen. Forslag og Anmærkninger til Negerloven med Genparter af Anordinger og Publikationer vedkommende Negervæsenet*, 1785. Quoted in Hall, *Slave Society*, 37.

106. Barzun, *Race: A Study in Superstition*, 45; cited in Stroupe and Fleming, *While We Run this Race: Confronting the power of racism in a Southern Church*, 21.

107. Quoted in Hall, *Slave Society*, 17.

Anders Sandøe Ørsted (1778–1860), the Danish privy councilor and celebrated jurist, played a significant role in slave trading. As late as 1802, he helped pass a verdict that allowed the export of an African slave from Denmark.[108] In the same year, he witnessed the emergence of a new law that fought *marronage* (runaway slaves): "After 1802, Denmark ruled itself out as a haven for escapees. A supreme court decision that year in the case of the slave Hans Jonathan decreed that the free soil of the mother country did not confer freedom on the enslaved."[109] Ørsted used to cite Roman and Nordic ancient natural laws in order to legitimize servitude and slavery.[110] He concluded that in the West Indies a free person who killed a slave was not guilty of capital offense.[111] The future (1842) Danish prime minister, Ørsted paid the Danish West Indies islands a visit in 1843–1844.[112]

During the first half of the nineteenth century A. S. Ørsted was also the most influential member of the royal cabinet. This founder of Danish-Norwegian jurisprudence also triumphed in placing Hans Lassen Martensen, the son of a ship captain in Flensborg, on the chair of the bishop of Zealand. It was not until he [Ørsted] was removed from his influential position, held from April 1853 until December 1854, that Kierkegaard addressed his thunder against the state church.[113]

A Prophetic Type of Christianity

> Nor was there anyone even far beyond the confines of Denmark who would attack, as radically as Kierkegaard did, the popular political-religious paradigm of State, church, and society, thereby risking the ultimate, even his own personal existence.[114]

Recently a Kierkegaard scholar from Canada, Abrahim Khan, has equated Kierkegaard with Gandhi and Gustavo Gutiérrez as a promoter of a prophetic type of Christianity with its cardinal feature of fearless

108. Green-Pedersen, "The Economic Considerations," 402 n. 1.

109. Ørsted, "Beholdes Herredømmet over en vestindisk Slave, naar han betræder dansk-europæisk Grund," 459–85. Quoted by Hall, 394.

110. Ibid., 34ff.

111. Ibid., 36.

112. Curtin, *Atlantic Slave Trade: A Census*, 46.

113. Kirmmse, *Kierkegaard*, 185, 189. Much of the material of this section has been taken from Kirmmse's *Kierkegaard*.

114. Kung and Jens, *Literature and Religion*, 193.

criticism of the existing order: "the religion of the solitary individual, an ideal type neither becomes institutionalized as do sectarian movements headed by charismatic leaders often become nor issues in the formation of a movement or a following."[115] Khan mentions the figure of the gadfly which irritates the self-complacency of the established order and keeps the political order under suspicion witnessing to a higher reality: "When a gadfly appears to remind that the individual is higher than the established order, there is an inevitable collision."[116]

The Dane thus embraces the Protestant principle as Tillich understood it: "a prophetic denunciation of a sacralized secular order,"[117] which in fact implies "an attitude of permanent vigilance against ideology that can be either secular or sacred."[118] We can clearly see how the Dane is promoting a prophet-king dialectic of alterity-totality, of God's justice and a fetishist system. Little wonder Kierkegaard provoked these words from an honest German writer:

> Søren Kierkegaard is one of those authors who often provoke their readers to anger, and these authors are constructive in their own fashion. You don't like them; there is no one you feel so critical as of them. But you read them again and again and you are annoyed and you admit to yourself angrily that this un-

115. Khan "Opposition within Affinity," 189.

116. Ibid., 197.

117. In this respect it is interesting to be aware of how Kierkegaard has been fatally misquoted. To mention one example, Charles Bellinger became excited in discovering Franklin Roosevelt's use of Kierkegaard. It was during World War II that Roosevelt became acquainted with the Dane at the suggestion of the Rev. and Canon Theologian of the Cathedral of "St. John the Divine" in New York, Howard A. Johnson. Some weeks later, Roosevelt recommended to Frances Perkins: "Kierkegaard explains the Nazis to me as nothing else ever has. I have never been able to make out how people who are obviously human beings could behave like that. They are human, yet they behave like demons. Kierkegaard gives you an understanding of what it is in man that makes it possible for these Germans to be so evil."

So far so good, but this is a partial truth and thus a partial untruth. In order to do justice to Søren Kierkegaard's thought, Bellinger should not have forgotten to mention that Roosevelt's "good neighbor policy" included his support for Latin American tyrants such as Trujillo, Somoza, and Batista. Frances Perkins, *The Roosevelt I Knew*, 148. Cited in Bellinger, "Toward a Kierkegaardian Understanding of Hitler," 229 n. 12 (italics mine).

118. Khan, "Opposition within Affinity," 199.

pleasant person talks about things which are damnably important for you (*die einem verflucht nahe gehen*).[119]

We should take into consideration the fact that Kierkegaard never
read Marx's *Communist Manifesto*, published in 1848 but not translated
into Danish until 1852. Therefore, speaking about Kierkegaard's religious revolt, Löwith made an important remark on the Dane's different
social critique:

> Marx's economic analysis and Kierkegaard's experimental psy-
> chology being together both conceptually and historically: they
> comprise *one* antithesis to Hegel. They comprehend "what is" as
> a world determined by merchandise and money, and as an exis-
> tence shot through with irony and the "drudgery" of boredom.
> The "realm of spirits" of Hegel's philosophy becomes a phantom
> in a world of *labor* and *despair*. For Marx, a "German ideology"
> perverts Hegel's self-existed "idea," and for Kierkegaard, a "sick-
> ness unto death" the "satisfaction of the absolute spirit."[120]

José Porfirio Miranda[121] and Enrique Dussel,[122] on the other side,
lost a larger point due to the fact that neither of them made references
to Søren Kierkegaard's later period. Now Kirmmse, Nordentoft, and
Plekon have already documented the Dane's social critique, but it is
my contention that there is also an economic critique in Kierkegaard's
corpus that requires exploration. Let us bear in mind that Kierkegaard's
economic protest and his taking the side of the poor occur within the
larger attack upon Christendom.

Brilliant theologians have branded Kierkegaard a thinker who
never transcended the individual sphere.[123] In order to deal with
this charge, let it suffice to say that he deliberately wrote his *Works of*

119. Hesse, *Vivos Voco: A Review of Kierkegaard's Auswahl aus Sermon Bekenntnissen
und Gedanken*, 658ff.; quoted in Mustard, "Søren Kierkegaard in German Literary
Periodicals 1860–1930," 98.

120. Löwith, *From Hegel to Nietzsche*, 161.

121. "Kierkegaard never understood that Jesus Christ is the Messiah to the extent
that he is the Savior of all the poor and the liberator of all the oppressed" (Miranda,
Being and the Messiah, 56).

122. "Of all the critics of Hegel, Kierkegaard is the one who has more metaphysical
sense, but since he did not make a social critique he fell again in the support of the
current European *status quo*" (Dussel, *Método para una filosofía de la liberación*, 149;
my translation).

123. Niebuhr, *Christ and Culture*, 243ff. See also Bonhoeffer, *Ethics*, 197–98.

Love to counteract this misunderstanding of his thought. Even more important is the fact that when Kierkegaard approaches the theme of "Christendom," he is actually addressing the society and culture with which the church interacts. From the very beginning, Kierkegaard had the suspicion that Christianity was a mere accommodation to bourgeois society.

Kierkegaard was afraid of equating politics with the eternal truth: "[if] A policy which in the proper sense of 'eternal truth' were to make serious work of introducing 'eternal truth' into real life [it] would show itself in that very same second to be in the most 'impolitic' thing that can be imagined." (PV, 118) Kierkegaard was aware of the disastrous consequences of this marriage: "And this triumphant church, or established Christendom, does not resemble the church militant any more than a quadrangle resembles a circle. Imagine a Christian of those ages when the church was truly militant—it would be perfectly impossible for him to recognize the Church in its present perversion" (TC, 207).

In his attempt to separate the church from the state, Kierkegaard was not pursuing a kind of rejection of mundane policy. On the contrary, he was struggling for the preservation of the Christian message as a critical instrument within society. Instead of escaping from the world, he was denouncing the manipulation of religious speech.[124] According to Kierkegaard, what lies beyond the doctrine of the church are the Hegelian philosophy and its ideology that privileges the status quo of the aristocracy.[125]

In 1846 Kierkegaard wrote his most specifically political book: *Two Ages: A Literary Review.* He did so on the occasion of reviewing a contemporary novel. There he states his social analysis of society, which was influenced by the political changes of 1848–1849. The present age of the 1840s was the age of reflection and corresponded to the bourgeois conservatism: "In contrast to the age of revolution, which took action, the present age is an age of publicity, the age of miscellaneous announcements: nothing happens but still there is instant publicity" (TA, 70). This age was typified by Johan Ludvig Heiberg, the aristocratic Hegelian who subscribed to the ideology of the self-satisfied and to the glorification of the status quo. The age of revolution, on the contrary,

---

124. See, e.g., Westphal, "Kierkegaard as Public Philosopher," 41.

125. Kirmmse, *Kierkegaard,* 514.

was an age of passion and refers to the older generation of the 1790s when intellectuals were concerned with the notion of "being human." The personification of that age was the very author of the novel, Fru Gyllembourg. She was the most popular writer of prose fiction in Denmark and, ironically enough, J. L. Heiberg's mother. Kierkegaard was not against reflection in itself but opposed the ideology that reduced human beings to nothingness.[126]

Kierkegaard's support for the verdict in favor of the 1848–1849 constitution made him the champion of the "common man." At least in theory, the new church was the folk church (*Folkekirke*), and this renaming of the church was the circumstance for Kierkegaard to insist upon the urgent redefinition of the relation between church and state.[127] It is within this framework that we are able to understand Kierkegaard's sentence: "What Christianity needs is not the suffocating protection of the state; no, it needs fresh air, it needs persecution, and needs . . . God's protection."[128] Kierkegaard was not a reactionary person; he was a sharp observer of his time and welcomed the new sociopolitical form: "For is this not the law of confusion that governs recent European events? They wish to stop by means of a revolution a counterrevolution. But what is a counterrevolution if it is not also a revolution? And to what can we compare a revolution if not to a gadfly?" (LD # 260).

The Rich and the Poor

Crown prince Frederick VI promoted significant agrarian reforms. It was especially in the late 1840s, when important political changes took place in Denmark, that the "common person" was emerging. This new social class included the emancipated peasants who, with their new social status, took up occupations as artisans, farmers, workers, servants, and the like. Some scholars assert that Kierkegaard loved his neighbors

126. See, e.g., "The individual who was only in principle lost in the abstractions of idealism was in practice lost in the abstractions of modernization" (Elrod, "Passion, Reflection, and Particularity," 8).

127. "Kierkegaard's work is the last great attempt to restore religion as the ultimate organ for liberating humanity from the destructive impact of an oppressive social order. His philosophy implies throughout a strong critique of his society, denouncing it as one that distorts and shatters human faculties" (Marcuse, *Reason and Revolution*, 264–65).

128. AUC, 140.

not because they were lovable in themselves or because of a special intrinsic characteristic, but due to God's transcendent commandment: "thou shalt love thy neighbor."[129] But it is easy to miss Kierkegaard's point in *Works of Love*: in loving the neighbor one is rejecting the bourgeois ideology and seeking the Kingdom of God and its justice.[130]

From 1787 to 1807, King Frederick VI led relevant changes that affected positively the condition of the peasantry. The application of new technology, an educational program, cash incentives, the home consumption of potatoes (that freed grain for the market) contributed, but "[t]he first and most important precondition for success of the peasants reforms was the fifty-percent rise of grain prices in the principal reform period of 1788–1805, owing particularly to demand from England."[131] The system of great landlords, nucleated villages, and dispersed holdings took a new form with the agricultural reforms. That is why by 1807 approximately 60 percent of the shareholders transformed their status to independent property owners.

Despite the reforms, the cottager peasants remained at the bottom of the social scale: "The reparceling of copyholdings and the shift to self-ownership was an option which the better-off copyholders quickly seized, while those with less land or with less advantageous rent contracts often found it impossible to buy and were forced to join the ranks of the cottagers."[132]

The lucky children of the reform era (i.e., the better-off peasants) thus supported the interests of the great state owners and kept the cottagers as a resource of cheap labor. The sad Danes (i.e., the lower peasantry, which constituted one-third of the Danish population by mid-nineteenth century) were the subject of concern for Kierkegaard.[133] It was within this class that after 1850 religious sectarianism found fertile soil and in which a large-scale immigration to the New World took place.[134]

---

129. See Moore. "Religion as the True Humanism," 19.

130. See, e.g., Plekon. "Blessing and the Cross," 28.

131. Kirmmse, *Kierkegaard*, 12.

132. Ibid., 18.

133. Ibid., 20.

134. Ibid., 54.

Kierkegaard's personal experience was also helpful in his theological conversion to the cottagers. His father, Michael Pedersen (1756–1838), was a tenant of a church farm (*kierke, gaard*) in Sæding, Ringkøbing Amt, Jutland. At the age of eleven he had been sent to Copenhagen with a wealthy relative. Eventually he had become a rich businessman, but his rural accent and odd dress were constant reminders of his humble origin. Søren Kierkegaard's mother, Anne Sørensdatter, was initially the maid in the Kierkegaard home. When Søren *Aabye*, Kierkegaard's father, became a widower, he married Anne. Michael and Anne, as rural persons, did not have a middle names:[135] "Verily nothing has ever been farther from me than pretension to social superiority. Being myself of humble origin, I have loved the 'ordinary' person or what is spoken of as simple classes" (PV, 91). Kierkegaard used to have regular conversations with street people, including children.[136] But he did not limit himself to a kind of naive appreciation of the poor. He himself took the side of the oppressed: "The 'ordinary' person is my task, even if I continually have had to make a stand at the very top level of the cultured and distinguished world" (Pap. x 2 A48). Or still more clearly, he writes; "To *make oneself literally one* with the most miserable (and this, this *alone* is divine compassion) is for men the 'too much', over which one weeps in the quiet hour on Sundays, and at which one bursts with laughter when one sees it in *reality*" (TC, 63).

Kierkegaard powerfully, as we say today, chose solidarity with the economically most unfortunate. His acidic criticism of the church was directed, as we have many times repeated, against the ideology of the establishment.

On the theme of the imitation of Christ Kierkegaard also provides us with valuable enlightenment about the Christian commitment to marginalized people. Kierkegaard, much earlier than Bonhoeffer, was

---

135. "As far as is known, all previous generations of their families had automatically passed down the patronymic, i.e., the father's Christian name with the appropriate 'sen' or 'datter' suffix, to all children in a family. But Søren Kierkegaard's parents had now become city people and had appropriated the modern fashion of giving their children middle names that could commemorate any of various family members, or even of close family friends" (Kirmmse, "'Out with it!'" 42).

136. For Kierkegaard's lively character and sociability see Kirmmse, *Encounters with Kierkegaard*, 9: "Peasants and children are the only reasonable human beings with whom it is relaxing to spend time."

able to detect the Protestant overemphasis on faith to the detriment of the integral and responsible Christian praxis.[137]

In the midst of a conformist church that delighted in a bland theology, Kierkegaard's insistence on going back to the New Testament's demands of radical discipleship was certainly inadmissible to the church establishment.[138] In his book *The Practice of Christianity*, as well as in his later production, Kierkegaard thought of conversion as a real, new practice of justice and love: "for the ethical and ethico-religious are so very easy to understand, but on the other hand so very difficult to do" (CUP, 417).[139]

In consideration of the Golden Age economic-religious and social map, it is necessary to take into account that Kierkegaard's attack upon Christendom corresponds with his critique of the whole set of values of his particular society. The image of the pastor was not confined to a mere religious one. The association of the clergy with the state made the former an extension of the latter.

The confirmation certificate was the requirement which gave the peasant legal adulthood.[140] Only by means of this document were people able to get married, to enter into contractual relationships, to enter a guild, to change one's place of residency, to travel about the country, to enter a university, or to have access to the vast employment opportunities. As Kierkegaard briefly put it, this piece of paper was "the certificate the pastor issues, without which the boy or girl concerned cannot succeed at all" (MLW, 245).

Pastors often owned the largest independent farms in the parish. They often held the sole library in the community. One description of the activities of the local pastors is the following. Besides their church responsibilities, they were in charge of

> collecting taxes; taking the census; helping to administer military levies; keeping the parish register of births, deaths, marriages and confirmations; supervising and inspecting the local schools; encouraging agricultural innovation; supervising the poor relief system in the parish, a position in which the pastor could exercise great discretionary power; and, after 1841, serv-

137. See Plekon, "Protest and Affirmation," 50.

138. See Plekon, "Introducing Christianity into Christendom," 339.

139. See also Plekon, "Prophetic Criticism, Incarnational Optimism," 150.

140. Kirmmse, *Kierkegaard*, 50ff.

ing as chairman of the local councils under legislation which extended limited self-government to rural districts.[141]

In this light, when Kierkegaard addresses the issue of the clergy, he has in mind the symbol that represents the authority of the crown and the well-educated people. Pastors legitimized the establishment instead of reflecting the suffering Christ. The important role that they played in reinforcing the status quo had strong direct political implications: "'the pastor' pronounces a blessing on this Christian society, this Christian state, where one cheats as in paganism, and also by paying the 'pastor', thus the biggest cheater cheatingly makes out that this is Christianity."[142]

141. Ibid., 79.

142. Kierkegaard, *"The Moment" and Late Writings*, 185.

2

Kierkegaard on Economic Issues

Years of Transition, 1846–1852

In the end, therefore, money will be the one thing people will desire, which is moreover representative, an abstraction. Nowadays a young man hardly envies anyone his gifts, his art, the love of a beautiful girl, or his fame; he only envies him his money. Give me money, he will say, and I am saved.

—Søren Kierkegaard (PA, 40–41)

I am ugly, but I can buy for myself the *most beautiful* of women. Therefore I am not *ugly*, for the effect of *ugliness*—its deterrent power—is nullified by money. I, according to my individual characteristics, am *lame*, but money furnishes me with twenty-four feet. Therefore I am not lame. I am bad, dishonest, unscrupulous, stupid; but money is honored, and hence its possessor. Money is the supreme good. Therefore its possessor is good.

—Karl Marx[1]

THE EVOLUTION OF KIERKEGAARD'S THOUGHT WAS TIME-AND-SPACE bound. The Denmark of the 1840s experienced the transition from the feudal and agricultural system to the economy of liberal ideology. With the new government of 1848–1849 mercantilist capitalism was replaced by laissez-faire capitalism. Kierkegaard's own development from his earlier conservative position to his later critical attitude can be observed as far back as 1846. Alastair McKinnon has argued persuasively that the attack upon Christendom of 1854–1855 was not an isolated episode that took place at the very last period of Kierkegaard's life. According to

1. Marx and Engels, "Economic and Philosophic Manuscripts of 1844," 324.

this Canadian scholar, that critique was present at least as far back as the writing of the *Unscientific Postscript* in 1846.[2]

On March 30, 1846, Kierkegaard wrote his *Two Ages: The Age of Revolution and the Present Age*, which has been considered his most political book,[3] though Kierkegaard definitely arrived at a much more radical position during his final stage. This is not the place to analyze the content of *Two Ages*, yet I should mention a couple concepts that are relevant for our purposes. In this book, he addressed the issue of the revolution with an affirmative attitude. Kierkegaard elaborated a critical and dialectical appraisal of the revolutionary age. According to him, in view of the substantial political changes that were taking place in those days, a new society was emerging. True, there were losses and gains: the new society lost intensiveness (passion, character) but gained extensiveness (democratic government). Kierkegaard celebrated the new synthesis through his dialectical appraisal of the new form: "Generally speaking, compared to a passionate age, a reflective age devoid of passion *gains in extensity what it loses in intensity*. But this extensity in turn may become the condition for a higher form if a corresponding intensity takes over what is extensively at its disposal" (TA, 97; italics original).

For Kierkegaard, the dialectic of society consists of the fact that "[t]he individual is primarily related to God and then to the community, but this primary relation is the highest, yet it does not neglect the second" (Pap. VII 1 A20 n.d., 1846) (JP, 4110).

In order not to do violence to Søren Kierkegaard's thought, we must bear in mind that he was a careful maieutic thinker who knew how to place the forces of society in tension with the absolute, as he himself stated in 1848: "that I know nothing about sociality. The fools! . . . always when I have first presented one aspect sharply and clearly, then I affirm the validity of the other even more strongly" (Pap. VIII 1 A4) (WL, 18).

A year later, in the midst of the signing of the new constitution, Kierkegaard made a summary of his ideas, highlighting his social and political agenda: "In old times there lived only an individual; the mass,

2. McKinnon, "Kierkegaard's Attack on Christendom," 95–106.

3. "While most of his largely unsystematic social theory and criticism are located elsewhere in his books, journals, and letters, *Two Ages* remains one of the most explicit and concentrated of his writings in these areas" (Plekon, "Towards Apocalypse," 20).

the thousands, were squandered on him. Then came the idea of representation. Those who really lived were again only individuals, but the mass nevertheless saw themselves in them, participated in their life." And he concluded: "The last stage is: the single individual, understood in such a way that the single individual is not in contrast to the mass, but each one is equally an individual" (Pap X2 A265 n.d., 1849) (JP, 2019). Kresten Nordentoft has rightly pointed out that Kierkegaard's visualization and realization of this "final situation" is the key to understanding his whole corpus and his attack upon Christendom as well.[4]

Having mentioned the way Kierkegaard approached the social and political system, now let us proceed to verify the manner in which he deals with economic issues, again, from a structural perspective. By the same token, it would be very helpful to be aware that since Kierkegaard is a dialectical author, he deals with the subject of material poverty even when he develops the treatment of wealth (*Rigdom*) and money (*Penge*), always within the general framework of the attack upon Christendom.

I am personally interested in Søren Kierkegaard's postrevolution (1848–1849) period. I wish to emphasize that in order to do justice to his thought, the treatment of this subject should include the Danish journal entries that remain untranslated into English,[5] as well as the *Journals* available in English and his published books of the last years.

I would like to argue that some of Kierkegaard's economic ideas, as we shall see, are definitely useful and relevant for our current situation. But first, I must hasten to mention that during the years of 1846 to 1852 there is a clear turning point in Kierkegaard's emphasis.

Wealth and Poverty as Correlative Terms

> "what I have, another cannot have; the more I have, the less another has." (CD, 120)

Mammon (*Mammon*) means for Kierkegaard not only wealth but also prestige and power. In his *Christian Discourses* he refers to the unrighteous mammon as the earthly goods that necessarily do injustice to the poor: "All earthly and worldly goods are in themselves selfish, invidious, the possession of them, being invidious or envious, must of necessity

---

4. Nordentoft, *Kierkegaard's Psychology,* 252.

5. See Appendix B.

make others poorer: what I have, another cannot have; the more I have, the less another has." The nature of mammon is unrighteousness and inequality, therefore it: "cannot in and for itself be acquired or possessed equally, for if one is to have much, there must necessarily be another who gets only a little, and what the one has, the other cannot possibly have" (CD, 120).

Regarding the manner of acquisition of the relative goods, one can accomplish that by pure accidental means such as playing the lottery, inheriting a fortune, by the change in the value of the currency, by purchasing a piece of furniture from a dealer. Furthermore, in 1846, Kierkegaard made the concession that mammon also can be reached by hard work (CUP, 382). Nonetheless, what is sure is that mammon is unrighteous, i. e., unequal, ergo contrary to the gospel: "mammon, which has the quality of confirming the distinction between man and man and in an altogether indifferent way. For this is the very nature of 'money'" (Pap X 1 A 55 n.d., n.d. 1849) (JP, 2769).

For some who represent economic liberalism there is a correlation between the number of rich people and the welfare of their society. The more the wealthy people, the more benefits will their community enjoy because the profits will penetrate from the top to the bottom.[6] What is

6. John Maynard Keynes (1883–1946), the British economist for whom "what is rational for the individual and the firm is not necessarily rational for the government," played an important role in the constitution of the International Monetary Fund. In 1930 Keynes delivered a lecture in Madrid where he showed his cynical and macabre conception of wealth and poverty:

> When the accumulation of wealth is no longer of high social importance, there will be great changes in the code of morals. We shall be able to rid ourselves of many of the pseudo-moral principles which have hag-ridden us for two hundred years, by which we have exalted some of the most distasteful of human qualities into the position of the highest virtues. We shall be able to afford to dare to assess the money-motive at its true value. The love of money as a possession—as distinguished from the love of money as a means to the enjoyments and realities of life—will be recognized for what it is, a somewhat disgusting morbidity, one of those semi-criminal, semi-pathological propensities which one hands over with a shudder to the specialists in mental disease . . .
>
> I see us free, therefore, to return to some of the most sure and certain principles of religion and traditional virtue—that avarice is a vice, that the exaction of usury is a misdemeanor, and the love of money is detestable, that those walk most truly in the paths or virtue

lacking in this conception of society is Kierkegaard's dialectic in dealing with matters of wealth and poverty which are neither accidental nor fortuitous terms but dialectical ones. Wealth and poverty then, are not natural phenomenons but historical products: "the more I have, the less another has."[7]

Kierkegaard agrees with thieves in the sense that money is a great good, and also with slanderers in considering honor and reputation as great goods. But Kierkegaard disagrees with both for expropriating those goods from him as a person: "'O miserable, despicable mammon.' that is what his life expressed, 'miserable mammon,' with which a person defiles himself by hoarding, which he accumulates to his own ruination, which he possesses to his own damnation, in order finally to curse himself eternally in hell" (FSE, 177).

I have set the year 1846 as an important milestone in Kierkegaard's work but, from that does not follow that he was blind to some matters before that year. For instance, in 1842 he portrayed what was happening within the Danish elite for whom the theater, prostitutes, rides to Deer Park, funerals, and funeral eulogies would be free, since for them "money is always available," and therefore "everything is free in a way" (E/O I 287).[8] What was at stake was the absolutization of money, as the opening quotation of this chapter reflects.

---

and sane wisdom who take least thought for the morrow. We shall once more value ends above means and prefer the good to the useful. We shall honor those who can teach us how to pluck the hour and the day virtuously and well, the delightful people who are capable of taking direct enjoyment in things, the lilies of the field who toil not, neither do they spin.

But beware! The time for all this is not yet. For at least another hundred years we must pretend to ourselves and to everyone that fair is foul and foul is fair; for foul is useful and fair is not. Avarice and usury and precaution must be our gods for a little longer still. For only they can lead us out of the tunnel of economic necessity into daylight. (Keynes, "Economic Possibilities for our Grandchildren," 329–31)

7. Surprisingly enough, even Adam Smith saw the dialectical relationship between wealth and poverty! "Wherever there is great prosperity, there is great inequality. For one rich man there must be at least five hundred poor . . . and the affluence of the rich supposes the indigence of the many" (*The Wealth of Nations*, 709–10, cited in Meeks, *God the Economist*, 197 n. 31).

8. Apocalypse, on the contrary portrays a golden city where everybody walks on golden streets and by doing so is telling us that "[w]here everything is gold, the gold is no longer money. Everything is available" (Hinkelammert, *Sacrificios humanos y sociedad occidental*, 111).

The absolutization of the relative good of money is treated in *The Christian Discourses* and other works under the subject of seriousness of life. Kierkegaard confronts the overly busy person: "that busy man also must have been in the wrong when he argues that he had a great deal of business from the fact that he keeps five clerks and himself has no time to eat or drink" (CD, 59–60). These human beings, by having lost the dialectical character of wealth and poverty, have centered their life in business and money: "he slaves from morning till night, makes money, lays by, engages in financial transactions" (CD, 92).

Around the same time, Kierkegaard writes about the relative character of money and its difference from the reality of spiritual wealth: "even though a change, a currency change, may also occur in the external world, turning concepts, language, merit, etc. upside down, he who possesses spiritual wealth does not lose one whit of what he possessed— no, not even in all eternity" (LD # 274, 273, 189 to Conferenstraad J. L. A. Kolderup-Rosenvinge). The magnification of money, on the other hand, is carried out by the "people on the mountain" or the supervisors of Denmark's market economy, "the promised land of paid jobs," where morality consists of the fact that "everything revolves around a paid job" (Pap. VIII 1 A 417 n.d., 1847) (JP, 6077).

Kierkegaard noticed how money had penetrated dimensions foreign to it. Money had primacy even within conjugal relationships. For instance, he reports a fortune hunter who married a rich girl for her money; but she, in return, wanted to have the advantage of knowing that it was she who made him rich (TA, 38). Kierkegaard also writes about the scandalous contradiction of the wealthy who are increasing their treasure and declare their not having worries about making a living; however, the reality is quite different. These rich persons are compared with "someone who owned a costly collection of excellent medicines that he used every day to say as he pointed at the medicines: I am not sick!" (TA, 181).

Søren Kierkegaard de-absolutized the place that had been given to money: "If you make earning money into the earnestness of life, then you have fallen from Christianity" (Pap. X, 3 A 347 n.d., 1850) (JP, 1787). The relativization of money is another way of describing Kierkegaard's conception of wealth and poverty as correlative terms, and Kierkegaard's attack upon a wrongly oriented society as well. For him, secularism not only has to do with the lack of faith but also with economic matters: "the same secular-mindedness which expresses itself in amassing money because one believes neither in providence nor in himself. The greater the faith in God, the less one feels the desire to hoard" (Pap. X, 4 A 13 n.d., 1851) (JP, 1266).

The magnification of money is connected also with reduplication or double life. Kierkegaard examines the life of the academically educated and artistically trained, who live in style within the refined circle but who, above all are interested in having money, "and lots of it" through dishonest means.[9]

For Kierkegaard, in money matters there is always a tension: "the rich man's possession of money being a kind of envy which has taken this money from the poor, who perhaps in their turn envy the rich for it; for there is envy in both situations, because earthly riches is itself envy." (CD, 121) Nevertheless, money is to be shared: "Money is the numerator; mercy the denominator. But the denominator is still the more important" (Pap VIII 1 A 209 n.d., 1847) (JP, 2768).

Kierkegaard was aware of the irrationality concerning the logic of the mercantilistic economic system: "The first barrel of gold, says the capitalist, will be the most difficult to gain; when one has that, the rest comes of itself. But the first farthing, with the knowledge that one is beginning to lay up for abundance, is also earnest-money" (CD, 28). His *Christian Discourses* draws a line between the society's rationality in relation to wealth and the Christian point of view: "God does not, as though he were a capitalist, want his fortune to be increased by sagacious investments, but on the contrary, to have it administered in an entirely different way, if He is to be well pleased" (CD, 32). Kierkegaard concedes the existence of wealthy Christians but with the substantial qualification that wealth is to be shared: "the rich Christian realizes that they are God's, and that they are to be administered as far as possible in accordance with the proprietor's wish, administered with the proprietor's indifference to money and money value, administered by giving them away at the right time and place" (CD, 33). The tangible fruits of faith in God are measured by putting wealth to the service of people: "the rich Christian is in a position to have joy in his earthly riches, finding joy whenever he is granted opportunity to do some good with his

---

9. Kierkegaard, *Journals of Søren Kierkegaard*, 1201; Pap., X 4 A 214.

riches, that he can do another man a service, and by this same act can serve God" (CD, 35-6).

Kierkegaard realized that humans do not live on air. In fact, four times he quoted in his books the anxiety of the poor generated by past time: "for yesterday, in view of what he has eaten . . . and not paid for!" (CD, 350).[10] But it is God the great provider, who takes care of his people. Now, the greedy people who monopolize God's goods set themselves outside of God's reign: "He sows and reaps and gathers into barns, and the whole world is like his great storeroom. Boring people have had the boring idea of turning the whole world into one great barn in order to manage without God" (FSE, 184). That kind of people has forgotten the dialectical relationship between wealth and poverty: "what I have, another cannot have; the more I have, the less another has" (CD, 120).

The Romanticization of Poverty and the Established Church (den bestående kirke)

> If I am unwilling *à la* Mynster to idolize the establishment (and this is Mynster's heresy) and in my zeal for morality eventually confuse it with bourgeois mentality . . . Then I cannot personally reject what has so clearly been upon me as a task. (Pap. VII 1 A 221 January 20, 1847) (JP, 5961)

In a forceful analysis of Mynster's sermon: "Meditation upon the Fate of People with Disabilities," which was delivered during the spring of 1850, Søren Kierkegaard strongly opposed the romanticization of the disabled together with the idealization of poverty. From the start, he denounced that the sermon does not appeal to the suffering people; but to the "pleasant relief of the fortunate." Kierkegaard's sharp eye detected in this homily the transformation of life's misery into an ideal state of existence. The result is the mockery of the suffering people as well as the cunning legitimizing of indifference of the wealthy people.

What is at stake in Christendom is in fact a class issue. Throughout this entry Søren Kierkegaard unveiled the connivance between the clergy and the privileged class; the trivialization of the physically and mentally poor; the falsification of the gospel by the powerful; the correlation between the sociological setting of the preacher and his speech; the so-

---

10. Observation made by Pastor F. L. B. Zeuthen in a thank-you letter to Kierkegaard on the occasion of the publication of *Works of Love*.

cially loaded reading of the Bible, and so on, all of that in detriment to suffering people. Kersten Nordentoft has also convincingly argued that the institutionalized bourgeois and clerical ideology exercised a social oppressive influence that deprived the proletariat of its privileged place in Christianity.[11] This "area for psychological observation" addresses, therefore, economic, political, and theological agendas for further investigation. The radical Kierkegaardian position together with the fact that this *Journal* entry has not yet been translated in full into English deserves to be cited *in extenso*:

> "Meditation upon the Fate of the Physically Challenged"[12]
>
> Mynster's sermon "Meditation upon the fate of those to whom the usual capacities are denied"[13] is not really preached for the comfort of such suffering people. On the contrary, it is for the pleasant relief of the fortunate, so that they may go home from church armed against the impression caused by those suffering people.
>
> There is something cunning here. Mynster is of the opinion that he cannot completely ignore such suffering people, about whom the Gospel constantly speaks. Consequently, he treats the subject in such a way that in the final analysis he denies that the suffering indeed suffer. He does not preach to comfort those who are suffering. However he says to the fortunate: take comfort, things are not so bad; they also have their mild side. There are examples of the visually-impaired with a clearer mental-eye (e.g., I can think of Homer); that the hearing-impaired have been profound thinkers.
>
> Now that is preaching! This is truly a way of mocking the suffering people. On the other hand, the fortunate are obviously happy with such sermons, which tranquilizes them so completely in undisturbed pleasure, so that they may enjoy life on the grandest possible style, undisturbed by the misery of life —"It is not so awful. It also has its mild side."

11. Nordentoft, *Kierkegaard's Psychology*, 253.

12. Nordentoft and Plekon drew my attention to this passage: Nordentoft, *Hvad Siger Brand-Majoren?* 202; and *Kierkegaard's Psychology*, 253. Plekon, "Prophetic Criticism, Incarnational Optimism," 144–45. I also acknowledge Bruce Kirmmse's correction of my translation, and many vigorous insights.

13. *Prædikarne paa Alle Søn-og Hellig-dage i Aaret. af Dr. J. P. Mynster, Biskop over Siellands Stift, kongelig Confessionarius, Storkors af Dannebrogen en og Dannebrogsmand*, 211–24.

On the whole, here is an entire domain for psychological observation: the cunningness, with which human egoism, under the guise of compassion, seeks to defend itself against the impression made by life's misery, so as not to interrupt a greedy lust for life. This is *à la Goethe*. And Mynster has obviously also modeled himself after him.

But is this Christianity as well? Is it also a sermon about Him, the Compassionate One Who sought out such suffering people, putting Himself wholly in their place?

How often one hears sermons and speeches on this subject as well: that the poor are far happier than the rich isn't it so? —And this is done under the guise of compassion. It is presented so movingly: how happy the poor can live, free from all the burdens of wealth. Is this really a speech to comfort the poor? No!, this is a point which is most welcome to the wealthy. For then, they do not need to give anything to the poor, or not so much—the poor are in fact happier. Poverty has its beautiful side. The rich go home from church to their treasures, to which they indeed cling more firmly than ever, edified by the lovely lecture, which spoke the language of compassion.

But, is this Christianity as well? Is it also a sermon about Him, the Compassionate One Who in order to comfort the poor, Himself became subject to equal circumstances?

But, just as the "Christian State" in fact only knows one sort of crime —theft[14]— a terrible indirect testimony against "the Christian State," so do the privileged classes also have their priests who are like co-conspirators. They really know how to preach in such a way, that the enjoyment of life is not disturbed in the least.

Such priests practice the art of coming as close as possible to the Gospel, but in such a way as not to disturb the possession and enjoyment of all the earthly goods, or the sort of life which is busy acquiring and preserving these goods. If someone wanted to preach the Gospel to them for free, they would not put up with it. What matters to them is that "their priest" is in possession of more or less the same advantages as they themselves. His income should correspond approximately to theirs; his rank and office in society corresponding approximately to theirs; the house he runs corresponding approximately to theirs. He should be a knight of approximately the same orders. Thus, one believes that one has a guarantee that this is a man who

---

14. Theft in this capitalist, mercantilist context is reduced to that kind of theft that threatens private property—the exclusive privilege of the well-to-do classes.

would know how to show due consideration, a guarantee that he, in preaching the Gospel, is properly constrained, so that the Gospel remains undisturbed.

By the way, this is true of all social classes: in appearance, everybody wants their priest, in outward circumstances, etc., to correspond approximately to external conditions. Then, one is sure that he will not go too far. The middle-class priest can certainly speak zealously against the luxury of the aristocracy and so forth. It is even very pleasant to the bourgeoisie, who lack these conditions. But he must canonize the way of life of his own social class.

I have heard a priest speaking zealously against the most prestigious ecclesiastical positions. He was of the opinion that a priest should be paid, so that he is able to live decently, but no more. And how much is needed for that? Yes, it was approximately his own salary, to the penny. And he held a position, from which he does not expect to be removed.

I have heard a priest speaking zealously against the clergy receiving decorations of stars and ribbons. He believed, however, that one could be a knight of Dannebrog, without causing offense; naturally, he himself was a knight. (Pap. X 3 A 135 n.d., 1850) (my translation)[15]

Whereas the theater, the university, the church, and the media were mediators of culture in the city, in the countryside and provincial towns the clergy had a monopoly as cultural agents. For instance Hans Christian Andersen became familiar with literature through the libraries of two pastors' widows from Odense.[16]

Mynster was the symbol of religious power during most of Kierkegaard's life. The bishop exercised an enormous influence on Kierkegaard; however, even the *Unscientific Postscript* starts showing the process of a ruptured relationship. Kierkegaard rejects the professionals of religion, who have become mere workers who are seeking a salary from the state, and prestige and power as well: "having life in immanent categories instead of in God's relationship (CUP, 389, 404, 426). By 1846–1847, his *Purity of Heart* not only exhibits the break with

15. For the complete entry, see Appendix C. *Hvor ofte prækes og tales der ikke og-saa om: at den Fattige er langt lykkeligere end den Rige—og det gjøres under Skin af Medlidenhed; man fremstiller det saa rørende, hvor lykkeligt den Fattige kan leve, fri for alle Rigdommens Byrder. Er det nu en Tale for at trøste den Fattige? Nei, det er en Rigmændene yderst velkommen Vending.*

16. Kirmmse, *Kierkegaard,* 492 n. 11.

Mynster, but is also "a sign of Søren Kierkegaard's break with the reign-
ing view of life (of humanity, God, religion, the world, eternity) shared
by the cultured bourgeoisie."[17] The same year, 1847, Kierkegaard better
understood that his career has been damaged because he challenges the
social and political conditions of his society: "But now and from now on
my career as an author is truly not spectacular. It is perfectly clear that I
will be a victim." Kierkegaard denounced Mysnter's heresy of idolizing
the establishment: "Mynster has never been out on 70,000 fathoms of
water and learned out there; he has always clung to the established order
and now has completely coalesced with it" (Pap. VII 1 A 221 January 20,
1847) (JP, 5961). Little wonder Kierkegaard was considered a suspicious
and dangerous person by the Primate of Denmark.

Kierkegaard observes how the clergy is sanctifying the bourgeois
mentality and morality by seeking decorations, to be honorary members, to belong to certain clubs (Pap IX A 404 n.d., 1848)(JP, 2753).
Pastors are, in Kierkegaard's view, like "public prostitutes" who, do not
preach about the fact that people spit upon Christ but about the nonsense which says: "Be a nice, good, altruistic man and men will love
you—for Christ, who was love, was loved by men" (Pap. IX A 288 n.d.,
1848) (JP, 6254).

If some scholars support the idea that Kierkegaard promoted acosmism, he himself qualified this concept. According to him Christianity
is neither acosmism nor merely cosmism: "the kind of culture and education supposedly identifiable with Christianity is almost the kind of
culture that quite ingeniously is characterized by the phrase to possess
the world" (Pap. X 3 A 588 n.d., 1850) (JP, 2712). Kierkegaard disagrees
with Mynster's understanding of Christianity as almost the same as culture and education. Furthermore, if culture is identified with the bourgeois morality of pleasure, refinement, and the like, then, Kierkegaard
observes, this concept of culture is counter to Christianity. He then
proposes a different understanding of culture: "If Christianity is supposed to be culture, it must be the culture of character, or education and
culture aimed at becoming persons of character" (Pap. X 3 A 588 n.d.,
1850) (JP, 2712).

In addressing Mynster, Kierkegaard was aware of the fact that he
was not just the bishop of *Sjælland*, he was not just the authority of the

17. Ibid., 284.

Danish Church, and almost absolute ruler; he was the most prominent representative of culture in Denmark.[18] Consequently, the more direct break with the bishop developed in *Practice in Christianity*, consisting of the rupture between culture and religion at large. Since the Folk Church [*Folkekirke*] continued to be an absolutist institution, and the new regime became steadier and steadier; therefore, Kierkegaard considered this the appropriate time to articulate his critique.[19]

By 1851, he noticed how Christianity and bourgeois culture were inexorably intertwined: "Once the objection against Christianity . . . was that it was unpatriotic, a danger to the state, revolutionary, and now Christianity has become patriotism and a state church" (Pap X 4 A 126 n.d., 1851) (JP, 4209). Or still more specifically: "Once Christianity was an offense to the Jews and foolishness to the Greeks, and now it is—culture. For Bishop Mynster, the mark of true Christianity is culture" (Pap X 4 A 126 n.d., 1851) (JP, 4209) (Or Letter, 116-17). Kierkegaard calls this way of interpreting Christianity as Christendom (*Christenheden*), in contradistinction to Christianity of the New Testament or (*Christendommen*). Christendom then was the one related not only to a religious system but to the sociopolitical and cultural circles as well. Søren Kierkegaard's break with Mynsterian Christendom then, was a rupture with the whole social order and its golden-age elitism.

The Mimetic Desire of Appropriation[20]

> The tragedy of Christendom is clearly that we have removed the dialectical element from Luther's doctrine of faith, so that it has become a cloak for sheer paganism and epicureanism. We completely forget that Luther urged faith in contrast to a fan-

18. Hansen, *Revolutionær Samvittighed*, 118.

19. For Mynster's holistic or corporatist view of society (i.e., "everyone must remain orderly and in their place in accordance to their 'office and estate'"), see Kirmmse, *Kierkegaard*, 126, 381.

20. I am borrowing from René Girard the concept of the mimetic desire of appropriation. This is a pastoral instrument to unveil the hidden agendas of the competitive society based on the insatiability of acquisitiveness. According to him, human beings inherently possess a mimetic desire for obtaining what the others have. Nevertheless, it is possible to overcome that destructive desire, beginning by denouncing the way the mimetic desire is manipulated by the economic and political structures. See Girard, *La violencia de lo sagrado* [*Violence and the Sacred*]; Assmann, *Sobre los ídolos y sacrificios*. See also Illich, *Toward a History of Needs*.

tastically exaggerated asceticism. (Pap. X1 A 213 n.d., 1849) (JP, 2484)

Kierkegaard's thought was not immune to the significant social and political events taking place during the years 1846 to 1852. One clear example of that is the analysis he made to the mimetic desire of appropriation.[21] Humankind, by nature, has the desire to satisfy its needs. It is even legitimate once in a while to be indulgent: "Yet it is relevant here that even Christ approves a certain pious prodigality such as, for example, the lavishing of costly ointment on him. The observation that astringency is corrupting is appropriate here." (Pap. X 3 A 342 n.d., 1850) (JP, 14) However, the dominant class of society orients the mimetic desire of appropriation to false needs instead of toward real needs. The structure of the mimetic desire is nothing but to wish for an object not like the object *per se*, but because somebody else has the same desire.[22]

Hegel already articulated the decisive importance of "the system of needs" as the glue of modern society.[23] Nevertheless, he did not sound the alarm as Rousseau did, in denouncing how people are liable to enslave themselves by false needs and being oppressed by those who define the needs as imperatives, and who at the same time meet those needs of society.[24]

Kierkegaard is not denying "the system of needs"; he even puts the following words in God's mouth: "go and enjoy the finite" (CUP, 442–44). For him, God is related to the ordinary life. Moreover, if we doubt regarding the finite, how can I know that I made a good decision? The Dane quotes Luther's saying: "just trust God that this is a good decision and go and do it boldly, otherwise, you never will make any decision" (CUP, 438).

What is at stake is an essential view of life or existence [*Tilværelsen*]. His competitive society lacks a clear distinction between the necessary and the relative. His society does not discriminate between false and

---

21. I am using this concept anachronistically but for pedagogical reasons.

22. In a society built on the desires of the elite, the objects of desire are equated with the basic needs, as Friedrich Hayek firmly believed: "The luxuries of today are the needs of tomorrow" (Hayek, *Constitution of Liberty*, 42; quoted by Sung, *Market, Desire, and Religion*, 60).

23. Hegel, *Introduction to the Philosophy of Right*, 126ff.; cited in Meeks, *God the Economist*, 160.

24. Ibid., 166.

real needs: "There is a busyness, a busy working for and a busy talking about the necessities of life." To the opulent circles Kierkegaard stated: "And the more fortunate, the more favored person is only all too easily persuaded and beguiled by temporality, until it seems to him that things go so well for him that he does not need anything more" (TA, 309). Status and narrow-minded competition dictate control of power, rank, and wealth, and in the end displaces the absolute.

The rich, having lost perspective on reality by being immersed in a style of life based on artificial needs, build on a vertiginous anxiety of comfort, safety, fame, and money as ends in themselves: "the rich heathen knows of nothing to talk about except his mammon" (CD, 38). Kierkegaard illustrates his point in his story about the lack of the extensive view of the stars:

> When the well-to-do person is riding comfortably in his carriage on a dark but starlit night and has the lanterns lit—well, then he feels safe and fears no difficulty; he himself is carrying along the light, and it is not dark right around him. But just because he has the lanterns lit and has a strong light close by, he cannot see the stars at all. His lanterns darken the stars, which the poor peasant, who drives without lanterns, can see gloriously in the dark but starlit night. (TA, 310)

As a constant note in Kierkegaard's corpus, the clergy are in part responsible for providing moral validation to this confusion of what is a real need, for the authentic existence: "Therefore all you prudent pastors ought to say forthrightly: We have omitted and set aside the most important view of existence; what we preach is a prudential life and a philistine-bourgeois gospel especially inspiring to lottery-players" (Pap. VIII 1 A 145 n.d., 1847) (JP, 305).

In a society that promotes the insatiability of acquisitiveness where the desires are unlimited, and worst of all, where desires are confounded with needs, the concept of the vocation (*Bestemmelse*) will be redefined. Still more, the vocation will be reduced to having a job, and not in order to make a living, but to pursue the accumulation of objects.[25]

In accordance with Kierkegaard's constellation of values, one way to reach the universal is through the actualization of one's vocation. But

25. "Part of leisure time is converted back into work to generate the income required to buy the maintenance time required for many consumer goods. We are left wanting time" (Meeks, *God the Economist*, 222–23 n. 38.)

we have to discriminate between vocation and a limited "vocationalism," (PC, 393, n.84) where vocation is interchangeable with having a job, and furthermore it is measured by the salary one earns (JP, IV, 764–65).

At the aesthetic level, vocation has to do with the development of the particular talents with egoistic purposes. Whereas at the ethical-religious dimension one raises the question, "In the course of your occupation, what is your frame of mind, how do you perform your work?" At this stage, one does not evaluate vocation by immediate success, by being able "to make it," or by favorable results: "Therefore if a brazen person could bring himself to consider the most loathsome crime so he *could* execute it, then this would be what he was to do" (TA, 139)! Kierkegaard summarizes his position by pointing out that the occupations blessed by God are those that are consecrated to God's service regardless of the final results (CD, 306).

From the aesthetic perspective, equating God's call with a task (*Opgave*) or work (*Gjerning*) contains an ideological element. In this view, for example, a true Christian shoemaker would be recognizable "by having the most work to do, having the most assistants, and perhaps the king and queen and the whole royal house, or at least the clergy, had their shoes made by him" (PC, 215). Within this framework, to appeal to God is nothing more than to manipulate him, or in Kierkegaardian language, "to make the divine the superlative of the human" (Pap. X 4 A 487 n.d., 1852) (JP, 4949).

Kierkegaard blames Mynster for reducing the concept of vocation to pure intellectual deliberation where the religious is present by only ornamentally adding "God's name to it" (Pap. IX A 430 n.d., 1848) (JP, 5013). For Kierkegaard, the ethical-religious has to make a difference; for example, in the case of a merchant: "he ought to express that he is a Christian by not getting mixed up in this gray dishonesty which is the normal thing in the commercial world." The Bishop, on the other hand, still remains in the aesthetic sphere by compromising the gospel: "If Bishop Mynster had expressed the kind of conscientiousness which is specifically Christian, he would never have become bishop" (Pap. X 3 A 401 n.d., 1850) (JP, 5014).

Success as the result of God's call was very suitable for Kierkegaard's society, whose motto was: "Everything revolves about money" (Pap. VII 1 A 25 n.d., 1846) (JP, 2144). In that way the ossified bureaucrats baptized their bourgeois lifestyle built on class conventionalism: "What is regarded as real earnestness is a kind of training, the trained competence in being a husband, and office-holder, etc." (Pap. VII 1 A 165 n.d., 1846) (JP, 231). It is a life built on promotion: "Most men think that *earnestness* means to get an office, to be attentive to openings at a higher level which they can try to get, how they will make the move and what they then will do to adapt themselves." It is a life built on aggressive competition: "everyone strives and battles and grabs to become something. But this something is a departmental consultant or a fleet medical office, etc" (Pap. VIII 1 A 368 n.d., 1847) (JP, 233). It is a life built on immediate success and unlimited desire of acquisitiveness: "'I am only thirty-four years old and am already department head. I am only twenty-nine and already have a big business etc."(Pap. IX A 134 n.d., 1848) (JP, 6188). It is a life built on the mimetic desire dictated by the elite: "They think it is earnestness to move in exclusive society; they prepare more for luncheon with His Excellency than for communion" (Pap. VII 1 A 178 n.d., 1846) (JP, 232).

Kierkegaard reacted against a society centered in furious competition with each other. His critique embraced the economic sphere in a direct way. He denounced the evils of his time: "In the end mediocrity and finite prudence about earthly advantage will be deified, and it will be regarded as immoral not to have earthly advantage from one's efforts." Or still more clearly, "But it is not true that every individual who has made his life secure is supposed to insist defiantly that this kind of striving is the earnestness of life and that belonging to an idea is fanaticism—just the opposite, an admission must be made" (Pap. IX A 134 n.d., 1848) (JP, 6188).

He touched the structure that privileged the economic value: "Youthfulness is looked upon with favor during certain years, but then one is supposed to become earnest,—that is, be interested in money and finite things" (Pap. IX A 387 n.d., 1848) (JP, 235). And he drew a dividing line between the bourgeois ideology and the gospel: "if you make earning money into the earnestness of life, then you have fallen from Christianity" (Pap. X 3 A 347 n.d., 1850) (JP, 1787).

In a quotation already mentioned above, Kierkegaard declared, regarding the mimetic desire: "In the end, therefore, money will be the one thing people will desire, which is moreover representative, an abstraction. Nowadays a young man hardly envies anyone his gifts, his art, the love of a beautiful girl, or his fame; he only envies him his money. Give me money, he will say, and I am saved" (PA, 40–41). In the same book he wrote in 1846: "A revolutionary age is an age of action; ours is the age of advertisement and publicity" (SV XIV 65). Kierkegaard in his last years insisted on ringing the alert against a society that privileged success, wealth, competence, and the like as the marks of human beings.

In a time when God's commandment: "Do not make for yourselves images of anything in heaven or on earth or in the water under the earth" (Exod 20:4) was still strictly observed, Louis-Jacques Mandé Daguerre invented the first practical photographic process (the daguerreotype). This invention immediately raised a reaction. In 1839, a Leipzig news-paper published the following: "The desire of freezing the luminous reflection, is not only impossible, but blasphemy. Man was created in God's image and no machine invented by man will be able to freeze his image. The French inventor who believes he has succeeded can be called the most foolish of all fools."[26] In 1840, for the most famous Danish sculptor, Bertel Thorvaldsen, however, vanity was stronger than reli-gious belief: "the old man had had to sit absolutely still for a very long time—while making a pair of horns with the little and index fingers of his left hand in order to ward off the camera's evil eye![27]

Kierkegaard, on the other hand, never had his picture taken. Instead of that, he foresaw in an extremely enlightened way the role picture (Billede) cameras,[28] still being developed in that period, would play in the creation of wants, in advertising, in the never-ending buying busyness, and in the mimetic desire expressed by the modern slogan, "Keep up with the Joneses":

> By means of the daguerreotype it will be easy for everyone to have his portrait made—formerly only the distinguished were able to do this; and at the same time every effort is made to make us all look alike—therefore, only one single portrait is needed. (Pap. XI1 A 118 n.d., 1854) (JP, 4230)

The Gordian knot of the mimetic desire of appropriation then, consists of distinguishing between real and false needs, taking desire rather than need as the point of departure. If desire is the axis around

---

26. Batres, Ser o tener, 204–5.

27. Garff, Kierkegaard: A Biography, 464.

28. "Once buying is seen as a way of dealing with guilt, failure, the loss of self-esteem, and the fear of death, it will be elevated to the status of worship" (Meeks, God the Economist, 173).

which everything revolves, and if desire is by nature insatiable, then we will never be able to know what it means to have too much or too little.[29]

The Reserves of Christendom's Bank and Class Inequality

> Therefore I have always urged that Christianity is properly for poor people who perhaps toil and sweat the whole day and are scarcely able to make a daily living. The greater the advantages the more difficult it is to become a Christian. (Pap. X 3 A 714 n.d., 1851) (JP, 991)

> [Søren Kierkegaard] suspects, for example, that the doctrine of civic equality has an ideological element. He is familiar with the fact that members of different classes who behave towards each other in the name of Christianity as if they were nothing but men, do so generally, only in order to maintain the fiction of civic equality and thus better to preserve civic inequality.
>
> —Adorno[30]

In a *Journal* entry worthwhile quoting at length, Kierkegaard noticed the link that exists between the bourgeois way of life and the moral validation provided by the clergy:

> Let us assume that it became customary for a clergyman to have a business manager who would collect his money, tithes, offerings, etc., which is quite all right inasmuch as the business manager is in the clergyman's service. But let us suppose that this became an independent way of making a living and that such a business manager would pay the clergyman his wages and now himself made the plans and had only a financial interest in the pastor's standing with the congregation. What then? Well, this would result in the practice that the pastor, every Saturday night upon finishing his sermon, would go over to the business manager and let him see it. And the business manager would say: "If your Reverence talks this way, no one will come to church, and, damn it all, there goes the offering plate money, and in that case I can't guarantee much for this year, which, after all, is to your

---

29. "When one thinks from the standpoint of desires there are not limits. One pursues the limitless. And when one desires the limitless there is never anything left to share. There is never enough" (Sung, *Desire, Market and Religion*, 33).

30. Adorno, "On Kierkegaard's Doctrine of Love," 425.

own interest. No, you must butter up the congregation a little; let me tell you how. If I am not quite up to writing a sermon, I do understand very well the times we live in and what the congregation wants."

I imagine the pastor would flush with embarrassment and say: "Have I been appointed teacher in order to flatter the congregation and for you to earn money?" But the business manager answers: "I have no time for hysterics, high-mindedness, and all that. Everyone is a thief in his own job, and my job is to see to it that Your Reverence satisfies the times." The nauseousness of the moneyman's sniffing at the sermon and judging it commercially is revolting enough. (Pap VII 1 A 77 n.d., 1846) (JP, 2767)

Shortly after his *Concluding Unscientific Postscript* Kierkegaard's economic criticism is oriented toward a society and a church based on acquisitiveness and comfort as their main values: "As a rule the 'bread and butter' consideration plays a decisive role in the world; wherever this middle term drops out, men become irresolute." The heathen within Christendom or the "Christian in name only," together with the clergy are "traders" and seekers of "bread and butter." That state of affairs, in Kierkegaard's opinion, contradicts the essence of Christianity: "When, however, a private man is religious in a stricter sense and expresses his religiousness, he is regarded as mad. And why? Because the bread-and-butter middle term is lacking" (Pap. VII 1 A152).[31] In his *Edifying Discourses* Kierkegaard addresses people who have "married money" and know nothing but worldly comparisons (TA , 200), in order to have a conversion from their practice: "In eternity you will not be asked how large a fortune you are *leaving behind;* the *survivors* ask about that" (TA, 223).

Continuing to use commercial language, Kierkegaard speaks about the reserves of Christendom's bank: "The pastors preach indulgence and teach that renouncing everything is required only of some individuals." Those reserves have been increased due to the flexibility of the proclamation of the gospel: "The renouncing of all things has the spaciousness of freedom. God speaks something like this: It would give me great pleasure if you were to renounce everything for Christ's sake, but it is not absolutely demanded of you" (Pap. VIII 1 A 572 n.d., 1848) (JP, 3744) Kierkegaard, thinking in sociological terms, confronts

---

31. Kierkegaard, *Armed Neutrality*, 17.

the church members whose money sense is the most developed, and for whom it is convenient to have their pastors in luxury and opulence: "Just imagine the situation now when it is said (on the basis of experience): If a father has a son who otherwise is no good at studies, let him study theology; it is the most secure way to a living" (Pap. X 2 A 543 n.d., 1850) (PC, 346) (Pap. X 3 A 244 n.d., 1850) (JP, 3151).

In his *Judge for Yourselves* of 1851 (published posthumously in 1876), Kierkegaard was implacable. There he mentions the enormous funds of Christendom's bank. The salaried officials and the honorable people have "turned sufferings and blood into money, pecuniary advantage, honor, prestige, esteem" (FSE, 129). Such hard-earning working capital has been accumulated during three hundred years, thanks to the illusory assurance: "If it were required of me, I would be willing to forsake everything, sacrifice everything, for the sake of Christianity" (FSE 135). People have made use of these "assurances": "From generation to generation, while they continued the calm acquisition and possession of the things of this world" (FSE, 135). The assurance fund is an important part of the capital of Christendom's bank and, curiously enough, it is the Christian public who is most interested in not losing it: "Admittedly it is the proclaimers who make use of assurances, but perhaps it is the audience, the world, that profits most by forcing the proclaimers into this untruth so that Christianity will not become too earnest" (FSE, 136).

In antagonism with that version of society and Christianity, Kierkegaard was of the idea that the true disciple knows nothing about the "assurance fund": "the disciple is unconditionally in poverty," "he is literally indigent," "he has no money," "he has nothing." Or more concisely: "for a long time no one has made the confession that this whole business of one thousand clergymen is really not Christianity but a toned-down teaching—toned down a whole quality in comparison with genuine Christianity" (FSE, 133).

Now we must bear in mind that Kierkegaard is methodologically differentiating between Christianity (*Christendommen*) and Christendom (*Christenheden*), and this is not just a mere play with words. In fact, precisely that differentiation allowed him to be appreciative of the left-wing, free-thinking Hegelians such as Feuerbach and their contributions to the political revolution: "if you look more closely, you will see that they actually have taken upon themselves the task of defending Christianity against contemporary Christians." Kierkegaard categorically asserts that the problem with Christianity is to be found at the existential level: "it is wrong of established Christendom to say that Feuerbach is attacking Christianity; it is not true; he is attacking the Christians by demonstrating that their lives do not correspond to the teachings of Christianity" (Pap. X 2 A 163 n.d., 1849) (JP, 6523). Kierkegaard is challenging the whole politico-religious structure: "I am a man and I too, humanly speaking, love to live happily on earth." And he makes his point: "But if what one sees all over Europe is Christendom, a State, then I intend to begin here, in Denmark, quoting the price of being Christian so that the whole concept: State-Church, officials, livelihood, should be shaken."[32]

Contrary to popular thinking, Kierkegaard was not a solipsist thinker; he addressed reality with structural categories. In an early entry he pointed out: "Christ indeed has died for all men, also for me, but this 'for me' must nevertheless be interpreted in such a way that he has died for me only insofar as I belong to the many [the "ordinary" people]" (Pap. II A 223 April 6, 1838) (JP, 1976). A decade later he continued to use sociological terms: "One solitary man cannot help or save an age; he can only express that it is foundering" (Pap. X 1 A 171 n.d., 1849) (JP, 4157).

During the turbulent years 1848–1849, Kierkegaard increased his criticism of the aristocratic groups. Speaking about the "ordinary" person, he says: "how few are they who understand him and understand the callousness and cruelty of the class distinctions that ordinarily underlie associations with the 'ordinary' person" (Pap. X, 2 A 88 n.d., 1849) (JP, 6504). In those same days Kierkegaard bought Alexander R. Vinet's book on socialism that was published in Berlin in 1849: "I have now obtained *Der Sozialismus in seinem Principe betrachtet* by Vinet, *Übersetzt von* Hofmeister." In this respect, on the one hand Kierkegaard criticizes Vinet for favoring the public opinion over the single individual; on the other hand the Dane recognizes, "But nevertheless there is spirit" (Pap X 4 A 185 March 9, 1851) (JP, 4211).

In the analysis of his age Kierkegaard discovered how a "spiritual guerrilla war" is taking place in order to preserve injustice and inequality. The state does not have to take recourse to soldiers, police, diplomats, or political planners, but to pastors. In his opinion, the Reformation

---

32. Kierkegaard, *Kierkegaard's Journals*, 939; Pap., X 1 A 541.

seemed to be a religious movement, but in fact it was a political one; whereas this time: "everything appears to be politics but will turn out to be a religious movement" (Pap X 6 B 40 n.d., 1848(?)–49) (JP, 6256).

The blending of church and state, and the corresponding economic implications, led Kierkegaard to define the pastor in these terms: "What is a pastor? A pastor is one who is paid by the state to proclaim the doctrine of poverty. A pastor is one who is respected and honored and esteemed in society for proclaiming that we should not seek after worldly honor, esteem, and wealth" (Pap. X 5 A 164 n.d., 1849) (JP, 3139).

As we will see in detail further on, pastors were linked to the intellectual circles as their very appearance resembled the time they invested in "patterning the pastoral robe so that it would almost look like a professor's gown; this would be scholarly." But pastors also want to be in the parliament: "And this is embellished by the high-sounding name of working for the whole,—that is, staying in Copenhagen and enjoying oneself, whetting the appetite, voting, and all that.—And this is earnestness!" (Pap. X 2 A 357 n.d., 1850) (JP, 3140). For Kierkegaard, then, the clergy are important factors in the legitimizing of social and economic inequality: "those interested in the bourgeois corporation are canonized and of course they are canonized by the last clerical order to appear in Protestantism: the office-seekers or place-hunters."[33]

As the symbol of religious power Mynster started losing Kierkegaard's respect even as early as1847: "The only contemporary I have paid any attention to is Mynster. But Mynster cares only about holding office and administering, thinking that this is the truth" (Pap. VIII 1 A 414 November 20, 1847) (JP, 6075). By 1850, on the occasion of the publication of *Practice in Christianity*, their relationship practically ended. This book which addresses the credibility gap between what one says and what one does in Christendom[34] raised the following commentaries from Mynster: "The book has made me furious; it is playing a profane game with holy things," and "Yes, half of the book is an attack on Martensen, the other half on me."[35] These phrases were said on October 21 to Just Henrik V. Paulli, Mynster's son-in-law and Royal Chaplain since 1840. Under those circumstances Kierkegaard was prepared to

33. Ibid., 1134; Pap., X 3 A 463.

34. Hansen, *Revolutionær Samvittighed*, 110.

35. "My Conversation with Bishop Mynster October 22, 1850, after he had read *Practice in Christianity*" (Pap X 3 A 563 n.d., 1850) (JP, 6691).

face the state: "I considered it my duty to maintain the cause in such a manner that I might let the established order determine to what extent it would force me to go farther, by taking steps against me" (Pap X 3 A 563 n.d., 1850) (JP, 6691).

Kierkegaard did touch structures of power. In 1851, he stated that his agenda was not to improve himself as in the ascetic fashion: "Christianity did not come in order to develop the heroic virtues in the individual but rather to remove selfishness and establish love— 'Let us love one another.'" Now, to commit ourselves with others did not mean to side with the "property-owners, cultured, and possessors of power" but with the "ordinary" person: "Therefore I have always urged that Christianity is properly for poor people who perhaps toil and sweat the whole day and are scarcely able to make a daily living. The greater the advantages the more difficult it is to become a Christian, for reflection can so very easily take a wrong turn" (Pap. X 3 A 714 n.d., 1851) (JP, 991).

In opposition to associating the figure of the pastors with prestige, status, and political power, Søren Kierkegaard's thought addresses those who are being systematically excluded from history, namely, the politically poor. In the entry: "The Modern Profitable Proclamation of Christianity," he had the bourgeoisie in mind: "If you are 'nobody,' you must not get involved in preaching that the true Christian repudiates the world's honors, medals, ribbons, and titles. The congregation would cry: What exaggeration!" But Mynster and Martensen were his main target: "No, you must at least be a Knight of Denmark if you are to preach successfully and profitably about it to the edification, contentment, and enjoyment of the congregation,—And if you excel in this kind of preaching of Christianity, then you will become Your Excellency, which is, as the philosophers say, a necessary development." The upper class and the clergy then ended up embracing this contradictory rule: "by expressing just the opposite of what you depict beautifully and picture fascinatingly, your life should guarantee that the whole thing is a game, a theatrical treat—then the congregation declares: By God, that was a lovely sermon" (Pap. X 3 A 720 n.d., 1851) (JP, 4559).

If in the *Postscript* Kierkegaard reflects on the easy-to-learn but hard-to-apply formula of establishing "an absolute relationship to the absolute *telos*, and a relative relationship to relative ends" (CUP, 386), then in the entry of 1852, "Serving God, Rather than the King," Kierkegaard makes his earlier claim explicit. He declares that nothing is better and more distinguished than serving God: "Neither silk, nor velvet, nor gold, nor stars, and obviously, since this is a matter of serving God, He will also contribute on the greatest possible scale—To be sure, that is, if it were not even more distinguished that serving God is characterized by poverty and lowliness." With this important qualification Kierkegaard substantiates his point, regarding the politico-economic ideological ingredients of a pseudo-Christianity: "All illusion in Christendom, from the very first to the last, is due to the fact that the secular notion of distinguishedness has been substituted for the divine."[36]

In relation to Christendom, Kierkegaard would agree with Marx in considering it "the opium of the people," because he attacked bourgeois Christianity dialectically: "[Søren Kierkegaard] on the basis of a vision of revolutionary Christianity," Marx "on the basis of revolutionary atheism."[37] The other fact we should not lose sight of is Kierkegaard's political and economic dimension, which can be found in his very concept of the individual, as Forrester has already pointed out: "And even his individualism and scorn for the masses can well be interpreted as the desire that the masses should discover individuality just as in Marx the collectivist society is a condition of radical individual freedom."[38]

The Bourgeois Philistine (*Spidsborger*)

If you wish to love me, love the men you see.
Whatever you do for them you do for me.

—Jesus Christ (WL, 158)

I was dressed, and you stole my clothes.

—Jesus Christ[39]

36. "Guds Tjeneste frem for Kongens Tjeneste: Guds Tjeneste er den fornemste Tjeneste, ganske vist; selv-følgeligt er da Intet for godt for den, hverken Silke eller Fløiel eller Guld eller Stjerner, og selvfølgeligt, da det er Guds Tjeneste, vil ogsaa Gud give til efter den størst mulige Maalestok—ganske vist, hvis det ikke var endnu fornemmere at Guds Tjeneste var kjendelig paa Armod og Ringhed. Alle Bedrag i Christenheden ligefra det første indtil det sidste ligge i, at man substituerer det verdslige Begreb af Fornemhed istedetfor det gudelige" (Pap X 4 A 672 n.d., 1852; my translation).

37. Forrester, "The Attack on Christendom in Marx and Kierkegaard," 191.

38. Ibid, 193.

39. Words said to the Spanish conquerors, according to Bartolomé de las Casas;

During the years of 1846 to 1852, Kierkegaard articulated powerful social, economic, and political concepts within the broad context of the state-religion monism. In this subsection I propose a closer examination of the bourgeois philistine, who was Kierkegaard's interlocutor while the provoking gadfly elaborated his economic critique. In doing so, I will start by providing a general scope of the role the bourgeois philistine played in Kierkegaard's transitional works. I will also draw attention to some relevant themes linked with the bourgeoisie.

In Kierkegaard's Transitional Works

EDIFYING DISCOURSES (OPBYGGELIGE TALER)

The provoking Dane criticizes the market economy where the knowledge of the self derives from "his merits" and from "what abilities are entrusted to him." The self has become another commodity, a good of trade, an object of comparison in relation to the social value standards: "in this way what we call a person's self is also just like the value of money, and he who knows himself, knows to the last penny how much he is worth, and knows how to sell himself so that he gets his entire worth." In short, this knowledge of the self is dictated by the bourgeoisie exploitative interests (ED 4:29–30).[40] It is very revealing to read an early entry connected with the same topic: "The esthetic ideal is replaced by national taste, yes, town-and-class taste, and the most correct copy of it" (Pap I A 222, August 11, 1836) (JP, 853). In this respect, what John Douglas Mullen observes holds true: "Marx was not the only mid-nineteenth-century thinker to perceive that grand theories when 'seen through' can often turn out to be the productions of a class in service of the tastes of that class."[41]

Kierkegaard was keenly aware of the legitimacy of assuming a social role; nonetheless "What can be avoided is the absolute identification of oneself with the role."[42] The mature Kierkegaard continues opposing social roles that subsume individuals, but especially roles that are related to prestige and power: "The alleviation might be, for example: I

---

quoted in Hinkelammert, *Sacrificios humanos y sociedad occidental*, 170.

40. Cited in Nordentoft, *Kierkegaard's Psychology*, 87.

41. Mullen, *Kierkegaard's Philosophy*, 134.

42. Nordentoft, *Kierkegaard's Psychology*, 243ff.

am Chancellor, Knight of Denmark, member of the Cavalry Purchasing Commission, Alderman, Director of the Club" (Pap. XI 1 A 284 n.d., 1854) (JP, 200).

Works of Love (*Kjerlighedens Gjerninger*)

This book contains much of Kierkegaard's Christian ethics, develops important economic themes, and questions the whole framework of the new liberal ideals: "'Here lies a world which is for sale and only awaits a buyer'... But money is the world's god; therefore it thinks that everything which has to do with money or has a relationship to money is earnestness" (WL, 296).

Works of Love again is a transitional piece of work that does not represent the Dane's final thought. In this book, Kierkegaard discriminates between *Kjerlighed* ("love"), which excludes the possessive pronouns *mine* and *thine*, and *Elskov* ("romantic love") which implies love in return as in a trade relationship according to the world of money in the commercial world: "One pays out money in order to purchase this or that convenience; one pays the money but does not obtain the convenience—yes, in this way one is fooled. One makes a transaction of love; one pays out his love in exchange, but one gets no love in exchange—yes, in this way one is deceived" (WL, 223).[43]

Kierkegaard proposes the divine love, *Kjerlighed*, for which God is the middle term[44] and the neighbor is the first person one sees: "the next human being in the sense that the next human being is every other human being" (WL, 70). In this kind of love, to really love the unseen is demonstrated by loving the person one sees: "The more he loves the unseen, the more he will love the men he sees.... 'If you wish to love me, love the men you see. Whatever you do for them you do for me'" (WL, 158). This is, of course, contrasted with the mercantilistic mentality that isolated the selfish individual, as Kirmmse has correctly pointed out: "Kierkegaard's supposed asocial individualism is in fact conceived and

---

43. Nordentoft, *Kierkegaard's Psychology*, 393.

44. In a syllogism, the term which is contained in both premises is the middle term; the predicate of the conclusion is the minor term. The premise that contains the major term is the major premise, and the premise containing the minor term is the minor premise. The order in which the premises are stated does not, therefore, determine which is the major premise.

executed as an attempt to recall the variously competing and massing *homines oeconomici* to the possibility of being Neighbors."[45]

In *Works of Love*, Christianity is portrayed in contradistinction to a caste system based on social distinctions by virtue of birth, education, economic power, or the like. Kierkegaard promotes the equality of the eternal: "But, alas, in actual life one laces the outer garment of distinction so tightly that it completely conceals the external character of this garment of distinction, and the inner glory of equality never, or very rarely, shines through, something it should do and ought to do constantly"(WL 96). Granted, in 1848 Kierkegaard stated that "Christianity will not in partiality side with any temporal distinction, either the lowliest or the most acceptable in the eyes of the world" (WL 81, 80–83). However, as we shall see, this view will be modified especially during his radical final years.

CHRISTIAN DISCOURSES (*CHRISTELIGE TALER*)

The plain language of Kierkegaard's *Christian Discourses* describes the heathen as the heathen within Christendom, and "The Concerns of the Heathen" as the worries of the urban privileged class: "he who desires to be rich—his thought is constantly upon the ground, with his anxiety about earthly things; he walks with bowed head, looking constantly before him, if per chance he might find riches" (CD, 24).

At this point Kierkegaard is very careful in not spiritualizing or underestimating the crude reality of poverty. Kierkegaard's audience is quite specific: "The person I portrayed (in the first discourse on the cares of the pagans) as crudely talking about the earnestness of life is not, as one immediately sees, what is called a poor man—indeed, I could never imagine such a person talking that way" (Pap. VIII, 1 A 598 n.d., 1848) (JP, 6120) Without resorting to technical and philosophical terminology, the *Christian Discourses* addresses a wide range of economic issues, such as socially provoked financial concerns, absolutization of money, greediness and envy, the manipulation of social prestige, worries about tomorrow, activism, and the like.[46]

---

45. Connell, "Introduction," xviii, follows Kirmmse.
46. Ibid., 85ff.

The Sickness unto Death (*Sydomen til Døden*)

In this book, Kierkegaard deals with social typologies, the philistine being one of them. The "bourgeois philistine" (*Spidsborger*[47]) was an urban, middle-class businessperson[48] who "constituted the bulk of the bourgeoisie and of the literate public, yet they were not themselves tastemakers, but rather followers, consumers of the taste or ideology prepared by their Golden Age superiors in 'Culture.'"[49]

The Sickness unto Death draws very well the boundary line between *to have* and *to be*. To have, or to know oneself by externality, is to allow oneself "to be cheated of one's self by 'the others,'" "having become part of the multitude, a cipher, a copy, the others, a number." In this way it is much easier and safer to adjust to social (worldly) categories, to exist for others: "for in the world a self is what one least asks after, and the thing it is most dangerous of all to show signs of having. The biggest danger, that of losing oneself, can pass off in the world as quietly as if it were nothing; every other loss, an arm, a leg, five dollars, a wife, etc. is bound to be noticed" (SUDb, 62–63). Anti-Climacus named that sickness as despair, or more exactly, sin.

"Judge for Yourselves" (*Til Selvorøvelse*)

Kierkegaard continued using a more popular style to assert that consumers as well as producers of this mercantilistic mentality kept a tight

47. "*Spidsborger* itself is allied to the German *Spiesbürger*, and originally meant a free citizen (*Borger*) wealthy enough to be allowed to be part of the militia for the defense of the city and as such permitted to carry a spear (*Spyd*)" (Kirmmse, "Psychology and Society" 177–78 n.11).

48. At this point it is useful to make some clarifications. The philistine social category must not be confused with the aesthetic existence. For instance, it is helpful to remember how Lukács missed the whole point in characterizing Kierkegaard's aesthetic sphere as a kind of feeling and not as a kind of existence. Moreover, the Marxist scholar did not take into account Kierkegaard's two distinctions within the aesthetic way of being: The first one represents the person of immediate and unreflective relation to the world. This type of existence is not worth living according to Kierkegaard following Socrates, and is not a prerogative of the "aristocracy" but is open to everybody who owns an unexamined life. The second kind of aesthetic existence is exemplified by the persons who want to embrace all possibilities but end up committing themselves to nothing. This is not the romantic position; on the contrary, it is a criticism of the romantic inwardness of the "beautiful soul." See Hunsinger, "A Marxist View of Kierkegaard," 29–40.

49. Kirmmse, "Psychology and Society," 178.

relationship with the official bourgeois religion: "they whose career it was to proclaim Christianity found it necessary (out of love of mankind, to say nothing of self-love) to make Christianity commensurate with buying and selling. Thus it became only 'comfort.'" Or yet more: "But to sell Christianity as comfort in this way without life commitment —this is indulgence, is doing business with Christianity" (FSE, 132).

Culture as a Market Commodity

> I will leave behind me, intellectually speaking a not-so-little capital. Alas, but I know who is going to inherit from me, that character I find so repulsive, he who will keep on inheriting all that is best just as he has done in the past—namely, the assistant professor, the professor. (Pap. X 4 A 628 n.d., 1852) (JP, 6817)

Kierkegaard perceived the contradiction that exists between the intellectual and spiritual human capabilities, which are economically disinterested, and a society based on profit. As early as 1842, he wrote: "The same thing has happened in the world of the sciences as in the world of commerce. First one traded in kind; then money was invented; today in the sciences all transactions are in paper money, which nobody cares about except the professors" (Pap. IV A 6 n.d., 1842–1843) (JP, 3).

In the entry already quoted, "everybody is a thief in his own job," Kierkegaard makes his point straightforwardly by pointing out the role that money plays in the sphere of the spirit. He argues that in a parallel way in which the business manager of the church has power over the pastor, the money factor determines the power of the readers over the publishers, and the power of the publishers over the authors. Kierkegaard accuses the "publisher-effrontery" for regarding that "books are a commodity and an author a merchant." This is an immorality that corrupts the nature of this intellectual enterprise: "But without modesty there is no true intellectual-spiritual relationship; but how is the author's possible modesty to be of any good to the reader when it has to go through this medium of effrontery: money, money, money, the demands of the time, money, money." Kierkegaard's understanding of the true intellectual-spiritual relationship explains, in part, his assuming the roles of writer and publisher as we will see below: "the one who essentially carries out the intellectual undertaking should himself take over the financial side, not because of a possibly greater financial reward, far from it, but in order that there can be a little modesty" (Pap VII 1 A 77 n.d., 1846) (JP, 2767).

The commercialistic dimension of the church did not escape Kierkegaard's eye. Regarding the Bible societies, he states: "those vapid caricatures of missions, societies which like all companies only work with money and are just as mundanely interested in spreading the Bible as other companies in their enterprises: the Bible societies have done immeasurable harm."[50] For Kierkegaard, the capitalistic enterprise and scholarship are in connivance. The Bible is very easy to understand: "I open the N.T. and read: 'If you want to be perfect, then sell all your goods and give to the poor and come and follow me.' But scholarship helps us in our task of not wanting to understand, namely, not wanting to act accordingly: 'Good God, all the capitalists, the officeholders, and the pensioners, the whole race no less, would be almost beggars: we would be sunk if it were not for scientific scholarship!'" Kierkegaard reacts against the reduction of the Scripture to a doctrine that has to be interpreted by the Bible experts. Instead, without denying the value of scholarship, he affirms the existential dimension that is lacking: "the New Testament is very easy to understand, but so far I have found tremendously great difficulties in my own self when it comes to acting literally according to what is not difficult to understand" (Pap X 3 A 34 n.d., 1850) (JP, 2872).

Professors in theology have joined the mercantilistic ideology: "They write books and then books about books, and books to give synopses of the books—periodicals arose merely to write about them, and book publishers flourish, and many many thousands have jobs." Kierkegaard continues, "and not a single one of these hired hands even remotely resembled in his life a truly Christian existence." Knowledge then not only becomes a commodity but it becomes alienated from actuality: "I, Professor of Theology, Knight of Denmark, honored and esteemed with a fixed salary and free housing, an author of many learned books about Paul's three journeys" (Pap X 2 A 633 n.d., 1850) (JP, 3568).

In the entry "Sadness," Kierkegaard reflects on the rich man who amasses a fortune but does not know who is going to inherit it from him (Luke 12:20, Ps 39:6). From the intellectual perspective, Kierkegaard is

---

50. Kierkegaard, *Journals of Kierkegaard*, 847; Pap., IX A 442.

also leaving behind him a fortune but in his case he already knows who will inherit it from him: the professor (Pap. X 4 A 628 n.d., 1852) (JP, 6817). Kierkegaard disliked professors for buying and selling intellectual goods or, to say the same, for purporting to live at the level of the spirit: "In newspapers, in books, from pulpits, from podia, and in assemblies there is a solemnity, a pomposity—a pomposity that suggests that everything revolves around spirit, around truth, around thought," and actually, Kierkegaard argues, "Perhaps it does, too, perhaps. But perhaps everything nevertheless revolves around the job, around the career, perhaps. Is it the job, the career, that inspires the theological graduate, or is it Christianity? . . . or is it scholarship?" (FSE, 123).

Kierkegaard resisted assimilation into his mercantilistic, capitalistic society. He disapproved of the replacement of vocations such as an artist, a thinker, a teacher of ethics with the more attractive economic aspect of the traders. But he also perceived how art and scholarship surrendered to the money motive as well, turning into "even less than an out-and-out tradesman" (Pap. X 2 A 142 n.d., 1849) (JP, 980). Kierkegaard observes the way pastors and professors have used Pascal's thoughts but how, simultaneously they have done *epoge*[51] of his paradigmatic life: "This infamous, nauseating cannibalism whereby they eat the thoughts, opinions, expressions, moods of the dead—but their lives, their personal qualities—no, thank you, they want nothing to do with that" (Pap. X 4 A 537 n.d., 1852) (JP, 176).

Professors and in general the cultured spiritless who live in the social conventionalism of immediacy are the consumers of this market ideology: "Charming! As it says in the novels, he has now been happily married for several years, a forceful and enterprising man, father, and citizen, even perhaps an important man." Supposedly they own a self. Kierkegaard observes, "At home in his house his servants refer to him as 'himself'. In the city he is one of the worthies. In his conduct he is a respecter of persons, or of personal appearances, and he is to all appearances a person. In Christendom he is a Christian, one of the cultured Christians." However, here comes the thorny issue: "The question of immortality has frequently engaged him, and on more than one occasion he has asked the priest if there is such a thing, whether one would really

---

51. In other words, made abstraction of Pascal's life.

recognize oneself again; which for him must be a particularly pressing matter seeing he has no self" (SUD, 87).

In a context where the market is the final judge of values and where everything is for sale including the world of ideas and thoughts,[52] finally the very human being will be included as another commodity in the going rate: "When the National Pension Fund gets going, it would be entirely proper to list once every month the going rate or the market price of men: the government offers so much; the National Fund, so much." (Pap. XI 1 A 354 n.d., 1854) (JP, 3222)

In order to better grasp the social type of the "bourgeois philistine," allow me to introduce concepts and people that will be useful for defining the "bourgeois philistine."

The Cultured (Dannede) *and the Spiritless* (Aandløshed)

In this segment I will deal mainly with issues related to *De Dannede* ("the cultured") but in a dialectical way with the poor in the cultural sense or *De Udannede* ("the uncultivated" or "uneducated in manners"). During its Golden Age, the population of Denmark was 90 percent peasants. Copenhagen, on the other hand, had approximately 125,000 inhabitants, from which a narrow base belonged to the well-educated circle (*Dannelsekulturen*). The flourishing of the Golden Age from 1800 to 1850 was confined to the well-educated bourgeoisie.

Kierkegaard made important observations regarding Denmark's educational system. As early as 1837, he pointed out how the practical mind of his contemporaries was reflected in a seductive educational opportunism: "take quick correspondence courses which cover in fifty hours what otherwise takes three years," and you will become a successful businessperson (Pap. II A 4 n.d., 1837) (JP, 782). Kierkegaard subscribed to the Socratic method of education, but at the same time he praised other alternatives: "Grundtvig really made an invaluable observation when he said once in a conversation that instruction by questioning the child is wrong; it is the child who should be permitted to question" (Pap. X 1 A 647 n.d., 1849) (JP, 788). Nevertheless, Kierkegaard's main objec-

---

52. "There is a need for people who are willing to sell themselves, to offer themselves on the market. Take for example, the expression 'I don't believe what you say'; many people say today, 'I won't buy it.' That is to say, they are quite aware, although not consciously, that even exchange of ideas is a matter of the market, where either you buy it or you don't buy it" (Evans, *Dialogue with Erich Fromm*, 6–7).

tive went beyond the educational system; he was primarily interested in the formation of the character: "to bring up human beings is a very rare gift" (Pap. VIII 1 A 258 n.d., 1847) (JP, 787).

Kierkegaard branded the bourgeois philistines as spiritless. This characterization does not have to do with dullness, lack of talent, or the possession of a low intelligence quotient. Spiritlessness points toward the absence of self-knowledge and the deficiency in committing oneself to actuality. Hegel fits Kierkegaard's criticism:

> A thinker erects a huge building, a system, one that encompasses the whole of life and world-history, etc.—and if one then turns attention to his personal life one discovers to one's astonishment the appalling and ludicrous fact that he himself does not live in this huge, high-vaulted palace, but in a store-house next door, or a kennel, or at most in the janitor's quarters. If one took it upon oneself to draw attention with but a single word to this contradiction, he would be insulted. For so long as he can complete the system—with the help of his error—being in error is not what he is afraid of.[53]

The enlightened bourgeois norms of culture, then, were Kierkegaard's target in dealing with the underclass of the culturally deprived that, nonetheless were not spiritless.[54]

Kierkegaard was not promoting anti-intellectualism; he instead was unveiling the modern elitist and heretical version of gnosticism: "Certainly Christianity has never been a mystery, has in fact abhorred mystery, in the sense of being only for a few superlative people who have been initiated. No, God has chosen the poor and the despised (James 2:6)—but the initiation was not lacking." What matters for Kierkegaard is the articulation of knowing with doing: "It is not an intellectual initiation but an ethical initiation, personality's enormous respect for being admitted into the Christian community, a respect expressed not in assurances and frills but existential in action." The narrow circles do not have the monopoly of the gospel, because this is for everyone who follows Christ: "Therefore I never forget that in Christianity a shoemaker, a tailor, and a manual laborer is just as much a possibility as the greatest scholar and the keenest intellectual. Yes, in general the Church must

---

53. Kierkegaard, *The Sickness unto Death*, 74 (Hannay translation).
54. Norderntoft, *Kierkegaard's Psychology,* 240.

always expect its salvation from a layman, simply because he is closer to the ethical initiation" (Pap. X 2 A 341 n.d., 1850) (JP, 2793).

Kierkegaard warns his readers in relation to the spiritual goods of insight, knowledge, talent, aptitudes (CD, 123), which very easily can become an end in itself: "The learned man becomes more and more learned, but in an invidious sense, and at last so learned that no one can understand him, so learned that he cannot communicate himself" (CD, 124).

To reach actuality is also a matter of inwardness (*Inderlighed*),[55] but this term has misled more than one of Kierkegaard's critics. However, inwardness or, even worse, "interiority," was a daily used word that plainly meant intensity, passion, heartfelt sincerity, commitment, love, trust, and the like. That word did not have philosophical connotations; on the contrary, it was understood by the common reader. When he states that religious faith is a matter of inwardness, Kierkegaard is not referring to the purely personal, subjective level; on the contrary, he is encouraging us to make a decision[56] and to brave externality in a significant manner.[57]

In summing up, let us bear in mind that Kierkegaard embraced the church's doctrine, form of government, and liturgy. However, it is at the level of practice where he was critical: "The doctrine of the established Church, its organization, are both very good. Oh, but our lives—believe me, they are indeed wretched."[58]

55. "Inwardness" does not have to do with the subjectivity of the autonomous individual but with the intersubjective individual. See Westphal, "Levinas, Kierkegaard, and the Theological Task," 252.

56. See, for example Freud's concept of decision and the Oedipal: "Freud's real discovery, the tremendous power—possibly the greatest passion which exists in man or woman—of the wish to return to the womb, to mother's breast, to mother's lap, to that which is certain, to that which is protection, to that which does not force one to make decisions. You might say it involves escaping from freedom into the past—into the enveloping, protection, loving, warmth of the mother or of a person with a 'motherly' function. This doesn't mean necessarily the real mother. . . . However, this escape is at the expense of the full development of the person. Therefore it constitutes in some significant sense his rejection of his potential independence, his refusal to actualize his independence" (Evans, *Dialogue with Erich Fromm*, 71).

57. Nordentoft, *Kierkegaard's Psychology*, 241.

58. Kierkegaard, *Kierkegaard's Journals*, 1185; Pap., X 4 A 33.

I will now analyze some social institutions in order to better understand the discontinuity that existed between the theory and practice of the well-to-do and well-educated spiritless.

H. L. Martensen and the University

Søren Kierkegaard's attack upon the well educated included the aristocracy, the professors, and the Hegelian system. Martensen was the symbol of the academia besides being since 1845, the "handsome court preacher" who, with a straight face preached about the poor without committing himself to them (Pap. X 2 A 227 n.d., 1849) (JP, 3491).

In Kierkegaard's time the only university in Denmark was the University of Copenhagen, which had around two hundred professors. Due to the amalgamation of church and state, the 1300 to 1400 priests received university training.

Hans Lassen Martensen had a brilliant and successful career. His curriculum vita included being a court preacher, a member of the Royal Scientific Society, a knight of Dannebrog, and bishop of Zealand. Within the university, he started as a professor in 1837. The next year he became the successor of Kierkegaard's favorite deceased professor Paul Martin Møller. By 1840 Martensen was promoted to an Extraordinary Professor, and in 1850 acquired the rank of Ordinary Professor.[59]

Martensen's aristocratic personality was attuned to the narrow and exclusive audience to which he preached: "the noblest and most cultivated in the capital." On the occasion of criticisms raised against him for caring only for the elite, we can see his concept of culture and church: "[i]t must be noted that it is of great importance that the cultivated people are preached to, and it would be one of the saddest things if the cultivated remained outside the Church, alien and indifferent in relation to the Gospel." And he continues with his conservative views: "Culture is the highest power in society, and the preacher who can seize hold of the cultivated seizes hold of the most important part of society, which can influence the rest."[60]

In the entry "the age of saints is past; they are not created any more," Kierkegaard highlighted the connection between academia and the privileged classes. He mentions a person who is in the social register

---

59. Kirmmse, *Kierkegaard,* 170.

60. *Af mit Levnet,* [*From My Life*] 2:94. Quoted in ibid., 192.

due to his possession of an *honoris causa* doctorate, besides the fact of being able to marry his children to a major, a candlemaker, or a wholesale merchant: "In the everyday life of the world one can scarcely be a success if one is not in the social register or has no honorary degree" (Pap. IX A 475 n.d., 1848) (JP, 223).

Martensen established himself as the symbol of intellectuality as a professor of theology and well-celebrated lecturer. In 1849, with the publication of his *Christian Dogmatics (Den christelige Dogmatik)*—whose intended original title was: *Speculative Dogmatics*—he dispelled all doubts about his leading cultural role. While in the first half of the foreword Martensen attacked the left-wing Hegelians, the rest is devoted to rejecting the anti-intellectualism and individualism of Søren Kierkegaard. What Martensen proposes is "continuing progress toward the unity of faith and knowledge."[61] In the midst of those difficult years in which "all existence was disintegrating," Kierkegaard faults Martensen for sitting and organizing a dogmatic system in which the most important matter is "to determine where the angels are to be placed in the system, and things like that" (Pap. X 1 A 553 n.d., 1849) (JP, 6448).

The same year, 1849, at the Roskilde Ecclesiastical Convention, on October 30, Peter Christian Kierkegaard compared his brother's work as an author with the one of Martensen (Pap. X 2 A 273, 275) (JP, 6553, 54). Søren then broke with Peter and even on his deathbed refused to see him. A partial reason for the rupture was that Kierkegaard saw a lack of originality in his former professor: "Martensen really has no primitivity but permits himself to appropriate outright all of German scholarship as his own." But there existed more reasons: "If I am to be compared with Martensen *qua* author, it does seem to me that the essential difference ought to have been indicated, namely this, that I have sacrificed to an extraordinary extent and that he has profited to an extraordinary extent."[62]

One-third of Kierkegaard's *Practice in Christianity* was precisely against Martensen's theology, which was taken in tow by speculative Hegelianism; and in the other two-thirds he criticized Mynster (Pap. X 4 A 604 n.d., 1852) (JP, 6813). It is no wonder some Kierkegaard scholars have seen in the radical attack on the church a parallel attack upon

---

61. Ibid., 177.

62. Letter 240, S. Kierkegaard [December 1849])P. C. Kierkegaard. In *LD*.

Hegelianism: i.e., a reaction against the system that has subsumed the individual *(den enkelte)* at different levels.[63]

Kierkegaard's most widely sold book and the only one that saw several editions in the author's lifetime, *For Self-Examination*, has also speculative Hegelianism as its main target. Kierkegaard pointed out that whereas in the Middle Ages monastic-ascetic Christianity was the norm, in the mid-nineteenth-century professorial-scholarly Christianity was the fashion. The professor thus was the true Christian: "And with the professor came scientific scholarship, and with scholarship came doubts, and with scholarship and doubts came the scholarly public, and then came reasons *pro* and *contra*, and *pro und contra* were Germanized: *denn* [because] *pro und contra* allow *sich* [themselves] to say very much in the matter" (FSE, 194). For Kierkegaard, Christianity is not merely cognition but a sheer activity. Academia and the scientist are not the ultimate criterion of Christianity.

At this point it can be helpful to open a parenthesis and to realize the radicalization of Kierkegaard's thought in his last stage of life by observing his antagonistic relationship with Martensen during the final years: In December 1854, Martensen wrote: "Dr. S. Kierkegaard, whose Christianity is without Church and without history, and who seeks Christ only in the 'desert' and in 'private rooms.'" (AUCb, 362) In his autobiography Martensen observed that Kierkegaard "was only a humorist."[64]

Kierkegaard, on the other hand, on May 28, 1855, complained about a writer of *Kjøbenhavnsposten*, perhaps hired by the clergy: "On the occasion of my first article against Martensen, the paper declared me—in both prose and poetry—lunatic" (AUCb, 518). In August of the same year, Kierkegaard revealed Martensen's agenda: "What if this need is satisfied by becoming the royal court Chaplain? . . . It is four hundred rix-dollars[65] for twelve sermons, and thereby also the prospect of the bishopric is made more probable, which otherwise would remain very doubtful" (AUCb, 330). Now we can close the parenthesis and focus our attention on another "bourgeois philistine."

---

63. Hansen, *Revolutionær Samvittighed*, 129ff.

64. Kirmmse, *Encounters with Kierkegaard*, 199.

65. "The rix-dollar was worth about $5.00 in 1973 currency, contained six marks of sixteen shillings each" (Hong, MLW, 643 n. 261).

J. L. Heiberg and the Theater

Johan Ludvig Heiberg (1791–1860), the director of the Royal Theater, was part of the "rare few," or the creators of culture. He and Mynster and Martensen were the deans of the Golden Age school for philistine consumers of culture.[66] He was a multifaceted person who made inroads in many fields, as already mentioned above, and a pioneer in teaching Hegelianism in Denmark. He was a very prestigious person as Knight of Dannebrog and director of the Royal Theater for fifty years.

Heiberg's fame was increased by his being the husband of Johanne Luise Heiberg (1812–1890), the most celebrated actress in the country, who was mainly responsible for placing the theater in the center of Danish cultural life.[67] This is not the appropriate place to analyze Heiberg's life;[68] what interests us is the class and ideological agendas that Heiberg and Martensen had, as the most influential Hegelian philosophers and theologians of the refined class. They, as Kirmmse chose to emphasize, "have compromised Christianity by abusing Christian notions of God and the God-Man in order to deify their own aristocratic-conservative notion of a compound Christian-bourgeois culture."[69]

In effect, Heiberg's hierarchical view of society can be perceived in his conception of it as an organism: "The State is an organism . . . [In] an organism only what is organic has validity and rights. . . [In] the organism of the State nothing has political rights except the things that are themselves organized, thus estates and corporations."[70]

Regarding the issue of spiritlessness[71] (*Aandløshed*), or the state of being dead while yet alive, Heiberg agrees with Kierkegaard that it can be found with great frequency among the "bourgeois philistines"

66. Kirmmse, "Psychology and Society," 178–79.

67. Kierkegaard was inspired by her in writing *A Crisis in the Life of an Actress*. Furthermore, Heiberg was son of Thomasine Gyllembourg (1773–1853). Gyllembourg was born into a wealthy family of merchants and was the author of the novel *Two Ages*. In the review of that book, Kierkegaard suggests that *Fru* Gyllembourg was representative of the age of revolution whereas her son represented the age of reflection deprived of passion.

68. See Fenger, *The Heibergs*.

69. Kirmmse, "Psychology and Society," 186–87.

70. Heiberg, *Heibergs Prosaiske Skrifter*, 6, 270; quoted in Kirmmse, *Kierkegaard*, 161.

71. "As one more and more becomes spirit, it does not pain that one is not like the others. Spirit is precisely: not to be like the others." (AUCb, 344).

(*Spidsborgerne*). However, Kierkegaard disagrees with Heiberg in the sense that spiritlessness does not have to do with a lack of education but with a lack of will: "Self" is "spirit," and "the more will, the more self" (SVI XI 127, 142).[72] In *The Sickness unto Death*, Kierkegaard faults Heiberg for remaining trapped in Hegelian speculative intellectualism.

Kierkegaard perceived how in his day theater and church blended: "In paganism the theater was worship—in Christendom the churches have generally become the theater." Now the economic aspect played an important role since the pulpit, as a norm, contributed to "keeping an artistic" class distance: "it is pleasant, even enjoyable, to commune with the highest once a week by way of the imagination" (Pap. IX A 39 n.d., 1848) (JP, 6150). Kierkegaard's orchestration of preaching proposes "grace" as the major premise and true discipleship as the minor premise. However, he realizes the objections to his method: "But such a proclaimer, of course, is disturbing, for we want 'grace' to mean that we have the right to keep our money" (Pap. X 3 A 484 n.d., 1850) (JP, 3513).

Kierkegaard detected many analogies between the church and the theater: "Yesterday Dean John Doe, Knight of Denmark, appeared as guest at the Church of Our Lady. The house was sold out, filled to overflowing. Probably no one who was there will ever forget it" (Pap. X 4 A 90 n.d., 1851) (JP, 5040). Kierkegaard's suspicious character led him to define the church as a mere "theatrical entertainment and enjoyment," and led him to be on guard against its proclaimers: "—however impressively His Reverence declaims, however impressively he depicts, however much he weeps does not help—Fru Heiberg also can do all that" (Pap. X 4 A 227 n.d., 1851) (JP, 3519).

The "plump career-preachers" are, in Kierkegaard's view, pecuniarily motivated. In an entry he analyses Peter's sermon on "The First Day of Pentecost," based on the text of Acts 2: "The faithful lived in harmony together . . . and there where no poor among them; because they shared everything in common." Kierkegaard's economic consciousness praises the institution of diakonia of the early church on not having poor people among them by everything's being held in common. And Kierkegaard hastens to contextualize the Scripture: "—well, we have it in our power to bring it about. But I wonder if His

---

72. Kirmmse, "'Out with it!,'" 19.

Excellency is actually served thereby, or wishes it, or has any idea of what he is saying; or I wonder if the congregation does?" (Pap. X 4 A 330 n.d., 1851 (JP, 3522).

What is lacking is the commitment: "Every person always understands the truth a good deal farther out than he expresses it existentially [*existentielt*]. Why does he not go farther out, then?" (Pap. X 4 A 247 n.d., 1851) (JP, 2301). It is because for the official preacher, money, prestige, and esteem have primacy over the poor; that is the reason why "he draws the attention of the government, becomes a Knight, ranking with the cabinet ministers, gets permission to have the velvet on the left arm, etc." (Pap. X 4 A 495 n.d., 1852) (JP, 3525) Not surprisingly, the proclamation of Christianity has been entrusted to this kind of "speech experts" (Pap. XI 1 A 447 n.d., 1854) (JP, 3535).

It is inhuman cruelty and sadism, according to Kierkegaard, the way the cultured are mentally armed with a thousand prudential rules and evasions. As it has already been apparent, there are many *Journal* entries protesting against the opulence of the churches, but here we limit ourselves to a couple of them: "to preach in an elegant church to an elegant, honored, cultured gathering about those noble ones who suffered for the truth etc.—and the general effect is that the auditors have passed a pleasant hour and the speaker is admired." Kierkegaard faults this kind of preacher for obtaining "blood money" by means of turning the "martyrs into money"; but he goes on to blame the congregation because of their "brutish cruelty" in tolerating that way of preaching. This order of affairs is generalized all over Denmark, in the city and in the countryside as well: "there is no setting for the larger decision." Nevertheless, Kierkegaard is of the opinion that at least in the countryside the pastor "can see to humbling himself and his listeners under eminence and greatness so that it all becomes a little more than a pleasant hour." And Kierkegaard concludes, "But to preach this way in the great cities is treason against Christianity" (Pap. X 1 A 125 n.d., 1849) (JP, 3481).

The glorious moments lived on the stage keep a parallel with the church's weekly aesthetic intensifications as well. Kierkegaard mentions a pastor who, like an actor, feels a void when he does not perform. It is comparable with an addicted person for whom "it is not so easy to do without alcohol." The church and the theater are similar: "In a magnificent building where art and good taste have produced the aesthetic effect of pomp and ceremony, when the organ's magnificent voice has filled the vaulted room and the last tones die away—" Kierkegaard continues, "a speaker steps forth who now sets everything in motion to create the desired effect at that moment; he himself is fired up by perceiving how effective he is; he is intensified, etc." (Pap. X 2 A 149 n.d, 1849) (JP, 3488).

Kierkegaard's economic critique goes on to draw the ideal difference between a pastor and an actor. The former backs up the existential, what he expresses, with his words: "that the pastor is poor when he preaches about poverty, is derided when he preaches about suffering derision, etc.; whereas the actor simply has the task to deceive by doing away with the existential altogether—in the most profound sense the pastor has the task of preaching with his life" (Pap. X 2 A 149 n.d, 1849) (JP, 3488).

Mynster is another clear example of what a spiritless "bourgeois philistine" is. Nonetheless, I will return to him in the segment about the established church. Now let us move to a brief survey of the politically poor.

The "Ordinary" Person

> The people, the great majority of men, who must use most of their time in earning a living, in menial work—in regard to them it would be cruel to jack up the price. (Pap X1 A135 n.d., 1849) (JP, 236)

It is my contention that Søren Kierkegaard's economic agenda indeed challenged the structures that produced economic inequality. In the transitional years of 1846 to 1852, one can notice Kierkegaard's shift from the conservative to the more critical social and political paradigm, motivated in part by the general political transformations.

The *Concluding Unscientific Postscript* captures very well the need for the intellectual to be sensitive to the perspective from below: "[T]he wise person ought first to understand the same as what the simple person understands, and feel himself obligated by the same things which obligate the simple person and only then ought he go on to world-historical matters." The way culture was understood led Kierkegaard to state: "The more culture and knowledge, the more difficult it is to become a Christian" (SV, 1st. ed. VII, 131, 332).[73]

Kierkegaard detected the interplay between wealth and poverty: "Is it really so glorious to become *the* superior person no one else can become; is it not disconsolate instead! Is it so glorious to dine on silver when others starve, to live in palaces when so many are homeless," he continues, "to be a scholar no ordinary person can become, to have a name in the sense that excludes thousands and thousands—is that so glorious!" (TA, 226). Kierkegaard also was very sensitive to the poor. During his walking and in the midst of his intellectual activity, he used to talk to them, and what is more important, he listened to them (Pap. IX A 298 n.d., 1848) (JP, 6259).

Kierkegaard's ontological egalitarianism prevented him from assuming the gnostic positions that subordinate body to mind; menial work to mental activity; the illiterate to the literate: "humanness consists in this: that every human being is granted the capability of being spirit; it is not that nonsense about a company of brainy people; one often finds a simple man existing within the realm of spirit and a professor a long way away from it" (Pap. IX A 76 n.d., 1848) (JP, 69). For him, a servant-girl is, before God, as important as the most eminent genius. Kierkegaard himself acknowledged his "almost exaggerated sympathy for the ordinary people, the common man" (Pap. XI A 135 n.d., 1849) (JP, 236). However, together with that, he was unmasking the unfair and anti-Christian structures: "I wanted to live with the Common Man; it gratified me immeasurably to be concerned, friendly, kind, and attentive to that social class which simply is forgotten in the so-called 'Christian state'" (Pap. X, 2 A48, n.d., 1849) (JP, 6498).

Kierkegaard's egalitarianism guided him to take sides with the illiterate: "No, the cultured and well-to-do class, who if not upper-crust are at least upper-bourgeoisie—they ought to be the targets and for them the price ought to be jacked up in the drawing rooms" (Pap X1 A135 n.d., 1849) (JP, 236). To be congruent with his love for the common person, Kierkegaard broke with the bourgeoisie: "how could the Gospel, which is for the poor, possibly be for the elite!" (FSE, 43). The price consisted in sacrificing "every advantage of solidarity with the upper class" (Pap. X3 A 13 n.d., 1850) (JP, 6611).

---

73. Quoted by Kirmmse, *Kierkegaard*, 264.

The intellectual who flirts with ideas that are far from being actualized in his life filled the pages of the *Journals*. Take Eugene Sue, to quote just one example: "[he] has written his way to being a millionaire by describing the poverty and wretchedness of actual life. Indeed, I am grateful that he was in a position to give 50 dollars to the poor, that he was the lucky person to whom this enviable opportunity was offered" (Pap. X 2 A 392 n.d., 1850) (JP, 820).

The Vexing Gadfly and the "Ordinary" Person

> If Christianity would have held continually to the intensive, if no one had been allowed to call himself a Christian unless his life expressed equality with the wretched, well, then Christianity would have continued to be the salt of the world instead of being frightfully diluted in these millions and millions of Christians and rendered unrecognizable through politicizing evaporation. (Pap. X 4 A 541 n.d., 1852) (JP, 3201)

Kierkegaard, who belonged to "the movement party" during his transitional years played with words[74] in his diagnosis of his time. By analogy with the railroad trains that are stopped by means of a gadfly, Kierkegaard's gadfly sting is revolutionary in facing tumultuous European events: "They wish to stop by means of revolution and to stop a revolution by means of a counterrevolution. But what is a counterrevolution if it is not also a revolution? And to what can we compare a revolution if not to a gadfly" (LD # 260 #186. before August 20, 1848, to J. L. A. Kolderup-Rosenvinge)?[75]

Kierkegaard is promoting neither a politics of no intervention between religion and state nor a clericalization of the state. If the state, in Kierkegaard's view, takes religion for granted, then we will be drawn into the vortex of politics: "Any purely political movement which accordingly lacks the religious element or is forsaken by God, is a vortex, [which] cannot be stopped, and is a prey to the illusion of wanting a fixed point ahead, which is wanting to stop by means of a gadfly; for the fixed point, the only fixed point, lies behind." Kierkegaard is then reckoning a revolutionary role to religion: "And therefore my opinion

---

74. *Bremse* means both a "brake" or "to brake," and a "botfly" or "gadfly."

75. Janus Lauritz Andreas Kolderup-Rosenvinge (1792–1850), professor of law at the University of Copenhagen. The *Conferentsraad* is an honorific title.

about the whole European confusion is that it cannot be stopped except by religion" (LD, 262, # 186).

Two years later, Kierkegaard added more relevant data to his concept of the revolutionary gadfly. This takes place within the context of a self-complacent established order that presumes to have achieved total peace and security: in a word, the highest. Mr. Impudence, or the gadfly, thus has the mission of constantly preventing the established order from falling asleep or from self-deification: "Every human being is to live in fear and trembling, and likewise no established order is to be exempted from fear and trembling." The molesting gadfly, in this manner, is the religious revolutionary who addresses the political realm in a direct way: "Fear and trembling signify that there is a God—something every human being and every established order ought not to forget for a moment" (PC 88).

Kierkegaard himself, in addressing the self, articulates a social criticism by resorting to basic social typologies. In Kierkegaard's catalog of the levels of intensity for despair, he refers to the lowest degree of consciousness as being despairingly unconscious of having a self. The corresponding social type is spiritlessness (*Aandløshed*). To this group belong the literate people of the middle class. The well-to-do philistine (*Spiesburger or Spidsborger*) i.e., the honorable gentlemen who owns political power as well.

On the other side lies the "ordinary" person, the one who, before the constitution of 1848–1849, did not possess political personhood and after that date gained political power only theoretically. For this segment of society, the price of Christianity had to be reconsidered: "The people, the great majority of men, who must use most of their time in earning a living, in menial work—in regard to them it would be cruel to jack up the price. Here, however, a mildness and a consolation ought to be humanely provided" (Pap X1 A135 n.d., 1849) (JP, 236). Kierkegaard's ontological egalitarianism is well known: "I have always been indescribably inspired by the fact that before God it is just as important to be a servant-girl, if that is what one is, as to be the most eminent genius. From this comes also my exaggerated sympathy for ordinary people, the common man." Nevertheless, the Dane's social-class criticism is less-often quoted: "No, the cultured and well-to-do class, who if not upper crust are at least upper bourgeoisie—they ought to be the targets and for them the price ought to be jacked up in the drawing rooms" (Pap. X 1 A 135 n.d., 1849) (JP, 236).

In his *Concluding Unscientific Postscript* Kierkegaard was sensitive to the truth that the reality of oppression exists at different levels: "the cook says to the poor woman who comes on Saturdays: 'You may have forgotten what I can do,' namely, persuade the mistress not to give her any longer the week's leftovers." This man, on the other hand, is exploited as well: "and on Sunday we all go to church (with the exception of the cook, who never has time because there are always dinner guests on Sunday at his Honor's)." Churchgoers are also objects of manipulation: "Yet, one moment: we have arrived at church; with the assistance of a very authoritative usher (for the usher is especially powerful on Sundays, and indicates with a silent glance at so and so what he can do), we are severally assigned to our seats with reference to our particular position in society" (CUP 420). And finally, the church rulers are subservient of the mighty civilians: "The clergyman enters the pulpit—but at the very last moment there is a very influential man who has come late, and the usher must now exercise his authority . . . On Monday the clergyman is himself a mighty man, that we are all made to feel, except those who are more mighty than he" (CUP, 420).

Kierkegaard emphasized the heterogeneity of Christ with the established order but simultaneously noted the homogeneity of Christ with the common person, in whom "the best capacities are to be found" (Pap. IX A 340 n.d., 1848) (JP, 1016). N. F. S. Grundtvig sided with the happy Danes of the fairly well-off middle class whereas Kierkegaard took the cause of the sad rural and urban Danes. This element must be taken into account when we refer to Kierkegaard's metamorphosis of 1848. In the entry "An accounting of the attack of The Corsair," Kierkegaard confessed having achieved a change of perspective: "As an author I have gotten a new string in my instrument, have been enabled to hit notes I never would have dreamed of otherwise. I have achieved 'actuality' [*Virkelighed*] in a much stricter sense of the word." This was not a purely intimistic spiritual experience; this change was shaped by the political and social events of his time. This explains the presence of the "ordinary" person in his reported metamorphosis (Pap. X2 A 251 n.d., 1849) (JP, 6548). A year later he wrote down what "to achieve actuality" means. It includes the existence for every human being particularly for those who do not possess social entity: "On Sunday the pastor preaches about loving 'the neighbor'—but in so-called actuality every man as such has a certain relativity in which he lives; the others do not essentially exist for him." Or still more clearly, he states: "From a Christian point of view I do not have the right to ignore existentially one single man" (Pap. X 1 A 632 n.d., 1849) (JP, 4163).

Contrary to that of other Danish Golden Age members, Kierkegaard's agenda systematically included the excluded people: "The common man is my task, even if I continually have had to make a stand at the very top level of the cultured and distinguished world." Kierkegaard's concept of equality contained direct effects for the here and now: "I wanted to live with the simple man; it gratified me immeasurably to be concerned, friendly, kind, and attentive to that social class which simply is forgotten in the so-called 'Christian state.'" About the constitution of 1848–1849 Kierkegaard did shake up the establishment by raising the issue of "the scandalous wrongness of the existence of the poor":

> An oldish woman from Amager sits in Buegangen and sells fruit; she has an old mother whom I sometimes have helped a little. When I greet her, I essentially am not doing anything—but yet it would please her, it would cheer her up that every morning a man whom she must regard as well off came along and never forgot to say 'good-morning' to her and sometimes also spoke a few words with her. Really, what the state needs is just the kind of idler I was if it is to recompense in the smallest way for the scandalous wrongness of its existence. For everyone clutches at the higher, the more distinguished relativities in society—and when people reach that point, who cares about the common man of the land? An idler like that is necessary, or many of them; he is a copula. To the social class that generally has to stand and wait in anterooms and hardly gets permission to say a word, how encouraging in many ways that there is a man they invariably see on the street, a man they may approach and talk to freely, a man with hundreds of eyes particularly for the sufferings of that social class—and I was that man—and that in addition this is a man who has established himself in the elite world. (Pap. X2 A 48 n.d., 1849) (JP, 6498)

The Slaves, the Dregs of Society: The Excluded People

> To love human beings is to love God and to love God is to
> love human beings; what you do unto men you do unto God,
> and therefore what you do unto men God does unto you. (WL
> 351–52)

Works of Love not only shows Kierkegaard's dialectical concept of the
self and its relational character, but, more concretely, this book describes
Kierkegaard's siding with the trilogy of the widow, the orphan, and the
foreigner, which in biblical language corresponds to the poor.

In this work, Kierkegaard registered a meaningful reaction against
the Copenhagen elite for whom the "ordinary" person did not even exist: "this distinguished corruption teaches the man of distinction that he
exists only for distinguished men, that he shall live only in their social
circle, that he must not exist for other men, just as they must not exist for him." And again: "He must never be seen among less important
people, at least never in their company, and if this cannot be avoided, or
must appear as a stately condescension—although in the subtlest guise
in order not to offend and hurt." Kierkegaard detected in such attitudes
a kind of schizophrenia that allows rich people to keep their privileges
in their relationship with nonpersons:

> He must be prepared to employ extreme courtesy towards com-
> mon people, but he must never associate with them as equals,
> for thereby expression would be given to his being—a human
> being—whereas he is a distinguished personage. And if he can
> do this easily, smoothly, tastefully, elusively and yet always keep-
> ing his secret (that those other men do not really exist for him
> and he does not exist for them), then this refined corruption
> will confirm him as being—a well-bred man. (WL 85)

In the same year Kierkegaard wrote in his *Journal* about the in-
consistency between church doctrine and practice: "It is very moving
to preach on Sundays about Christ's associating with sinners and tax-
collectors—but on Mondays it is a crime to speak with an ordinary man,
with a servant girl." Before that order of things Kierkegaard went on to
brave the world of the invisible: "It is, as they say, imprudently stupid
to involve oneself in this manner with people instead of avoiding them
and keeping out of sight. How stupid Christ must have been" (Pap. VIII
1 A 314 n.d., 1847) (JP, 1011).

Kierkegaard's insistence on articulating the gospel with reality can guide us in order to see the economic implications of the same. In one entry from 1848, he throws light on the subject. According to him, Christianity has to penetrate the whole of life. The mission of the clergy is not to show up on Sundays and entertain their audience with lectures on Christian dogmas and then to deny and forget about all during weekdays. Kierkegaard was a sharp observer of contradictions in actuality: "I am eminently attentive to how things go in the world." For instance, regarding the story of the rich man and Lazarus, he pointed out that preaching about compassion involves the danger of risking one's reputation in the midst of a frivolous society and yet to be genuinely compassionate, have money to give to the poor, and not only that but truly have a heart in your bosom, be kind to every poor and needy person (Pap. IX A 381 n.d., 1848) (JP, 6270).

One is compassionate not in order to get rid of the poor, quite the opposite—in order to become a friend: "be willing to talk with the poor on the street, be willing to let yourself be addressed by him on the street: in short, be in truth tender and compassionate." It also means to question social honorability: "The frivolous majority will grin every time they see you standing in conversation with a poor man . . . the shrewd fellows who aspire to finite goals will consider you mad, not so much because you give money this way as because you are losing and diminishing your reputation" (Pap. IX A 381 n.d., 1848) (JP, 6270).

Thus in 1848–1849 Kierkegaard was not talking of merely spiritual or eternal equality but of economic and social likeness as well: "Just as Christ tells the rich young ruler to sell all his goods and give to the poor, so one could also speak of the requirement to give all his rank and dignity (that is, the earthly, temporal) to the poor in order to express equality" (Pap X 1 A 269 n.d., 1849) (JP, 4158).

A. G. Rudelbach is known in the Kierkegaardian circle for his book *On Civil Marriage*[76] *(Om det borgerlige Ægteskab)*. However, regarding Rudelbach's earlier and often-ignored work, *On the Constitution of the Church,* Kierkegaard expressed very enlightening economic judgments.

---

76. Written by A. G. Rudelbach on January 1851. In this book. the author, himself a Grundtvigian, argues in favor of the separation of church and state, and in doing so quotes Kierkegaard's work in order to back up his point. Kierkegaard immediately responded in his *Open Letter to Dr. Rudelbach* in order to emphasize his dissent with Grundtvigians and with any other party as well. See Kirmmse, *Kierkegaard,* 419ff.

It was due to the reading of this book that Kierkegaard commented on Acts 3:6:

> "Gold and silver I do not have, but I give you what I have; stand up and walk," said Peter. Later on the clergy were saying: "Gold and silver we have—but we have nothing to give." (Pap. X 1 A 672 n.d., 1849) (JP, 384)

In this book, Kierkegaard continued his reflection on the correspondence which must exist between Scripture and the "ordinary" person: "In Christendom life is completely unchristian also in terms of what it means to live together with the common man and what this involves." Kierkegaard praises *On the Constitution of the Church* for something very specific: "This book has the merit of having shown that the state church gave rise to or contributed to giving rise to the proletariat." And still more clearly:

> In this respect my life is like a discovery—alas, in a certain sense I can say that it is a dearly purchased discovery. It is unchristian and wicked to base the state on a substructure of men who are totally ignored and excluded from personal association—even though on Sunday there are touching sermons about loving "one's neighbor." (Pap X 1 A 669 n.d., 1849) (JP, 4164)

Kierkegaard's concept of equality then had to necessarily revisit the doctrine of the church itself:

> The definition of "Church" found in the Augsburg Confession, that it is the communion [*Samfund*] of saints where the word is rightly taught and the sacraments rightly administered, this quite correctly (that is, not correctly) grasped only the two points about doctrine and sacraments and has overlooked the first, the communion of saints (in which there is the qualification in the direction of the existential [*Existentielle*]). Thus the Church is made into a communion of indifferent existences [*Existentser*] (or where the existential is a matter of indifference)—but the "doctrine" is correct and the sacraments are rightly administered. This is really paganism. (Pap. X 4 A 246 n.d., 1851) (JP, 600)

Or to say the same thing in a different way, contrary to the early church, we converted the Eucharist into the real body of Christ and the Church into the mystical body.[77]

The Dane has been faulted for being "incredibly insensitive and oblivious about the inhuman institution of slavery and the caste system, and its relationship with Christianity and European and North American history."[78] This criticism was raised from his comments in *Works of Love*: "the times are past when the powerful and prominent alone were men, and the others—human slaves and serfs. We are indebted to Christianity for this" (WL, 84). A word on this charge must be said.

Kierkegaard not only used slave metaphors meaningfully, but he used them before he started his literary career: "It seems as if I were a galley slave chained together with death; every time life stirs, the chain rattles and death makes everything decay—*and that takes place every moment*" (Pap. II A 647 n.d., 1837) (JP, 5256). Later, in *Works of Love*, he also denounced the institution of slavery, associating it with the idolatry of money:

> Because earnestness is to make money; to make lots of money, even if it is by selling men—this is earnestness; to make great amounts of money by contemptible slander—this is earnestness . . . Money, money—this is earnestness. So we are brought up, from earliest childhood, trained in ungodly money-worship. (WL, 296–97)

The following year (1848) Kierkegaard noticed how A. S. Ørsted knew more than his opponent, Melbye the greengrocer, about current events, particularly about the abolition of black slavery in the Danish West Indies. On July 3, 1848: "[Melbye] declares in his platform that among other things he intends to work especially for the abolition of Negro slavery—Superb! It is as though someone were to state in his platform that he intends to work especially for the building of a railroad between Copenhagen and Roskilde . . . which had already opened the year before."[79]

---

77. See Cavanaugh, *Torture and Eucharist*, especially chapter 5, "The True Body of Christ" (205–52). See also Cela, "Cuerpo y solidaridad," 65–66.

78. Jegstrup, "Kierkegaard on Citizenship and Character," 252 n. 24.

79. *LD* 274, # 189, to Conferentsraad J. L. A. Kolderup-Rosenvinge, 1848.

Kierkegaard was sensitive to this social evil: "if a traveler saw how slaves groan under the chains, he would become aware, his sympathy would be aroused, and he would give a vivid description of the dreadfulness of slavery" (TA , 244).

In a *Journal* entry of 1851, Kierkegaard seems to be aware of the connection between the slave, plantation economy and the incipient industrialized economy: "Even the Portuguese recognized how helpful tolerance was in trade—to their great advantage. I really believe that this is the explanation: trade and shipping companies and railways and all worldly sociability, tolerance is in all their interests—long may it flourish!"[80] Kierkegaard traces the problem even to the first centuries of Christianity. The annoying gadfly includes in his *Journals* an entry on slavery in the time when Christendom emerged: "Then they knocked down what it means to be a Christian, and the rich and the powerful, who wanted to enjoy life—they too became Christians. And then—perhaps out of shame—a little was done for slaves and the poor" (X4 A 541 n.d., 1852 (JP, 3201).

Kierkegaard's sharp eye noticed the introduction of contradictions: "the rich and powerful Christians at times quote Paul on poverty! What insolence!" In order to be congruent, Kierkegaard suggests the following: "being a Christian is going to be merged with the enjoyment of life, then much, much more must be done for the poor and the suffering" (X4 A 541 n.d., 1852) (JP, 3201).

Kierkegaard is not interested in perfecting himself to a certain point but in working for others, emphatically for those who live at the edges of society: "I have therefore always urged that Christianity is really for the poor, who perhaps toil and moil the whole day long and hardly get a living. The more advantages that one has, the more difficult it is to become a Christian, for reflection can so easily take a wrong turn."[81] The entry "The Gospel is Preached to the Poor" should be quoted at length:

> When a king, e.g., wants to partake in a meal with poor people, then he has the decency (and this is quite royal) to eat of the same dishes, drink of the inferior wine or beer—if he does not want to do that then he will hold himself distant, because he realizes that it would be insulting to want to sit at the table with them without expressing equality.

80. Kierkegaard, *Kierkegaard's Journals*, 1188; Pap., X 4 A 66.

81. Ibid., 1170; Pap., X 3 A 714.

So it is with Christianity. It is not a doctrine about God's accepting and loving the poor, the dregs, the miserable, the unfortunate—No!, Christianity is this very act, that God in Christ is in solidarity with the dregs.

But if we behave differently, we actually insult the poor with our preaching of Christianity. For being one rich, powerful, fortunate, and wishing to proclaim Christianity—not to mention having gained this by preaching Christianity—this is in fact to insult the poor. (Pap X 4 A 671, n.d., 1852) (my translation)[82]

The Sickness-Poverty Correlation

I am arguing that during the years 1846 to 1852, and due to local and continental political events, Kierkegaard's mind was shifting from a conservative *Weltanschauung* to a new way of approaching reality. My claim states that in these years that I have branded as transitional, the vexing gadfly confronted economic issues especially under the central idea of Christendom. Therefore, in the period from 1852 to 1855, when Kierkegaard broke with Christendom, his radicalization was also perceived regarding his economic judgments. I am going to strengthen my point by dealing with Kierkegaard's treatment of physically sick and physically healthy people.

Many semantic distinctions (ontological, psychological, material, voluntary, simulated, and so forth) can be made about the issue of poverty. *Poverty* is an equivocal term that Søren Kierkegaard's attentive ear perceived.[83] What is more, in his use of language, he made significant differentiations among words. He did not deal exclusively with *Armod* ("poverty") but also with *Fattige* ("the poor"), which includes *Lidende*

82. "Evangelium prædikes for de Fattige: Naar en Konge f. E. vil deeltage i et Maaltid med fattige Folk, saa har han da den Sømmelihed, (og det er just kongeligt) at har han da spiser af samme Rette, drikker af den daarlige Viin eller Øllet—vil han ikke det, saa holder han sig borte, thi han indseer, at det jo var at fornærme at ville sidde tilbords med dem og ikke udtrykke Ligheden.

Saaledes med Christendommen. Den er ingen Lære om at Gud antager sig og elsker de Fattige, de Ringe, de Elendige, de Ulykkelige—nei Christendommen er selve denne Handling, at Gud i Christo gjør sig lige med den Ringe.

Men vi gjøre det anderledes, vi fornærme egentlig den Fattige ved vor Forkyndelse af Christendommen; thi selv riig, mægtig, lykkelig at ville forkynde Christendommen, end sige at have opnaaet dette ved at forkynde Christendommen —det er egentlig at fornærme den Fattige."

83. See, e.g., *Øieblikket*, # 6 (1855), AUCb, 203.

("the suffering"), *Ulykkelige* ("the less fortunate"), *Elendige* ("the wretched," "the miserable"), *Forurettede* ("the injured"), *Krøblinge* ("the crippled"), *Halte* ("those with limps"), *Spedalske* ("the leprous"), and *Dæmoniske* ("those possessed by the demonic")(X,4 a 578 n.d., 1852) (JP, 4685). The way Kierkegaard uses each of these different terms goes beyond the scope of the present investigation. Nonetheless, in this subsection I will recapitulate the entries related to one aspect of poverty, i. e., the poverty of health, as it appears at different levels throughout Kierkegaard's corpus.

The Copenhagen of Søren Kierkegaard was a city of tremendous social problems. For instance, if we are to believe historical demographers' statements that there is a correspondence between life expectancy and quality of life, then from 1840 to 1844 this city had a very low life expectancy: the average for men being thirty-four years and thirty-eight years for women.[84] For instance, the city authorities had a workhouse, *Ladegaarden*, for the indigent, the homeless, and criminals. (Letter 70, n.3)

In a revealing *Journal* entry Kierkegaard contrasts the quality of life in the city and the countryside in ancient times. In the latter, the inhabitants' diet consisted especially of vegetables, and they really believed in God's will divulged through dreams; in the former, dreams were associated with demons. Applying this contrast to his generation Kierkegaard asserted: "the slight significance attributed to dreams in our era is consistent with the spiritualism which constantly emphasizes consciousness; whereas that more simple era piously believed that the unconscious life in man is both the paramount and the most profound aspect" (Pap. X 2 A 258 n.d., 1849) (JP, 781).

Kierkegaard has numerous entries relating to health in which he shows his vocation to nurse the sick. In this respect, he also faults the priesthood for opting for wealthy people, for seeking financial security, and for completely forgetting about the poor, the suffering, and the sick. Let us be precise. Kierkegaard did not connect Gethsemane with sickness, with cares about next year, with what one was going to eat, or with cares about "what one ate last year but still has not paid for,"[85] or with

84. Garff, *Søren Kierkegaard: A Biography*, 539.

85. The country pastor Zeuthen, on the occasion of thanking Kierkegaard for his *Works of Love*, called Kierkegaard's attention to the fact that: "there is also an anxiety for *yesterday*, with respect to what one has eaten—and not paid for" (Pap. VIII A644, May 17, 1848; cited in TC, 115 n. 1).

other human contingencies (PC 113) Nonetheless, what he says about health and illness is still relevant for our purposes.

Having experienced himself a "lack of wellness" throughout his life, Kierkegaard addressed the issue of poor health in a significant way. It is correct that the Dane's health was weak in general; he possessed a kind of physical deformity and was sometimes depressed. However, Theodor Haecker has demonstrated that the repercussions of Kierkegaard's corporeality did not determine his spiritual outlook.[86]

The Dane took a critical distance regarding his sickness. In *The Sickness unto Death*, Kierkegaard himself appeared as the editor while using the pseudonym of Anti-Climacus as the author. Now shortly after having finished writing such psychological work, he was aware of his bodily limitations: "My energies, that is, my physical energies, are declining; the state of my health varies terribly. I hardly see my way even to publishing the essentially decisive works I have ready." In spite of this, he tried to make his contribution to society in positive terms: "It is my judgment that here I am allowed to present Christianity once again and in such a way that a whole development can be based on it" (Pap. IX A 227 n.d., 1848) (JP, 6238). In his *The Sickness unto Death*, Kierkegaard embraced the content of the book and therefore perceived himself in despair. At the same time, his pseudonym declared himself "recovered" from the sickness unto death. Anti-Climacus is Kierkegaard's "better self" and the one who makes the diagnosis of the sickness.[87]

However, Kierkegaard addressed health issues related both to individuals and to sociological structures. He was concerned with nursing the sick, with sheltering the less fortunate, with burying the dead: in brief, with social solidarity.

Kierkegaard never entertained romantic notions that denied the benefits of medical science.[88] What was at stake was his reaction against medical science that overshadowed the realm of religion and faith. He was averse to the kind of statistical natural-scientific epistemology that "merely states accurately how we are, the stock exchange rate, the market price—in order, through sagacious familiarity with this information,

86. Haecker, *Der Buckel Kierkegaards*.

87. Nordentoft, *Kiekegaard's Psychology*, xiv.

88. It is interesting to notice how in those days physicians and dentists did not have a monopoly in the field. Barbers still performed a number of surgeries (*LD*, document 5, n. 4).

to be able both to protect oneself against and to make use of people, to score a success, to win advantages in this world." The nature of this knowledge, in Kierkegaard's opinion, only seeks "to gain permission to be suspicious, with a kind of (scientific) good conscience, if on a rare occasion something superior should show up" (FSE, 157).

Kierkegaard had his own physician, Dr. Oluf Lundt Bang (1788–1877). Kierkegaard was also in very good terms with his nephew Henrik Sigvard Lund, (1825–1889), Nicole Christine's son. Henrik was a physician who was an intern at Frederiks Hospital during Kierkegaard's last days. In fact, during his uncle's funeral, he spoke against the appropriation of Kierkegaard's body by the established church. In 1855, Ilia Marie Fibiger (1817–1867), a Danish writer and philanthropist, was the head nurse at the same Frederiks Hospital, and she too diligently took care of Kierkegaard on his deathbed. For instance, regarding *For Self-Examination*, she had declared that it surpassed everything she had ever read with the exception of the New Testament (LD # 289, n.1).

Kierkegaard thus did not reject medical science per se. He was very much against the usurpation of roles: "Pastors are no longer spiritual counselors—physicians have become that; instead of becoming another man by means of conversion one becomes that nowadays by water cures and the like—but we are all Christians!" (Pap. X 2 A 238 n.d., 1849) (JP, 3137).

Kierkegaard's criticism of medical science can be extended to the whole scientific system, which considers religious knowledge a grotesque, underdeveloped form of knowing. This positivism has, in Kierkegaard's view, penetrated everything, including the realm of faith: "in our day the physician is the spiritual advisor. People even have a perhaps groundless anxiety about calling the pastor, who quite possibly in our day would talk somewhat like a physician anyway—so one calls the physician . . . For what is an anguished conscience?" And the physician answered: "such thing does not exist anymore, is a reminiscence of the childhood of the race" (FSE, 201–2).

Hypochondria and the Market

In the provoking gadfly's estimation, "[t]he bourgeois-philistine's" style of life is built on the idea of health as another market commodity. That was so real that the obsession with being healthy constituted one distinctive mark of that age. However, Kierkegaard's dialectics enabled him to provide psychological treatment for the people who were really sick and at the same time to unveil the hypochondriac society that pursued health as an end in itself.

In an earlier entry Kierkegaard had identified the bourgeoisie's two central concerns: beauty and health. For the handsome count and the beautiful countess, their perspective of life was derived from the fact that "they were the handsomest couple in the whole land" (E/O, II 185–86) And for them, health was considered "the most precious good" (E/O, II, 187) In regards to health, Kierkegaard warns the upper class against a sickness characteristic of them: "[The] Hypochondriac worries that one's heart is not beating properly, that one is constipated, etc." (Pap. VII 1 A 248 n.d., 1845–1847) (JP, 99). In the *Unscientific Postscript* he unveils the real values of the upper class: "a good living, a pretty wife, health, a social position on a level with an alderman—and then, too, an eternal happiness; which is as if one were to suppose the kingdom of *heaven* to be one among the kingdoms of this *earth*, and to seek information about it in a textbook of geography" (CUP, 350).

In adding more distinctive notes to the self, Kierkegaard noticed the way in which the spiritless, namely, the immediate person identifies the self as inessential to the spirit:[89] "For the immediate person doesn't know himself; he quite literally only knows himself by his coat, he knows what it is to have a self—and here again we have the infinitely comical—only in externals" (SUD, 84). Now without undervaluing the good of health, we agree with John Douglas Mullen in the sense that Kierkegaard's diagnosis fits very well our current bourgeois spiritless magnification of health in an idolatrous manner: "Hypochondria will be the prevailing neurosis. Literature on health, disease, death, dying, cure, and miracles will be devoured. The warriors against death (the doctors), the makers of miracles, will take on the character of priests, the forces of good in battle against evil (disease, death)."[90]

A case study can be mentioned in order to illustrate this point. Søren Kierkegaard's deep psychological techniques can be observed in relation to his brother Peter Christian's wife. Henriette Kierkegaard

89. "To have or to be spirit in the nineteenth-century meant 'to be spirited' i.e., 'to have a mind of one's own,' to be independent, self-controlling. To have spirit is associated therefore with freedom and self-knowledge" (Mullen, *Kierkegaard's Philosophy*, 167, n. 4).

90. Ibid., 84, 82ff.

(whose nickname was Jette) suffered serious hypochondria symptoms. She spent a great deal of time in bed with harsh mental depressions. Soon after one visit to Jette and Peter at Pedersborg near Søro, Søren, Copenhagen's "greatest peripatetic,"[91] continued encouraging his sister-in-law to go out to walk, as he himself used to do for an hour and a half sometimes:[92]

> *Above all, do not lose your desire to walk: every day I walk myself into a state of well-being and walk away from every illness; I have walked myself into my best thoughts, and I know of no thought so burdensome that one cannot walk away from it.* Even if one were to walk for one's health and it were constantly one station ahead —*I would still say: Walk!* Besides, it is also apparent that in walking one constantly gets as close to well-being as possible, even if one does not quite reach it—*But by sitting still, and the more one sits still, the closer one comes to feeling ill.* Health and salvation can be found only in motion. If anyone denies that motion exists, I do as Diogenes did, I walk. If anyone denies that health resides in motion, then I walk away from all morbid objections. *Thus, if one just keeps on walking, everything will be all right.* (LD # 150. Søren Kierkegaard) ([1847] Henriette Kierkegaard) (See also JP, 6063)

Shortly after writing this letter, Kierkegaard continued the treatment by noticing: "And now you are confined to bed again." This time Kierkegaard explains to Jette the close connection between physical illness and the "deeply painful, and slowly consuming worry" of imagining oneself abandoned by others "who probably never give one a thought." Kierkegaard asks his patient to banish the worry of being "afraid that whatever one has to say or write will not be good enough." In his view, this is the cause of Jette's constantly bedridden and monotonous life. He urged her to be "actively engaged in life," to not consider worrying a necessity, to go beyond her small rooms and have frequent airing out, to inhale "good and beneficent and gentle and soothing thoughts" (*LD* # 167, Søren Kierkegaard [December 1847] to Henriette Kierkegaard)

Kierkegaard demands that the sick person take control of herself— "That which determines the direction of one's thoughts lies basically

---

91. Christensen, *Peripaterikeren Søren Kierkegaard*, quoted in Hong, TA, x.

92. The only times Kierkegaard stopped his walking was when he was honored by the conversation with ill people regardless of the fact that after that, Kierkegaard usually lost all his mental material generated while in motion.

in one's own self"—and to take a dialectical distance from her sickness, "He who has a tendency to melancholy, for example, most probably always finds unhappiness. Why? Because melancholy lies within him." Therefore he appeals to the element of faith[93] in his eradication of illness: "*To have faith is constantly to expect* the joyous, the happy, the good." Consequently, he addresses her straightforwardly: "You are in some measure always suffering—hence the task lies right here: Divert your *mind, accustom yourself by faith to changing suffering into expectation of the joyous. It is really possible.*" Faith means potentiality, and this means future: "What is required is this flexibility in the quiet of the mind, which, wherever things go wrong for one, in that very instant begins all over again and says, 'Yes! Yes! Next time it will work'"(LD #167).

Kierkegaard the dialectician, in front of the sick, recommends diversion and self-love: "I consider it *my duty to say to every sufferer* with whom I come into contact: *See to it that you love yourself.* When one is suffering and unable to do much for others, it is easy to fall prey to the melancholy thought that one is superfluous in this world, as others perhaps sometimes give one to understand." Kierkegaard puts it bluntly: "The one must remember that *before God every person is equally important, without reservation equally important;* indeed, if there were any distinction, then one who suffers the most must be the closest object of God's care" (LD # 167).

Kierkegaard closes his work session by making his sister-in-law feel that she is the subject who supports him and not the other way around, as an object of pity: "Take care of yourself, dear Jette. Happy New Year! Thank you for concluding the old one so beautifully by thinking of me."[94]

---

93. See also the entry about Hugh of St. Victor's essay "The Seven Gifts of the Holy Spirit": "Two opposites struggle with each other; the remedy and the illness, the remedy for you and the illness against you. There is no healing without resistance to the illness; one does not have a hard time of it unless there is resistance to the remedy. The hard time you are going through is the struggle between the opposing factors" (Pap. X 2 A 353 n.d., 1850) (JP, 1653).

94. LD, # 167.

To Die and to Be Buried

> Immortality itself can be selective: only the select spirits climb
> to the heavenly domain.
>
> —Carlos Fuentes[95]

A detailed study of health care during the Golden Age is beyond the
limits of our investigation. In this section I would only like to highlight
the link between economic power and the last phase of human life, i.e.,
death, as found in Kierkegaard's writings.

Up until 1842, Kierkegaard had reflected on social inequality even
in relation to the action of being buried. Based on Luke 16:19–25, he
writes of the pomposity of the rich funeral: "he was *buried*, the rich man
died and was buried, the animal dies—its body rots away, and no one
pays any attention to it; (this is why the poor want so much to be buried).
At his departure, the glory of the world gathers around him; he is again
clad in costly linen, and in a large procession they *carried him*." This
pomposity is contrasted with the marginalization of the common person: "—the poor man also died; he was not buried; perhaps was thrown
aside because in death he lay in the way, just as he had in life, perhaps
in order to clear the way for the magnificent funeral procession—he
was carried away by angels" (Pap. IV B 176 n.d., 1842–1844(?)) (TA,
429–30). In another context, Kierkegaard ironically observes the contradiction of such an event: "and yet a burial place is the least a person
can possess" (Pap. VII 1 B 157:5 n.d., 1846) (TA , 379).

In 1847 Kierkegaard witnessed a splendid funeral ceremony with
military honors at Garrison Cemetery. Only invited guests were able
to enter whereas the huge mob was obstructed by the police; then "the
gate was locked, quality was confirmed"; it consisted of "touch and go;
everything depended on getting the gate shut and confirming the yawn-
ing abyss, the *qualitative difference,* this *distinguendum est inter et inter*"
(Pap. X I A 561 n.d., 1847) (JP, 3563).

Two years later Kierkegaard wrote about the qualitative difference
between the rich and the poor, as it is perceived in the distinction of
dying and being buried. It seemed as if not even death is capable of
abolishing the purely human qualifications. While Pastor C. H. Visby
was reading the list of births and deaths of "Our Savior's" church, he

---

95. Fuentes, *El Naranjo*, 138.

reported that the number of deaths included exclusively the "buried." For Visby, this meant a logical distinction; for Kierkegaard, this raised these comments: "How inhuman to identify dying with being buried! No wonder poor people are so concerned about being buried" (Pap X 1 A 2 January 2, 1849) (JP, 3215)!

Kierkegaard questioned Visby's New Year's sermon by exclusively addressing the people who probably would not celebrate the next New Year's Day instead of drawing the distinction "between those who would die and those who would be buried during the year just beginning." Kierkegaard was sensitive to the poor person who just heard that the ones who cannot afford to be buried do not exist, and he himself "could not expect to be buried because the welfare department will bury him? O inhumanity" (Pap X 1 A 2 January 2, 1849) (JP, 3215).

If, on the one hand, the death of the poor had been trivialized, on the other hand, the biblical message had been commercialized. In *The Practice in Christianity* Kierkegaard faults the clergy for flattering the mourning with Scripture. By being equated as a widower with Abraham, the husband feels moved to economically gratify the priests even though "There is naturally not a trace of sense in the discourse, or the pastor's conception is neither Abraham nor the widower." The church, in a blasphemous attitude, celebrates the pastor's speech "since each one expects his turn to come—should one not then be willing to pay ten rix-dollars for coming to resemble Abraham so easily!" (PC, 108). In any event, what Johaness Metz has noticed about the concept of death within mercantilistic-capitalistic society holds true:

> According to Kierkegaard, our love and mourning for the dead is the only form of love that cannot be included within the framework of a society based on exchange and the satisfaction of needs. For this reason—(and that is why Kierkegaard made this criticism of the middle-class Christianity of his own period)—community with the dead has been thrust further and further into the background.[96]

The Sick "Ordinary" Person and Encapsulation

Kierkegaard's contemporaries were well aware of the *privilegium flebile* (privilege of the miserable) or the *privilegia pauperum* (privileges of

---

96. Metz, *Emergent Church*, 38.

the poor), which included among other rights the one of being helped in sickness.[97] At the level of practice, it was a different story; the sick simply did not exist.

Works of Love contains an analysis of the use of language in relation to the feast that was offered to the maimed, the lame, the blind, and the like, of Luke 14:12–13. According to Kierkegaard, what is understood by "feast" in the common language-usage is the gathering together of "friends, relatives, rich neighbors—who can repay one's hospitality." But in the Christian sense, he continues, what makes the banquet or feast is precisely the getting together with the crippled and the poor (WL, 91).

It seems as if there would be a kind of class encapsulation[98] in which the bourgeoisie abstract themselves from the presence of the suffering people. They are the "catchpenny writers" who steal money out of the poor pocket, and they scorn the suffering and at the same time "hide behind their aristocracy." Kierkegaard, on the other hand, does not wrap himself away from the sick; they existed before him as they exist before God: "Alas, yes, I admit it, it has concerned me very much and very sincerely to recognize each and every poor man who recognized me, to remember to greet each and every servant with whom I have been related in the slightest way, to remember that the last time I saw him he had been ill and to ask how he was." Kierkegaard did not close his self's door behind him in respect to the oppressed class: "Never in my life, not even when most preoccupied with an idea, have I been so busy that I could not take time to stand still if a poor man spoke to me" (Pap. VIII 1 A 452 n.d., 1847) (JP, 6085).

Kierkegaard had no room for empty rhetoric. There was a correlation in his thought and deeds, as the passage about the carpenter shows. Frederik C. Strube was a cabinet maker from Iceland. Based on the census register for February 1, 1850, Strube, his wife, and two daughters were living in Kierkegaard's apartment on the corner of Rosenborggade and Tornebuskegade. In a thank-you to the physician S. M. Trier for taking care of Strube, Kierkegaard demonstrated his openness ("I have allowed him to go on living with me, because I felt it would distress him very much to have to move now.") and his sensitiveness for nursing

97. LD # 216, from the Conferensraad J. L. A. Kolderup-Rosenvinge—August 1, 1849.

98. For an analysis of the concept of encapsulation in Kierkegaard's works, see Nordentoft, *Kierkegaard's Psychology*, 223ff.

the sick ("Indeed, you will please remember, if that time ever comes and he has a relapse: then I am to inform you at once and then he will be admitted to the hospital as quickly as possible." (Letter 192. S.K.) [1848]) S. M. Trier. Søren Kierkegaard's draft) (Pap. X 2 A 10 n.d., 1849) (JP, 6489 n. 2454).

In connection with John the Baptist's doubts about whether Jesus was the person they were waiting for (Luke 7:23), Kierkegaard noticed how, contrary to Christendom, Christ unequivocally pointed to "the miracles (the lame walk, the blind see, etc.) and to the doctrine itself (the gospel is preached to the poor)" (TC, 97).

However, the relationship of those who constitute Christendom to the sick is one of ignorance, avoidance, and encapsulation. In a *Journal* entry Kierkegaard quoted *De ira*, III, 17, 3–4, seeking to illuminate his argument: "Seneca tells of a man on whom a king took revenge by having his nose and ears cut off, by having him generally mauled, and then locked up in a cage where he was unable to stand upright." Through this story Kierkegaard highlighted the tragedy of losing the capacity of being scandalized, because "after leaving him in there amid his own excrement—people finally ceased to have pity on him because he was so loathsome. Wonderful pity!" This is another way of "playing dead" or of attempting to protect oneself against the presence of the sick: "with the utmost circumspection we keep the lepers, the insane, the demoniac, the publicans, and flagrant sinners far outside human society—and yet it was precisely to such people Christianity was proclaimed" (Pap. X3 A48 n.d., 1850) (JP, 3498). Encapsulation is a method of defense that can be useful at the social and class levels by hiding the ugly side that distresses us: "True Christianity would shock everybody, as it once did, because in proclaiming consolation for such horrible sufferings it embarrasses society by pulling out these horrible sufferings for a day, something we usually defend ourselves against so that we may remain ignorant of them—we Christians!" (Pap X 3 A 48 n.d., 1850) (JP, 3498).

The Doctrine of Temporal Retribution

In the period we are dealing with (1846–1852), the provoking Gadfly is very suspicious of the old ideology that equates sickness with having committed sin, and poverty with the result of being a sinner. Obviously, the second part of the doctrine of retribution states that the healthy and the wealthy people possess those goods because of God's grace.[99]

Kierkegaard's agenda for nursing the sick is neither sentimental nor egoistic. He urges his readers "to seek the company of the cripples, the despised, the sinners, and the publicans," but simultaneously challenges the suffering people to resemble Christ: "at the very moment you yourself are suffering most of all, simply think about consoling others. . . . The task is not to seek consolation—but to be consolation" (Pap. VIII 1 A 432 n.d., 1847) (JP, 1841). Kierkegaard as a therapist worked with psychosomatic illness. He detected the sickness of the body and of the spirit. For example, in the parable of the ten lepers the physical sickness "reveals its own identity. The leper did not need to be told that he was sick." But sickness of the spirit was subtle: "that ingratitude was a sickness never occurred to them." In this case, as in everyone, the *psyche* and the *soma* are dynamically interrelated: "The danger with sickness of the spirit is just that a certain degree of health is required in order to become aware and to know and acknowledge that one is sick" (Pap. X 2 A 103 n.d., 1849) (JP, 4329).

Narrative can again fit our purposes of explaining the matter. Hans Peter Kierkegaard (1815–1862), Søren Kierkegaard's first cousin, who lived at Købmagergade 45, was severely crippled from birth, though he possessed a fine and alert spirit. For Søren, suffering was not an end in itself. Having in mind his cousin, Kierkegaard made an important distinction: "But by those who suffer we are thinking of those whom life itself seems to have assigned to quiet and, if you will, useless sufferings, useless because the sufferings do not benefit others, do not benefit any cause, but instead are a burden to others and to the sufferers themselves" (TA, 79).

Søren visited Hans Peter sporadically, but he addressed Hans Peter in his letters: "Above all do not forget your duty to love yourself, do not permit the fact that you have been set apart from life in a way, been prevented from participating actively in it, and that you are superflu-

---

99. This doctrine can be located as far back as the times of the book of Job, where his friends, the theologians, insist on justifying God and on condemning Job, following the formula, sickness and poverty equals a sinner: "It is very comfortable and tranquilizing, especially for people who possess big properties in this world; at the same time, the end result is the poor people's resignation, with a sense of guilt" See Gutiérrez, *Hablar de Dios desde el sufrimiento del inocente*, 64.

ous in the obtuse eyes of a busy world." Kierkegaard tried to counter-act a society for which the handicapped were marginalized by being considered unproductive: "above all do not permit this to deprive you of your idea of yourself, as if your life, if lived in inwardness, did not have just as much meaning and worth as that of any other human being in the loving eyes of an all-wise Governance, and considerably more than the busy, busier, busiest haste of busy-ness—busy with wasting life and losing oneself" (LD # 196. Søren Kierkegaard)[1848](Hans Peter Kierkegaard) According to his friend Hans Brøchner, Kierkegaard pro-vided to Hans Peter "an awareness of being essentially equal to those whom nature had equipped more fortunately."[100]

Petronella Ross's testimony is also worth quoting. She was a deaf writer known by her pseudonym of Fr. Godtkfær. Her permanent resi-dence was located in a small house for women on the island of Falster, south of Zealand. This place was one of the church-sponsored chari-table shelters named as convents, designed to serve women of the no-bility. At the time she wrote this letter she was taking care of her sick mother in Copenhagen. On the occasion of "The Cares of Lowliness," she addressed Kierkegaard about the healing experience obtained while reading him: "Thank you, good doctor, for every shaft of light with which you enlighten the dark lives of your fellow man, 'dark,' I sup-pose, because the eyes are not truly open." Or again: "I should go to the bookseller and choose among your works. I cannot hear your homilies, and you do say something that fortifies me" (LD # 280, n.5 Petronella Ross—July 12, 185—Søren Kierkegaard).

Kierkegaard denounced the way in which the cruel "values" of his society shaped religious speech. "It would seem easier to proclaim Christianity to those who lead happy lives, are healthy and prosperous, enjoy life—than to proclaim it to cripples, the sick, malcontents, etc." But Christian discourse is quite different: "If Christianity is to be preached in truth to the happy, those who enjoy life, then Christianity becomes a kind of cruelty." Christianity is heterogeneous to the market's laws of prosperity and success: "But the point is that people would rather enjoy life etc.—and that is why they are even afraid to look at a cripple, and in-sane person, a beggar; they wish to keep on being ignorant of him—and then to proclaim Christianity to the favored!" (Pap X 1 A 644 n.d., 1849)

---

100. Kirmmse, *Encounters with Kierkegaard*, 245.

(JP, 6469). Kierkegaard was an organic intellectual deeply immersed in actuality:[101] "O, I have seen this much too close at hand. My own soul has been in fear and trembling" always raising burning questions: "But then is not Christianity for all, is it only for those who are sick and full of sorrow, for those who labor and are heavy laden?" "Is it a mistake to want to make everybody Christians?" And still again: "These problems have occupied me very much. I sometimes use the advice I give myself: 'Does it concern you? Do you not need Christianity?' Then I answer Yes, and look after myself" (Pap X 1 A 644 n.d., 1849) (JP, 6469).

The following year (1850) he partially answered one of his questions by placing Jesus within his economic and social context: "Tell the child that he was love, that he came to the world out of love, took upon himself the form of a lowly servant, lived for only one thing—to love and to help people, especially all those who were sick and sorrowful and suffering and unhappy" (PC, 176).

Kierkegaard's conception of his age consisted in affirming his society's sickness unto death and the connivance of the scientifically and scholarly trained clergy who had learned "to suffer all the rudeness of the sick without being disturbed, no more than the physician is disturbed by the patient's abusive language and kicks during the operation." During the transitional years of 1848 and 1849 Kierkegaard was skeptical about healing his spiritually sick generation through the new democratic regime: "just as a patient, when he himself is supposed to point to the area where he suffers, frequently points to an utterly wrong place, so also with the generation. It believes—yes, it is both laughable and lamentable—it believes that a new administration will help" (Pap X 6 B 40 n.d., 1848(?)–49) (JP, 6256). However, let us recall that for Kierkegaard it was unthinkable to visualize a new administration without first having dissolved Christendom.

Kierkegaard is direct in favoring the sick: "If Christianity relates to anyone in particular, then it may especially be said to belong to the suffering, the poor, the sick, the leprous, the mentally ill, and so on, to sinners, criminals" (Pap. X2 A27 n.d., 1849) (JP, 386). Within the religious-political monolithic entity, on the contrary, the sick "have been removed from life so as not to disturb—earnest Christendom." Whereas Christ was the pastor of the sick and never marginalized them; the pas-

---

101. For Gramsci, all intellectuals are organic; all of them are in league with one segment of society. In the case of Kierkegaard, he sided with the "ordinary" person.

tors in Christendom, nonetheless "go on living in secular security; there they decorate life; 'they assuage the sorrows and ennoble the joys'—this they do, and, most curious of all, they do it according to a fixed price" (Pap. X2 A27 n.d., 1849) (JP, 386). Kierkegaard opposed the stronger members of society who not only controlled the meaning of the gospel but isolated the sick from Christianity as well:

> Christianity in Christendom fares as a weak child who is given something and then a couple of stronger children come and grab it. These all too intensely secularized people whose entire life and way of thinking are secular, they take possession of Christianity, grab all its consolation served up in the form of human sympathy—and those unfortunate persons who especially ought to have the benefit of Christianity are shoved aside. (Pap. X2 A27 n.d., 1849) (JP, 386)

Kierkegaard goes further to analyze sin-sickness: the oppressive doctrine of temporal retribution, which makes the physically and mentally poor the very ones responsible for their sufferings. To link sin with sickness and sin with poverty is in fact a sinful act, as to judge by externals or results: "if someone is a cripple or is deformed or has an unfavorable appearance—then to judge that he is an evil person; if someone is so unfortunate as to get along badly in the world, so that he amounts to nothing or is down and out—then to judge that *ergo* he is a bad person." Kierkegaard makes his point straightforwardly: "What an exquisitely contrived kind of cruel enjoyment to want to feel one's own righteousness in relation to someone who is suffering by explaining his sufferings as God's punishment upon him" (PC, 19–20).

Kierkegaard's Concreteness

> I was born in 1813, in that bad fiscal year when so many other bad banknotes were put in circulation, and my life seems most comparable to one of them. There is a suggestion of greatness in me, but because of the bad conditions of the times I am not worth very much. (Pap. V A 3 n.d., 1844) (JP, 5725)

Throughout this chapter I've been trying to show that the years 1846 to 1852 were years of transition for the final years of 1852 to 1855, when Kierkegaard broke with Christendom and radicalized his social and political positions. I have also claimed that under his attack upon

Christendom, the vexing gadfly did address economic issues in his writings and in backing those up by siding with the "ordinary" person as well. Consequently, in this section, I am going to focus my attention on Kierkegaard's concrete life within Golden Age Denmark.

Regarding concreteness, a contemporary social philosopher and psychologist firmly believed that "If philosophers in general talked more *ad personam*, that is to say, more in reference to what philosophy means in my life and in your life, then indeed critical thinking would, philosophy would, be much more obviously a field of great personal significance."[102] Concreteness was, without any doubt, the most salient mark of Kierkegaard's work. According to "Søren Kierkegaard: In order to experience and understand what it means to be a Christian, it is always necessary to recognise a definite historical situation. I start with the idea that Kierkegaard is right . . . The situation without the recognition of which Christian theology does not know whereof it speaks, is for us in this country first of all 'after Auschwitz.'"[103]

It is a known fact that Søren Kierkegaard was not affiliated with any political party at any point of his life. Nevertheless, he made significant contributions to this domain,[104] especially in taking the side of the population that did not have political power: the sad Danes. By "political poverty" I am referring to that great majority of the Danish population, which was taken for granted in matters of political decision making. It is true that with the shift from an absolute monarchy to a constitutional monarchy as it culminated in the constitution of June 5, 1849, the poor classes gained access to universal male suffrage. However, if class privileges were canceled on the one hand, rank and class divisions did not disappear on the other (see LD # 216 n. 5). Since the harsh reality for the majority of the people remained untouched, Kierkegaard took up the cause of the economically and politically poor: the "ordinary" person.

Let us recall that Kierkegaard did not write about the ideal political theory. This will become apparent through my method of placing his work within his particular sociohistorical context, i.e., within the incipient industrialization of mid-nineteenth-century Denmark. However, as

102. Fromm, *Art of Listening*, 69.

103. Metz, "Facing the Jews," 26.

104. Cf. Kirmmse, *Kierkegaard*, 405–22.

a general principle, I concur with Kirmmse's analysis of Kierkegaard's *via negativa*: "In Kierkegaard's view it is neither possible nor permissible for a Christian psychology to specify what a culture and a society ought to be, for the task of fulfilling the promise of the human spirit is an open-ended and individual one." Kirmmse continues, "However, it is possible to specify what a culture ought *not* to be, and this negative, limiting, political prescription took the form of the indictment of Golden Age Christendom, which Kierkegaard necessarily included as an important part of his greatest psychological work, *The Sickness unto Death.*"[105]

Kierkegaard's social critique was colored by the concreteness of his situation, which, in turn, made it very relevant, as Adorno chose to emphasize: "Many of his positive assertions gain the concrete significance they otherwise lack as soon as one translates them into concepts of a right society."[106]

Kierkegaard distanced himself from the scientific optimism of his generation; instead he addressed the social problems of massification, anomy, centralization, proletariatization in western Europe.[107] He foresaw the magnitude of the events that were taking place in his country "Now we are in the process of beginning somewhere else" (Pap. VIII 1 A 108 n.d., 1847) (JP, 4116) and in Europe as well, which came together with the disturbances because of food scarcity and high prices: "I must attach great significance to the bread-riots around Europe this year; they indicate that the European constitution (as a physician speaks of a man's constitution) has completely altered; in the future we will have internal disturbances" (Pap. VIII 1 A 108 n.d., 1847) (JP, 4116).

Kierkegaard was conscious of the urban overpopulation difficulties ("people are squeezed together in the big cities") of humans becoming dehumanized: "From his very infancy a man receives no impression of himself. In the big cities one has a greater impression of a cow than of a man, for in the country there are two, three, or more cows to one man, whereas in the big cities there are 1,000 men to one cow" (Pap. VIII 2 B 87 n.d., 1847) (JP, 655).

105. Kirmmse, "Psychology and Society," 192.
106. Adorno, "On Kierkegaard's Doctrine of Love," 423.
107. Hansen, *Revolutionær Samvittighed*, 95.

Alongside mass production appeared the standardization of humankind: "The real crime, the one people regard as the worst of all and punish cruelly, is to be not like other." Kierkegaard asserted that in antagonism to the animals where the class is superior to the particular, "—In respect to men, on the contrary, the qualification is that each one should not be like the others, should have distinctiveness" (Pap. IX A 80 n.d., 1848) (JP, 70).

"The advance of civilization, the rise of the large cities, centralization . . . have given all life a completely wrong direction." Furthermore, they have also emerged with the mediation of the press, which has represented a danger against the existence of the people. Sociologically speaking, the media contributed to "an increase of the inorganismic in the states. This becomes the public, and here is also the proletariat." The church is another social institution, which, in Kierkegaard's view, has privileged one segment of society to the detriment of the "ordinary" person:

> Meanwhile there are 1,000 clergymen who have turned Christ into money, make a living out of "the truth suffers in the world." And these clergymen are or aspire to be knights of the Order of Denmark etc. And the whole country is Christian, that is for sure, and now we are going to have a synod called together to reform the Church. Good heavens! (X 2 A 7 n.d., 1849) (JP, 4166)

Writer and Publisher

> According to the dialectic of the idea, to serve [tjene] an idea, which in my simple thinking is something different from earning [tjene] money and esteem. (Pap. VII 1 B 216 n.d., 1846-47) (TA , 364)

Some people have concentrated upon the idea of Søren Kierkegaard as a bourgeois. That is partially understandable for different reasons, the most important being that Kierkegaard himself wanted for us to believe this idea. Since the aim of this essay is to investigate the economic ideas of this thinker, and since Kierkegaard, the bourgeois, has become a commonplace, a word must be said regarding his own fortune (Formue).

One purpose of Kierkegaard's famous walks was to create the public image of himself as an indolent person and then to take distance from his pseudonyms. In fact, when he was very busy proofreading *Either/Or* and writing religious discourses, he changed the method: Every evening he "stopped at the theater for ten minutes—not one minute more." He continues, "I counted on there being several gossips at the theater who would say: Every single night he goes to the theater; he does not do another thing. O, you darling gossips, thank you—without you I could never have achieved what I wanted" (Pap. X 5 A 153 n.d., 1849) (JP, 6332). That kind of behavior of walking by the theater each night gained him the bad reputation of an irresponsible idler and a loafer, of a no-body who was "lacking in earnestness." However, he was aware of being highly industrious, working with his mind while walking, observing, talking (Pap. VII 1 A 107 n.d., 1846) (JP, 5894). Furthermore, he set defi-nite daily hours for his work and followed those with "unconditional obedience" before God: "From the very beginning I have been as it were under arrest and every instant have sensed the fact that it was not I that played the part of master, but that another was Master" (PV, 69).

Other purposes of his walks were for health and socialization; these were not as obvious: "I know very well that Heiberg and the like Christianly explain my walking the street as so much vanity—that I do it to be seen. I wonder if it is also to be seen that I walk about even more, if possible, in Berlin, where not a soul knows me?" (Pap. VIII 1 A 163 n.d.,1847) (JP, 6013).

Regarding his "lack of earnestness," his refusal or half-attempts to get a job, etc., on the one hand, it was also the guise he wished us to inherit: "An essential part of my work was to give the appearance of living in abundance" (Pap. VIII 1 A 170 n.d., 1847) (JP, 6015). On the other hand, however, he held an opposite concept of earnestness of the bourgeois mentality. Kierkegaard was freer in his use of money. He never speculated with it, not even tolerated earning interest, because of his religious convictions.[108] He gave away some money to charity [*godgørende*] again, not caring about his own personal reputation: "In situations where my silence will make me seem worse than I am, I should be silent—for instance, giving alms in secret" (Pap. X 2 A 43 n.d., 1849) (JP, 3985). Kierkegaard was very sensitive to the unfortunate: "There is no one, no one here at home who has sympathy with the poorer classes as I do" (Pap. VIII 1 A 254 n.d., 1847) (JP, 6045). He altruistically used

108. Kirmmse, *Encounters with Kierkegaard,* 181.

his money in his profession as an author, with the qualification that he did not side with the elite (Pap. X 2 A 586 n.d., 1850) (JP, 6594).

The public image of the bourgeois Kierkegaard thus has to be balanced with the one of him as free of airs of superiority and in possession of a historical consciousness: "Verily, nothing has ever been farther from me than pretension of social superiority (*Fornemhed*). Being myself of humble origin, I have loved the 'ordinary' person, or what is spoken of as the simple classes" (PV, 91). He closes his *My Point of View* with a revealing sentence that throws light on some of his public attitudes: "I have in a light-minded way made sport of worldly honor and prestige, that by impairing possibly my own worldly prestige I have at the same time contributed to impair worldly prestige in general" (PV, 92).

Kierkegaard himself considered that he shared his fortune with humankind through publishing his books. This is to a certain degree true, according to the general research on this issue.

In the classic book *Kierkegaard og Pengene*[109] (*Kierkegaard and Money*), we find that on August 1, 1838, when his father died, Søren Kierkegaard inherited a considerable sum of money, which, by October 2, 1855, when he fainted in the street, or by November 11, 1855, when he died in the hospital, had already been used up. In seventeen years, his fortune was gone.

Kierkegaard's ethical scruples regarding the commercialization of the intellectual work, along with his privileged economic situation, led him to also be a publisher. He wrote thirty-eight books, but only nine of them reached a second printing in his lifetime: one example of a book that saw a second printing was *Either/Or*, which was sold out in two years. His best-known books today did not have a good reception. For example, only fifty copies of the *Unscientific Postscript* were sold during its first four years. The average number of copies for each title varied between 500 and 525, with the exception of *The Concept of Anxiety* and *Fear and Trembling*, which sold 250 copies each; and five out of six *Edifying Discourses* sold 300 copies each. Besides the expense from the low quantity of copies, all his complimentary copies had gold edges and black leather. (LD # 268 n. 6).

Kierkegaard also hired secretaries such as P. V. Christensen (1819–63) who copied *Either/Or* (Letter 188. Søren Kierkegaard) [August

---

109. Brandt and Rammel, *Søren Kierkegaard og Pengene*.

1848]) J. L. A. Kolderup-Rosenvinge), and in order to have more leisure time, Kierkegaard employed male servants. Kierkegaard had to pay his proofreaders, but he decided not to charge a fee in the publishing costs for his own time and work (Pap. X 1 A 584 n.d., 1849) (JP, 6458). What allowed him to accomplish such enterprise was his inheritance (Hong V, 516, n. 905).

Christian Peter Bianco Luno (1795–1852) was Kierkegaard's main book printer, and Carl Andreas Reitzel (1789–1853), was Kierkegaard's main distributor. P. G. Philipsen was another bookseller and publisher Kierkegaard consulted in order to get better deals.

In 1846 after finishing his *Concluding Unscientific Postscript*, Kierkegaard attempted to close his career as an author: "I ought not be a writer any longer" "I repeat, this is final" (Pap. VII 1 A 4, February 7, 1846) (JP, 5873). However, Kierkegaard's attack on the media and the political transformations that were taking place provided him with new perspectives for his writing.

Kierkegaard's Unprofitable Life

> My dear reader, as you can see, this does not quickly lead to profit. That will take place only after my death when the oath-bound tradespeople will appropriate my life additionally to their provision of salt-barrels.[110]

Kierkegaard opposed a culture whose center was posited in the acquisition of money as the ultimate goal of life. Kierkegaard's fortune helps us to better appreciate his analysis of his society as well as his siding with the unfortunate people.

King Frederick VI was directly responsible for the Danish state of bankruptcy of 1813, in the same year Kierkegaard was born. The king insisted on Danish neutrality during the Napoleonic Wars. Once the allies achieved victory, Denmark not only suffered inflation but also lost Norway the following year. After England's furious attack on Copenhagen in 1807, Denmark printed a huge amount of unbacked

110. Last number (# 9) of *The Moment, Samlede Værker (SV)* 19, 323, my translation:

> *Min kjere Læser, Du seer, det gaaer ikke løs paa Profiten; det bliver først Tilfældet efter min Død, naar de eedfæstede Næringsdrivende ville tage ogsaa mit Liv til Indtægt for Saltmands-Tønden.*

currency. Consequently, by January 5, 1813, the currency notes backed with silver were replaced with the new rix-dollar notes, which were worth only one-sixth of their value.

Later the new currency dropped 1:100. It was not until 1818 with the creation of the National Bank, independent from the government, that economic stability was reached. Kierkegaard's father, however, survived the economic crisis. Shortly before the devastating year of 1813, "he transferred a large portion of his capital into guaranteed gold-convertible bonds and thus emerged relatively unscathed from the catastrophe, having in fact enhanced his relative position vis-à-vis many older, wealthier families in the city."[111] By the time of his death, he not only left an inheritance for his children but also established a trust fund of three thousand rix-dollars for his brothers and sisters. (LD # 66 n. 2).

Søren Kierkegaard himself confessed his melancholy and money as his main reasons for writing (Pap. VIII 1 A 641 n.d., 1848) (JP, 6132). Furthermore, he declared his writing to be a form of therapy (Pap. VII 1 A 222 n.d., 1847) (JP, 5962). However, he subordinated these two elements to a higher cause (Pap. VII 1 A 229, January 24, 1847) (JP, 5966). Comparing himself to his relative Wilhelm Lund, who in 1832 settled down in Lagoa Santa, Brazil, "lost to the world, absorbed in excavating antediluvian fossils," Kierkegaard wrote: "so I live as if outside the world, absorbed in excavating Christian concepts—alas, and yet I am living in Christendom, where Christianity flourishes, stands in luxuriant growth with 1,000 clergymen, and where we are all Christians" (Pap. X 3 A 239 n.d., 1850) (JP, 6652).

His writing had the distinctive notes of being uninterested in both money and prestige. He was aware that his proofreader was earning more money than he. In fact, Kierkegaard's first attempt to conclude his activity as a writer was by the consciousness of being an intellectual who addressed the problems of his society and not as a writer who was in the service of the status quo: "By accommodating myself I could perhaps become popular with the public, but that I do not want—so I shall not be an author at all" (Pap. VII 1 B 211 n.d., 1846) (JP, 5881). In his *Journals* he mentions how George J. B. Carstensen (1812–1857), the founder of the recreational park of Tivoli (1853) and of several newspapers, wanted to make Kierkegaard's intellectual work a part of his

111. Kirmmse, *Kierkegaard*, 260.

business enterprise: "In Denmark I have been offered an enormous fee to write in the papers (when Carstensen had *Figaro* or *Portefeuillen* he once offered me 100 rix-dollars a printed sheet for an article against Heiberg)—" however, Kierkegaard observes, "I have paid out rather much for the publication of one or another of my big books, the fruit of hard work for a year or a year and a half" (Pap. X 3 A 99 n.d., 1850) (JP, 6624).

Kierkegaard thus maintained a critical distance from his money. He was an author of independent means but at the same time an intellectual committed to a kind of Christianity antagonistic to a culture that revolves around conventional advantages and economic profit (Pap. X 2 A 550 n.d., 1850) (JP, 3142). Kierkegaard realized that he was ruining his financial future by putting his own money into his publications (Pap. X 2 A 10 n.d., 1849) (JP, 6489), but he continued enduring his financial sacrifices (Pap. X 2 A 25 n.d., 1849) (JP, 6493).

Kierkegaard's financially unprofitable life, on the other side, contained a wealth of new and fresh perspectives at different levels, of which he was also aware: "That I am an author who definitely will bring honor to Denmark is indisputable; that I have lived *qua* author practically at my own expense with no subsidy from the government or the nation" (Pap. IX A 169 n.d., 1848) (JP, 6204) On an international level, he did not succeed, because having been born in a market town and writing in a language that did not possess political and cultural power: "it was my fate to be an author—in Denmark. Such an author-existence in any other country would have been the path to wealth—in Denmark it cost me money" (Pap. X2 A619, n.d., 1850) (JP, 6603). At the domestic level, Kierkegaard's unprofitable life was linked to the fact that he was an outsider with respect to the intellectual elite. He himself contrasted his life with Martensen's advantages: "he is a professor, has an important office, has a velvet front—or stomach-piece, is a knight—while I am nobody, have put out money on my own writing" (Pap. X 2 A 596 n.d., 1850) (JP, 6595). Martensen represented the "system." He and his "circles" controlled the general tenor of the opinion, whereas, Kierkegaard goes on: "I was a nobody and remained a nobody, but I devoted myself to what for me was the costly—financially as well—pleasure of being an author in Denmark" (Pap. X 6 B 171 n.d., 1851) (JP, 6748).

In a rhetorical question relating to *publici juris*, Kierkegaard asks: why does an author make his writings public property? He wants to be sure that everybody understands the nature of his books as ethical-religious, and he is therefore pecuniarily disinterested: "I have never published any book for that reason [monetary], and even if I had, I certainly would soon have learned from experience that my books are not money-makers." (PC, 297) In fact, contrary to this money-based, bourgeois ideology, Kierkegaard considered the highest reward of his life the unprofitable one of not having received payment, money, honor, or reputation in his Christian authorship (PC, 306).

Let us be precise, Kierkegaard did not have the vocation for material poverty. He was aware of this, and this recognition was the source of his humility: "—the extraordinary in terms of character, the capacity to live in poverty etc.—that I do not have." He realized that his private means prevented him from living in poverty and from becoming self-sufficient and arrogant: "So it seems that I ought to stay within my limits and try to safeguard myself somewhat in finite respects" (Pap. X 4 A 339 n.d., 1851) (JP, 6771). More clearly he stated: "the fact that I have had the privilege of being able to live independently. I am fully aware of this and for that reason feel exceedingly inferior to men who have been able to develop an authentic life of the mind and spirit in actual poverty" (Pap. IX A 43 n.d., 1848) (JP, 6153).

Kierkegaard lived fairly well, particularly during the period from 1838 to 1848. His lifestyle as a single man was expensive. He lived in "the second floor" for "the better class" of Copenhagen, the *Belle-Etage*.[112] And when he and his brother Peter sold their house, Kierkegaard rented expensive apartments (Pap. X 2 A 10 n.d., 1849) (JP, 6489). Consequently, he was far from promoting an ascetic life: "It will be made to seem as if I wanted to introduce pietism, petty and pusillanimous renunciation in things that do not matter. No, thank you, I have never made the slightest gesture in this direction," he declares. "What I want is to incite in the direction of becoming ethical people, witnesses of the truth, wiling to suffer for truth and to renounce worldly shrewdness" (Pap. X 3 A556 n.d., 1850) (JP, 3319). In any event, Kierkegaard's understanding of the ethical character completely differed from the class ideology of the well-to-do, as it was expressed by the clergy in general and by the court preacher's opulence in particular: "If one is brash and wants such ostentatiousness to be earnestness, a fantasy existence *a la* witness-of-

---

112. Nordentoft, *Kierkegaard's Psychology,* 395 n. 14, translator's note.

the-truth, then a protest is due" (Pap. IX A 201 n.d., 1848) (JP, 3135). He also discriminates between having and earning wealth in relation to the preaching of the gospel: "if I imagined myself to be wealthy and then wanted to proclaim that it is blessed to do without, a proclamation which, however, is always more forgivable that earning wealth by proclaiming that it is blessed to do without" (Pap. X 4 A 674 n.d., 1852) (JP, 6825).

Kierkegaard rejected asceticism for being too closely associated with meritoriousness, and he said of himself: "a more altruistic disinterested author Denmark has hardly ever had" (Pap. X 2 A 544 n.d., 1850) (JP, 6593). His economic situation was not an end in itself; on the contrary, it permitted him to focus all his energies on his struggling with the social institutions: "but one needs the counterweight of not having economic worries" (Pap XI 2 A 12 n.d., 1854) (my translation).[113] His inheritance allowed him not to have a formal job; however, his concept of work and of money was quite different from the socially acceptable norm: "One very rarely sees a man who is conscious about himself and lucid about what he does—who works himself into poverty with such diligence and hard work" (Pap XI 2 A 34 n.d., 1854) (my translation).[114]

The political and economic crisis of 1848, especially the Slesvig-Holstein war with the Germans also drained Kierkegaard's capital: "Then I began the publication of *Christian Discourses*. While I sat reading the proof, the insurrection in Holstein and all that trouble broke out" (Pap. X 1 A 202 n.d., 1849) (JP, 6376). He lost money by buying government bonds (seven hundred rix-dollars) (Pap. IX A 375 n.d., 1848) (JP, 6268) However, his project of life persisted: "But now when I am able to understand how extraordinarily much has been entrusted to me and of what benefits I have—it seems to me, since I do in fact still have money— that I ought to stay put" (Pap. X 3 A 98 n.d., 1850) (JP, 6423). During his last years, Kierkegaard became more careful about his money. It was shortly before his death that he withdrew the last portion. (PC, 398, n. 62).

---

113. "men den Modvægt behøver man, at man ikke har oeconomiske Bekymringer."

114. "... Sjedent, sjeldent er det vistnok see: et Menneske, der med den Bevidsthed over sig selv og Klarhed over hvad han gjør, flittig og anstrentget—arbeider sig in i Armod."

To sum up, Kierkegaard did not idealize poverty: "One thing is quite arbitrary and that is to make poverty into piety, as though poverty were something in itself." He continues: "It is quite a different matter when poverty is related to an idea, in the service of which man places his life."[115] Neither did Kierkegaard idealize asceticism: "Yet it is relevant here that even Christ approves a certain pious prodigality, such as, for example, the lavishing of costly ointment on him. The observation that astringence is corrupting is appropriate here" (Pap. X 3 A 342 n.d., 1850) (JP, 14). Kierkegaard protested against the bourgeoisie who, on the one hand, receive earthly wages from the state and, on the other, preach: "He who does not give up everything he possesses cannot be my disciple." Kierkegaard calls this practice a double crime: "How do we have the audacity to preach such truths to people, yes, even merely to read them, we who not only do not give up everything we possess but struggle to gain more? But if our consciences condemn us, should we therefore hide what is written?" He argues: "No. I will not make myself guilty of a double crime, I will confess, confess before the entire people what the gospel says and what I still have not fulfilled" (Pap. X 4 A 121 n.d., 1851) (JP, 3162).

Kierkegaard's wealth helped him to avoid compromise with the structures he did not believe in: "Only when I accept an official position can Mynster more easily make his interpretation prevail" (Pap. X 4 A 511 n.d., 1852) (JP, 6795). But at the same time, he was self-critical: "I love this earthly life all too much, would like to have a comfortable life, humanly speaking, to have diversion, to enjoy life, etc. Ah, but I perceive that in the strictest sense Christianity demands something altogether different" (Pap. X 4 A 33 n.d., 1851) (JP, 6727). And he made a concession: "But precisely because, deeply humbled, I confess my inferiority, I have realized that Christianity permits me, at least for the time being, to live in this manner" (Pap. X 4 A 33 n.d., 1851) (JP, 6727).

However, Kierkegaard committed his life to denouncing the discontinuity between theory and practice: "The doctrine in the established Church and its organization are very good. But the lives, our lives—believe me, they are mediocre." And in so doing, he was a radical thinker. He did not assume a reformist position; he adopted a revolutionary attitude: "But do not incur new guilt by wanting to reform the

---

115. Kierkegaard, *Kierkegaard's Journals*, 1124; Pap., X 3 A 306.

Church when Christianity is no more" (Pap. X 4 A 33 n.d., 1851) (JP, 6727). No wonder H. P. Andræ perceived it very well:

> Søren Kierkegaard lies in the hospital . . . very sick —paralysis of the legs as a consequence of tuberculosis of the spine marrow. This awakens concern doubly at this time, because, with his writings against Mynster, Martensen, and the clergy—or, perhaps to express it better, against the whole outer form of the worship of God—he has aroused a great sensation, and it is certain that his writings, which have a large readership, including many theologians, will sooner or later have a revolutionary impact upon matters concerning the Church.[116]

Jesus Christ Economically Located

A relevant issue related to the vexing gadfly's concreteness is Søren Kierkegaard's social depiction of Jesus as a poor person. This is not the place to analyze it in full; however, let it suffice to say that Søren Kierkegaard's portrayal of the doloristic Jesus (the poor, the humble, the lowly) contrasts with the classical Christologies of the nineteenth century, which pictured him as the gentle good shepherd, as the little baby of Christmas, as the risen and glorified Christ, as the judge, as the ethical teacher.[117] Kierkegaard's sharp eye saw how the alliance of Christianity with the cultured, the privileged, the well-to-do, ended up reducing Jesus to a well-educated man. In Kierkegaard's belief structure, in the very act of Jesus's birth, there is a historical identification with the poor: "He is born in poverty and wretchedness. One is almost tempted to believe that it is not a human being who is born here—he is born in a stable, wrapped in rags, laid in a manger—yet, strangely enough, already as an infant he is persecuted by the rulers in power so that the poor parents must flee with him" (FSE, 58).

Kierkegaard's insistence on the existential has to do with his critique at the level of practice. Consequently, the doctrine of Jesus Christ has to be approached from that dimension as well: "It is all very well that by living only in certain select circles one is able to live securely, aloof

---

116. Andræ, *Geheimraadinde Andræs politiske Dagbøger* [Madame Privy Councilor Andræ's Political Diaries], 111, quoted in Kirmmse, *Kierkegaard*, 483.

117. See, e.g., Plekon, "Introducing Christianity into Christendom," 344.

from the crowd etc.—but does one have the right to live this way? Did Christ live this way?" (Pap. VII 1 A 212 n.d., 1846) (JP, 4114).

The poor Jesus Christ differs from the steady-salaried and honorable clergy whose maxim is, "Too little and too much spoil everything." Jesus was a lowly servant, despised, mocked, and spat on. On the other hand, the clergy's life depends on economic security, social prestige, and religious power: in sum, the priest "is a joker" (SUDb, 124).

In his *Practice in Christianity*, Kierkegaard develops the famous concept of contemporaneity [*Samtidighed*] with the degraded Christ, who took the form of a slave. Let it suffice to add that Kierkegaard is thinking neither of Christ manifested in his glory—because nobody would be offended by glory (PC, 65)—nor of an abstract Christ or of a man in silk, but of the degraded Christ who had no room in a society that had domesticated the absolute transcendence of religion. Now, the offense of contemporaneity with Christ has to do with Kierkegaard's social and economic critique of the socially sanctioned reasonableness of the establishment. In this respect, the two gadflies had to pay the price: "Like Socrates, Christ was executed as an infidel because he refused to recognize the established order as the criterion of virtue and goodness."[118] Christ was an offense to the political system; therefore, Kierkegaard highlighted "what 'the truth' had to suffer in every generation and what it must always suffer," by not backing off from the collision between piety and the established order (TC, 87, 37).[119]

Jesus's social and economic location is well described in *Judge for Yourselves*: "He belonged to nothing and to no one, was in no alliance with anything or with anybody, was a stranger in this world, in poverty and lowliness, without a nest, without a den, without a place where he could lay his head" (FSE, 167). This evidently is the counterpart of official Christendom: "Let it be as the preachers proclaim—namely, that Christianity is the gentle comfort, a kind of insurance for eternity" (FSE, 190).

Kierkegaard resisted a kind of culture that was divorced from Christ as the prototype (*Forbilledet*). A culture for whom Christ was understood in purely ideal terms denied even the humorous and pedagogic element of his life, as one hymn expresses: "How he weeps who

118. Westphal, "Kierkegaard as a Prophetic Philosopher," 6.
119. Quoted in ibid.

never laughs" (Pap. X 1 A 673 n.d., 1849) (JP, 1855). Kierkegaard's concept of the "totally Other" does not point beyond the present order but in contradiction to the same. In his *Christian Discourses* he conceives of Christ as the witness to the truth and the Prototype or the Pattern who lived expelled from human society (CD, 127). The disciples of Christ were also economically and socially located in the simplest condition. They were repudiated and despised as imitators of him who remained faithful to lowly people, starting with his own relatives: "He let Himself be born in poor and lowly circumstances, yes, in dishonor, and thereupon as a child lived with the simple man He called His father and with the despised maiden who was His mother." In his entire life, Jesus Christ dissociated himself from the powerful circles: "That thereupon He wandered about in the lowly form of a servant, not to be distinguished from other lowly men even by His extraordinary lowliness, until He ended in the utmost wretchedness, crucified as a criminal—and then, to be sure, left behind Him a Name" (CD, 45).

However, in order to avoid being an imitator of Christ, a defense mechanism is introduced: "we cannot resemble him absolutely because he is the Savior and Reconciler of the race," and alongside the risk of overemphasizing our impossibility of resembling him, thus: "His being the prototype almost evaporated as something altogether too transcendent. This, however, must not be done" (Pap. X 1 A 132 n.d., 1849) (JP, 693). Within this framework, Kierkegaard places the ill-oriented intellectual enterprise of his contemporaries (mere accommodation) by providing "reasons" to get people to accept Christianity without financial jeopardy: "He has the reason that it is his bread and butter, and he must take care to speak in such a way that the congregation is not niggardly with the offering. In short, he has the reason that he himself is stuck in the same worldliness as the congregation" (Pap. X 4 A 393 n.d., 1851) (JP, 3165).

The problem with the abstract and transcendent Christ of Christendom is that humanity never reaches actuality: "A Christian in the volatilized sense, a Christian such as we are, is one who accepts the doctrines, rests in grace, but does not in the more rigorous sense enter into 'imitation.' To such a Christian Christ is the Savior, the Redeemer, but not in the stricter sense 'the prototype'" (Pap X 4 A 296 n.d., 1851) (JP, 6761).

In his exceptional study of Golden Age Denmark, Bruce Kirmmse has already substantiated the fact that the political domain does have room in Kierkegaard's work. Concerning *The Two Ages,* the principle of association is authenticated: "the principle of association can be valid for the political and social purposes of material prudence."[120] And in general, in relation to a state that has subsumed the effects of the Christian faith, Kierkegaard points out the transcendence of the same: "The proper sphere of politics is much more modest indeed, namely, the making, by the human community, of such arrangements for its material well-being as seem prudent. To promise to deliver more is to spawn monsters that attempt to cut the individual off from his ground of being in God."[121] Nonetheless, regarding the notion of God's majesty put in abstract and irrelevant terms by the intelligentsia, Kierkegaard chooses to underline the other side: "In a certain sense it would certainly be an injustice to our age to say that it has no conception of respect for God in the sense of approaching God too closely and minimizing him. No, it is rather the opposite." Kierkegaard continued with his univocal language: "God has been made so majestic and has been so fantastically infinitized that he really has been smuggled out of everything to some point infinitely distant from actuality" (Pap. X 5 A 47 n.d., 1852) (JP, 2561).

---

120. Kirmmse, *Kierkegaard,* 393.
121. Ibid., 313.

Kierkegaard on Economic Issues

The Radical Final Years, 1852–1855

first money, and then you can have your child baptized; first money, and then earth will be thrown on your coffin and there will be a funeral oration according to the fixed rate; first money, and then I will make the sick call; first money, . . . and then the Kingdom of God. . . . And the whole thing remains with the first: money.

—Søren Kierkegaard (AUC, 235–36)

For Germany the *criticism of religion* is in the main complete, and criticism of religion is the premise of all criticism.

—Karl Marx[1]

MY OBJECTIVE HERE IS TO SHOW THAT WITHIN SØREN KIERKEGAARD'S critique of Christendom, economic issues are a significant factor in the Kierkegaardian theological discourse and not merely a footnote in his works. I have already pointed out how Kierkegaard's mind was shaped by a particular historical womb: the Danish *Belle Epoque* or Golden Age. However, I have also substantiated the fact that there did exist an evolution of Kierkegaard's thought, articulating the social, economic, and ideological elements of his time and space.

The young Kierkegaard up until 1846 held very conservative political views. Nevertheless the mature Kierkegaard began moving in a different direction from that year 1846 forward, due to the Danish and European social and political movements' taking place. I have labeled the years of 1846 to 1852 years of transition because if, on the one hand

1. Marx, "Contribution to the Critique of Hegel's Philosophy of Right," in *Early Writings*, 43.

there is a visible rupture in Kierkegaard's *Weltanschauung* (worldview) during those years, on the other hand the years of 1852 to 1855 introduce us to a prophetic Kierkegaard, who clearly broke with the political-religious monism, i. e., Christendom. The definitive Kierkegaard of the period between 1852 and 1855 orchestrated his assault on the establishment without making any concessions.

His assault upon Christendom is radicalized, manifested by his virtually abandoning pseudonymity and by addressing his audience en masse. Kierkegaard's critique of economic issues was also radicalized. This clear shift is indicated by the way he worked with social and structural metaphors, as well as in the manner he uncovered the hidden presuppositions of religion and politics.

The Voluntary Silent Stage: 1852–December 18, 1854

> By considering the priest one is led to the conclusion: Christianity is hardly the truth, but profit is the truth. (AUC, 271)

Kierkegaard's Paradigm Shift

Denmark's new government of 1848–1849 officially stated that its social institutions of church, university, and theater now belonged to the "ordinary" person, no longer to the crown and the rare few.[2] As time went by and no substantial change took place, it is not surprising that by the end of 1852, Kierkegaard emerged with a radically new way of facing his society.

Granted, Kierkegaard stopped going to church by December 18, 1854,[3] but from that does not follow that this date is the landmark of his decisive rupture. Let us recall the fact that on Sunday May 18, 1851, he preached for the last time at Højmessen in Citadellets Kirke, and that regarding this last sermon, he wrote in his *Journals* about the clergy: "fat preachers earning their livelihood who are also decorated Knights of Denmark"(A, 330).[4]

---

2. Kirmmse, *Kierkegaard*, 381.

3. Plekon, "Kierkegaard and the Eucharist," 214–36.

4. Kierkegaard held a *cand, theol.* degree; he lacked the Episcopal "collatio" or conference, the royal or ecclesiastical/governmental issuance of the call and ordination by the bishop. However, he was eligible to be called and to preach, he even considered "the possibility of preaching extempore, that is, without a previously prepared manuscript,

In a similar way let us take into account that it was on Friday, May 28, 1852, when he took communion for the last time.[5] Furthermore, from September 1851 to the beginning of 1852, Kierkegaard wrote his *Judge for Yourself* that remained unpublished until 1876. There he elaborated his concept of becoming sober, through which he "launched an all-out attack on the church."[6] Nevertheless, Kierkegaard's withholding that book shows his awareness of his new radical position. Finally by the same token, Nordentoft observes how Kierkegaard in his *Journals* of 1852 and 1853 leaves behind his own old-fashioned conservatism, the antidemocratic and antisocialist character that he espoused during the 1840s.[7]

Let us remember that Kierkegaard remained silent from 1852 until December 18, 1854, when he openly assaulted the church in the prestigious newspaper *The Fatherland* (*Fædrelandet*). Throughout those three silent years, however, he added seven more large volumes to his *Journals*. Johannes Sløk interprets this period of silence as the time of rushing for a new order of political, social, and ecclesiastical realm, specifically under the conservative A. S. Ørsted, the finance minister from April 1853 to December 1854.[8]

It may be well to open an explanatory parenthesis to look at the old Kierkegaard and to observe how people such as Stanley R. Moore[9] have missed the mark every time they associate the late Kierkegaard with misanthropy. The fact that Kierkegaard reflects an ascetic tendency and hostility to sex during his last years is not primarily related to the repudiation of that dimension, but to a new and radical way of the "*posing of the problem*, conditioned by the political, social, and ecclesiastical developments of the period."[10] Kierkegaard is dealing then with the tension between church and state:

---

and one would suppose without memorization of such text" (Plekon, "Kierkegaard's Last Sermon," TMs [photocopy]).

5. Plekon, "Kierkegaard and the Eucharist," 218.

6. Kirmmse, *Kierkegaard*, 442.

7. Nordentoft, *Kierkegaard's Psychology*, 251.

8. *Da Kierkegaard tav*, 1–78, cited in Plekon, "Kierkegaard's Theological Fullness," 17.

9. Moore, "Religion as the True Humanism," 17.

10. Nordentoft, *Kierkegaard's Psychology*, 64–65 (italics original).

> It is then no longer a case of the role of sexuality and love in the personal development of the single individual, but of the relationship between Christianity and bourgeoisified "Christendom," between the preaching of Jesus and the official institutions and the society which has exploited this for its own advantage.[11]

Kierkegaard's target thus is not home, sensuality, or sex in themselves. All of them play a subordinate role; what he is counteracting is "the sacrosanct notion of *the home,* the clerical-erotic, Christian-familial miasma as the climate which fostered the most luxuriant growth of self-deception and hypocrisy, and the atmosphere of diluted bourgeois morality which guaranteed the growth of all these phenomena."[12]

Closing this parenthesis on the supposedly insane last years of Kierkegaard, we returned to our social, political and economic themes. The dominant note in Kierkegaard's post-1852 writing boldly opposed the establishment (*det Bestaende),* which theoretically was overcome in the revolution of 1848. Instead of that order of things, he fought for a dynamic society:

> Precisely those men who are preoccupied with the desire to enjoy life, make a brilliant career in the world, precisely those men find it of utmost importance that there be no movement whatsoever on the religious. As soon as "the spirit" begins to move, existence [*Tilværelsen*] becomes so uneasy that a person cannot pull himself together and make a career in the world. Therefore it is very important that everything stay the same, that the religious should be appropriated from the previous generation exactly as it was, at most with only a few minor modifications. (Pap. X 4 A563 n.d., 1852) (JP, 1000) (Pap 5 A 125, 126, 147 et al.)

Jesus, The Man in Silk

> In the magnificent cathedral the Most Honorable, Right Reverend Privy-General-Superior-Preacher to the Royal Court, the chosen favorite of the refined world, appears before a select circle and preaches *greatly moved* upon the text he himself selected: "God has chosen the poor and despised of this world."

11. Ibid., 65.
12. Ibid.

And nobody laughs. (Øieblikket, no. 6 "Short and Sharp" my translation).[13]

Church members who deny their responsibility for the needy in any part of the world are as guilty of heresy as those who deny this or that article of faith.[14]

Søren Kierkegaard's sharp eye perceived the treatment that his society applied to the person of Jesus. From being a "loser" Jesus was now recognized as a "winner": "So the 'way' has now become a different one, not that of the New Testament: in humiliation, hated, forsaken, persecuted, condemned to suffer in this world—no, the way is: to be admired, acclaimed, crowned with garlands, accorded the accolade of knighthood as the rewards of a brilliant career"(AUCb, 21).

Kierkegaard's axiological egalitarianism is attuned with his Christology: Jesus Christ is, in Kierkegaard's opinion, the mistreated, dragged, crucified, who witnessed the truth in poverty, lowliness, abasement. The Galilean was hated, abhorred, insulted: "his daily bread perhaps he did not always have, so poor was he, but the daily bread of persecution he was richly provided with every day. For him there was never promotion, except in an inverse sense, downward, step by step" (AUC, 7).

Within this framework, Kierkegaard introduces a new conceptual "system": Indeed, it is not for nothing that the Dane has been vindicated as "The first theologian in the modern period to take the revolutionary turn in Christology away from the bankrupt christologies of the Enlightenment and romanticism, away too from those of bourgeois *Kulturprotestantismus.*"[15]

The Jesus in silk of the clergy contrasts with Jesus the poor, humiliated, mocked, and spat upon. The affluent and spacious churches contradict preaching the doctrine for naught, in poverty, in lowliness, in renunciation: "preaching is of course a livelihood, the surest way to

---

13. *I den pragtfulde Domkirke fremtræder den Høiævædige Geheime-General-Ober-Hof-Prædikant, den Fornemme Verdens udvalgte Yndling, han træder frem for en udvalgt Kreds af Udvalgte, og prækiker rørt over den af ham selv udvalgte Text "Gud har udvalgt det i Verden Ringe og Foragtede"—og der er Ingen, som leer.*

14. Visser't Hooft's *Memoirs,* 363; quoted in Duchrow, *Alternatives to Global Capitalism,* 38.

15. Plekon, "Introducing Christianity into Christendom," 344.

bread and steady promotion becoming Your Excellency, using the police against others" (AUC 19).[16]

The Heresy of Prosperity

The heresy of prosperity, plainly stated, consists of the naive understanding of wealth without taking into account the poverty on which it
is built. To prosper—this heresy boldly preaches—is a matter of wanting. Everybody can succeed financially.

I have already highlighted the fact that Kierkegaard was a dialectician who addressed, within the broad theme of Christendom, the issue
of wealth and poverty as correlative terms. If we fail to detect that they
are intertwined, we won't be able to see that what lies behind poverty
is misery, and ultimately, death:[17] "the day in which absolute poverty
would want to be eliminated, it will be necessary for the nations to obey
the sovereign commandment: you shall not kill."[18] Consequently, I am
dealing with the topics of wealth and poverty from this theological
perspective.

Once prosperity has been baptized by religious leaders then, in
gratitude, the upper crust will reward the clergy, but it is also true in
relation to other social institutions: "Money, power, and the like, these
are what count in the world. Art and scholarship and all such higher
things must put up with bowing and scraping before money." And
Kierkegaard continues straightforwardly: "If a wealthy man wants to
make a contribution, he is bowed to and feted as an art connoisseur
and patron of poets, although he understands neither art nor poetry
at all" (Pap. XI,2 A 54 n.d., 1854) (JP, 2570). Those kinds of people who
are unable to see other dimensions of reality deserve this judgment of

---

16. In the 1840s Mynster led a campaign against the Baptists in order to arrest
them and to baptize their children against their parents' will. Fortunately, the new king,
Christian VIII, did not back up the bishop. In January 1842, Orla Lehmann, a student
committed to liberalism, was sentenced to three months of imprisonment "for having
impugned royal authority in a speech a year earlier, when he had expressed skepticism
that absolute monarchy was in the best interests of the peasantry" (Kirmmse, *Encounters
with Kierkegaard*, 320). See also Garff, *Søren Kierkegaard: A Biography*, 318).

17. "Poverty which in the last analysis means early and unjust death, destroying
persons, families, and nations" (Gutiérrez, "Theological Language: Fullness of Silence,"
193).

18. Perroux, *Le pain et la parole*, 267. Quoted in Gustavo Gutiérrez, "Una teología de
la liberación en el contexto del tercer milenio," 132.

a contemporary scholar: "If somebody is an idiot, is an emotional idiot, an artistic idiot, he doesn't understand a thing, he is not capable of seeing anything except a practical value of cents, then we call him today a very clever man."[19]

In antagonism to the heresy of prosperity, late in 1851, Kierkegaard still had in mind the unrealistic ideal of becoming an ordained pastor, but one must hasten to add that he wanted to be a pastor for the poor and forgotten people: "If Christianity relates to anyone in particular, then it may especially be said to belong to the suffering, the poor, the sick, the leprous, the mentally ill, and so on, to sinners, criminals . . . Rarely do they have a pastor, and then he is a mediocre one." (Pap. X, 2 A 27 n.d., 1849) (JP, 386) Or better yet: "My desire has always been to preach to the common man. But when the journalism of mob vulgarity did everything to present me to the common man as being demented, I had to give up the desire for a time, but I shall return to it again" (Pap. X, 3 A 714 n.d., 1851) (JP, 991).

Kierkegaard's premature death or his half attempts to become a rural pastor did not allow him to achieve such a goal. Nevertheless in his career as an author, he sided with needy people: "There is certainly no one living in the Kingdom of Denmark with the feeling that I have for individuality. A servant girl, a watchman, a cabby, absolutely every man was to me of infinite value. And I know (as no one else in Denmark) how to talk to absolutely everyone and idealize them in conversation."[20]

On the other hand, the heresy of prosperity is based on a style of life that denies the essence of the proclamation and charges of Christianity. In the dialogue: "You must die to the world—that will be ten dollars," the novice asks: "Who gets the ten dollars?" and the pastor answers: "Of course I get it; it is my wages; after all, I and my family have to make a living out of proclaiming that one must die to the world . . . it is very necessary for me and my family to spend the summer in the country in order to recuperate, etc" (Pap. X 4 A 627 n.d., 1852) (JP, 3169).

In another narrative[21] i.e., "Preaching and money," a parson stated: "Thou shalt die unto the world.—The fee is one guinea." The neophyte

---

19. Fromm, *The Art of Listening*, 80.

20. Kierkegaard, *Kierkegaard's Journals*, 1854 (1367); (Pap., E.P. IX p.221).

21. Kierkegaard considered himself "the philosopher of story-telling," but he was a "major consumer of narrative genres." In 1850 there is a turning point from his earlier stage as destroyer of narratives to his final period as an builder of narratives. The young

reacts: "well, if I must die unto the world I quite understand that I shall have to fork out more than one guinea; but just one question: who gets the guinea?" and the Parson concludes: "Naturally I get it, it is my living, for I and my family have to live by preaching that one must die unto the world. It is really very cheap, and soon we shall have to add for considerably more." The justification is the same: "If you are reasonable you will easily understand that to preach that one must die unto the world, if it is done seriously and with zeal, takes a lot out of a man. And so I really have to spend the summer in the country with my family to get some recreation."[22]

Kierkegaard denounced the heresy of prosperity in 1849: "It is one thing to be a prophet (*profiteri*) of a faith, a science, a capability, and something else to make a profit (*profit*) on it" (Pap X 2 A 5 n.d., 1849) (JP, 2770). Again Kierkegaard uncovered the heresy of prosperity at the end of his life with a lapidary sentence: "By considering the priest one is led to the conclusion: Christianity is hardly the truth, but profit is the truth" (AUC, 271).

Translating this attitude into sociological terms represents also a huge profit. Take, for instance, the figure of the professor: "A man of understanding can never become a Christian; the most he can achieve, through the power of imagination, is to play with the Christian problems ... they become scholars, scientists, make everything copious and complicated, and drown therein the essential point of Christianity." Kierkegaard continues: "the human aggregate is transformed into the very opposite of what it must become in true Christianity, something one profits from just plain financial profit etc., or something from which one has the profit of an admiring chorus" (Pap XI 2 A 436 September 23, 1855) (JP, 6966).

Kierkegaard is convinced that the gospel is preached to the poor and that they are infinitely more important than the king. The priest, however, privileges the king. Instead of giving money to the poor, the priest is a receiver of stars, ribbons ... and a steady salary: "For when the king is a Christian, then the group of mighty ones who are his associates

---

Kierkegaard made a half-way use of narrative "in a kind of mental coitus interruptus. He dare not allow the narrative to have its obvious effect. It must at most 'make aware'" (Bjerg, "Kierkegaard's Story-Telling." 111–25).

22. Dru, *Kierkegaard's Journals*, (1267); (Pap., X 4 A 627).

follow him at once" (AUC 36). In Kierkegaard's commercial language, the clergy are a mercantile class; the shopkeepers, (AUC, 48) Christian counterfeiters, (AUC, 148) soul-traders or soul-sellers (AUC, 152). The church is like a shop where the traders know their business: "for Christ's judgment after all is surely decisive, inopportune as it must seem to the clerical gang of swindlers who have taken forcible possession of the firm 'Jesus Christ' and done a flourishing business under the name of Christianity" (AUC, 117).

Grundtvig, the Danish reformer who took the side of the "happy Danes," the peasants who profited from the land reforms, distanced himself from the "sad Danes" of the countryside and from the inner cities as well. Kierkegaard classified the Grundtvigians, including his brother Peter, as defenders of the established order because of their interest in money: "The Grundtvigians also support the idea of separation of church and state; consequently, it has been exclusively money matters which have captivated them in passionate love, and filled them with warm enthusiasm for the establishment" (Pap XI 3 B 188 n.d., 1855) (my translation).[23]

Numbers, success, progress, money are what count in the reign of God. Kierkegaard observes in the section "The Pastoral Oath" that seeking first the reign of God does not correspond with the pastoral model: "It takes the student four years to graduate, then he becomes a graduate. Now he has to wait four or five years before he gets appropriate seniority. Then he seeks. And finally he gets an appointment and a job—this is seeking the kingdom of God *first*" (Pap. XI 1 A 389 n.d., 1854) (JP, 3179). Kierkegaard's reading between lines sees the matter in a clear way: "First the Kingdom of God.' But does not the clergyman's whole activity rather follow this law: Money first of all, and then.—Whatever he involves himself with, it is: May I first ask for my money—and then." According to Kierkegaard there is in the New Testament an inverted process regarding the clergy advancement: "One would begin with 1,200 dollars and after being fifteen years, for example, in service, would get only 800, and soon the biggest and richest appointments would go to the beginners" (Pap. XI 1 A 390 n.d., 1854) (JP, 3180).

---

23. ". . . Men Grundtvigiarnerne have tillige den Thesis Adskillelse af Kirke og Stat, saa det altsaa ene og alene er det Pecuniaire, der i inderlig Kjerlighed fængsler dem til og varmt begeistrer dem for det Bestaaende."

Ludvig, a theological candidate who agreed to receive 150 dollars less than he requested, throws more light on this point. When the dean introduces him to the congregation he assures them that Ludvig has "an unprejudiced eye for earthly profit." Then the Dean preaches on "Lo, we have left all and have followed Thee": "and then he explains to the congregation that precisely in times such as ours there must be men like that as teachers, and in connection therewith he recommends this young man, of whom he knows how near he has been to drawing back for the sake of 150 dollars" (AUC, 208ff).

The power of providing moral validation for prosperity puts the clergy in an advantageous situation: "what helps the priests to cheat more than any other class in society is precisely the fact that they are so closely associated with religion. If such a thing could be done, he would gladly give a good shilling to obtain ordination, for that would pay brilliantly" (AUC, 206–7)

Money matters played a central role in the confrontation between the state church and the sects. The official clergy, in Kierkegaard's judgment, had the religious-economic monopoly, along with prestige and power: "But if profit with respect to religion is reprehensible, then the official clergy are much worse than the sect-makers, inasmuch as the official clergy have profit assured in a different way, and in addition also have the profit of honor and esteem" (Pap. XI 1 A 584 n.d., 1854) (JP, 3184).

To turn everything upside down is the antidote against the sickness of his society. The Christian method consists of seeing "everything inversely" (CD, 155). In 1849 he passed judgment on Mynster's exquisite palace: "It is shameful how we have used even the essentially Christian for refinement in worldly things. We crave worldly things—as much as any pagan—but we also cover it up with Christian disdain for all worldliness. Thanks, that means harvesting twice" (Pap X 1 A 600 n.d., 1849) (JP, 3061).

In his two last years Kierkegaard continued the critique of the heresy of prosperity: The bishop's palace, the clergy's long robes, the splendid churches, generate a psychological effect in the people. The nearness of God is perceived by appearances, by the phenomenological. People are "deluded by sense-impressions"; consequently, they are "prone to judge true Christianity by sense-impressions" (AUC, 175). Nevertheless, that is a falsification of the Christianity of the New

Testament, because God's logic of nearness and remoteness is inverse to ours: "the more the phenomenon, the appearance, expresses that God is very near, the farther away he is." God was closer to actuality when Christians were refugees and persecuted in the time of the catacombs, and inversely God was distanced from actuality when in the sphere of appearance the splendid and thousands of churches emerged. God was nearer at the time of the universal priesthood and more remote when the mighty clergy was created because "God relates inversely to phenomenon." The same happened with the increase and embellishment of doctrine through monstrous systems: "get a permanent committee of pastors and professors to make the doctrine more strictly accurate—excellent—in order to get farther away from God" (Pap XI 2 A 51 n.d., 1854) (JP, 3099). Pastors and professors, in their seeking profit, have a hidden economic agenda in their interpretation of Scripture, and furthermore they pursue honor.

God's paradoxical and inverse relation with actuality, however, uncovered ulterior motives: "we build huge edifices for him, and hundreds, yes, thousands of pastors and bishops, deans and professors, are summoned together in an enormous Church council, convinced that when such a colossal body is assembled and sits at unbelievable cost to the state—that God is present" (Pap XI 2 A 51 n.d., 1854) (JP, 3099). In the late Kierkegaard the accumulation of money, the heresy of prosperity, and, in general, the callousness toward economic sins constitutes the denial of God.

Economic Sins

Kierkegaard was not an ascetic. He realized that it was impossible for the clergy to live on nothing: "'But are you perhaps thinking that a person can live on air, or does Christianity perhaps think that it is illicit to work for a living?' By no means, not in the remotest way" (JFY 124). Kierkegaard has in mind the pastor's dignity [*Værdighed*], the dignity of His Reverence [*Velerværdighed*] or of His Right Reverence [*Høiværdighed*] and then he questions their incredible salaries, just like any other secular career. He illustrates the point in his entry "Judas and money," where he portrays Judas's economic sins—as a modern, refined, and highly cultured person who knows how to profit from the church. Judas established the calculating conditions for betraying Jesus: "I want a certain fixed sum yearly. I am a young man, well and strong, having in all human probability the prospect of a long life before me—and I wish to lead an agreeable existence (married and with family) with rich opportunity for enjoyment. That is the price."[24] In summing up, Kierkegaard seeks honesty: "One cannot live off of nothing. This one hears so often, especially from priests. And precisely the priests perform this trick: Christianity actually does not exist—yet they live off of it" (AUC, 182).

In considering the matters of wealth and poverty, I am aware that throughout history economic sins have been overshadowed by other sins. Wealth and poverty are, in general, a theme of reflection relegated to a segment of the field of social ethics. Nevertheless it is my contention that these economic topics are central to the doctrinal corpus of the Christian church. To this respect, the life and thought of Kierkegaard is enormously relevant. He did take into account the economic sins:

> A man who tricks and swindles day in and day out but otherwise is an extremely cultivated gentleman belonging to the society of the cultivated—if he has the bad luck to get drunk once—heaven help him, it is an irreparable loss, and he himself condemns it so severely that he perhaps, as they say, never forgives himself, while it probably never occurs to him that he should need to be forgiven for all the tricks and frauds and dishonesty, for all the spiritually revolting passions which make their home within him and are his life. (Pap. XI 2 A6 n.d. 1854) (JP, 4049)

To mention the economic sins is another way to address the issue of conscience and money. Regarding the practical character of an Englishman, Kierkegaard quoted from Schopenhauer: "to have a conscience was such an expensive way of life that his circumstances did not permit it." And immediately the vexing gadfly recounts a story his father told him concerning a person with a practical conscience, whose motto was: "it would almost be better not to have a conscience":

> In the old days when district judges and bailiffs were the gracious lord's sometime coachmen or servants, these subjects were still given a kind of examination, in which the chief administrative officer of the country questioned them—and the whole thing operated on "bribery." At such an examination the examiner said to the candidate: "What do you understand by

24. Ibid., (1342) (Pap., XI 1 A 374).

conscience?" The candidate answered in a low voice: ["]I have a fifty-pound tub of butter in the carriage." "Fine," answered the examiner. "Quite correct, but still not adequate." "I have . . ." "Fine, fine, but still not completely adequate." "I have ten dollars in cash." "Excellent!" (Pap. XI 2 A7 n.d., 1854) (JP, 3362)

I have been arguing that within Kierkegaard's growing critique of the church and Christendom, economic ideas are of major significance in Kierkegaard's late writings. In order to substantiate this claim, I have to widen the analysis to the economic sins of prestige and power that work together with economics: "'Had the Apostle Paul any official position?' No, Paul had no official position. 'Did he then earn much money in other ways?' No, he didn't earn money in any way. 'Was he at least married?' No, he was not married. 'But then really Paul is not a serious man.' No, Paul is not a serious man" (AUC, 181).

Kierkegaard's society did not address economic sins simply because there were not such sins where the absolutization of money has taken place. On the contrary, "by the power of money" there was lots of success in having million of Christians: "That thing about eternity is definitely the cleverest of all inventions, when it gets into the right hands, the hands of practical people; for the Founder, unpractical as he was, had a wrong notion of what Christianity is" (AUC, 147).

Golden Age Denmark was Christian in name because in practice it was a negation of Christianity: "Thus in a very short time—triumph, triumph, triumph!—perhaps 30 to 40,000 Christians." Kierkegaard addressed his thunder against the cross-bearers who ran the enormous Christian houses of prostitution. Under the name of progress, he argued, the church does not care about economic sins, namely, about the people who have "scarcely a piece of dry bread in his house" (Pap XI 3 B 175 n.d., 1855) (JP, 3213).

The commercialization of the ministry constitutes an economic sin. Kierkegaard called the priests civil functionaries like every other employee—nonetheless, with more benefits: "this profession may be considered one of the most agreeable and the most highly honored" (AUC, 23). Kierkegaard's claim was that the manipulation of prestige, the pursuit of power, and the pecuniary motivation as they were observed within Christendom were but a way of playing Christianity. Profit, rank, titles, decorations; being admired, acclaimed, crowned with garlands, accorded the accolade of knighthood as the reward of a brilliant career; seeking wealth and luxurious enjoyment of the most exquisite refinements, all of that demonstrates, paradoxically, the denial of God (AUC 8, 21, 70, 71).

The mouthpiece of state religion has equated God's governance with the state of well-being of the fortunate. Kierkegaard, who delved into motivations, presents us another perspective. Kierkegaard compares the economic sins of the clergy with that of Ananias and Sapphira, in the sense that private property and wealth are not the indefensible things; what is at stake is the appearance of piety and their public image of committed Christians: "As far as I am concerned, the clergyman is welcome to take a tenth instead of a twentieth or thirtieth—but he may not pretend that it is Christianity he actually wants if it is the tenth that he wants" (Pap. X 4 A 622 n.d., 1852) (JP, 3168). The fact is that material comfort demands spiritual comfort. And in a society where taxes were for the sake of the supreme value (i.e., money and "the security of property"), why not raise more taxes, Kierkegaard's irony asks, for eternal salvation: "This provides a certain sense of security as well and therefore has a tranquilizing effect" (Pap XI 2 A 111, n.d., 1854) (JP, 4501).

Kierkegaard energetically denounced the concept of justice in his time. In his society, where money and private property were supreme goods,[25] evidently sin was confined to theft. However, for Kierkegaard, the greatest sinner is not a thief but the reduction of sin as theft itself.[26] The person who believes that theft is the only form of sin is unrighteously identified as a pious, admired and God-fearing person: "he wins a double advantage: worldly goods—and at the same time the glory, the halo of the saint, and the corresponding respect and deference" (AUC, 250–51)

At this point we have already seen the breadth of vision and depth of penetration with which the irritating gadfly has within his attack upon the church and Christendom unveiled economic sins. In closing

---

25. Fromm has pointed out the equivocal way in which property has been classified as private or public, nationalized or socialized. He proposes to discriminate between functional or nonfunctional property. Functional property satisfies real personal and existential needs; this kind of property does not have an exploitative character. The nonfunctional property, on the other hand, Fromm also calls exploitative or dead property, in the sense that it is oriented towards a pathological need. In the first case, to have means to use; in the second, to have means to possess. Cf. *Del tener al ser; caminos y extravíos de la conciencia*, 33, 36.

26. Kierkegaard, *Kierkegaard's Journals*, 1363; Pap., E.P. IX p. 214.

the discussion of private property, a last quotation is in order: "'Is this a just rule? What has become of divine justice?' Encroachment upon the property of others, thievery, fraud, in short, everything that has to do with money (the god of this world), is punished, punished severely—so severely are crimes punished in this . . . righteous world!" (AUC, 252).

Providence (Forsynstro) and the Retribution Ideology

> "The rich man in his castle,
> the poor man at his gate;
> God made them, high or lowly,
> and ordered their estate."
>
> —Miss Humphreys, 1848.[27]

> But this prompts the old atrocity again—namely, the idea that the unfortunate, the poor are to blame for their condition, that it is because they are not pious, are not true Christians. Consequently they are supposed to have not only suffering but guilt as well, and the rich have not only pleasure but piety in addition. (Pap. X, 4 A 578 n.d., 1852) (JP, 4685)

Let us begin by noting that it was Kierkegaard, rather than Max Weber, who was the first intellectual who saw the ideological link between economic success and spiritual elevation. Søren Kierkegaard's economic judgments, then, can throw much light on issues such as the gospel of wealth, the idealization of poverty, and so forth.[28]

In previous years Kierkegaard had criticized the paradigm of Jewish piety, which adheres strongly in the material: "according to the ratio: the more pious one is, the better it goes for him on earth, the longer he lives, etc." (Pap. IX A 424 n.d., 1848) (JP, 2217). In fairness to Kierkegaard, however, let us remember that his main target was Christendom rather than Judaism. Kierkegaard's agenda is to show the ideological elements that exist in this connection between financial success and the Christian faith. With this in mind, he takes the occasion from Cicero's *De natura deorum*, book 2. The concept of God reflected here is of that who is concerned exclusively about weighty matters and ignores the insignificant: "There is a providence which is concerned about the whole and also

---

27. Mullin, *Wealth of Christians*, 132.
28. Nordentoft, *Hvad Siger Brand-Majoren?* 203.

about individual men—but, note well, superior men" (Pap X 4 A 442 n.d., 1851) (JP, 3062).

Cicero's way of thinking is, Kierkegaard continues, a frightful denial of God: "How in all the world would I dare to believe that God is concerned about me if he is concerned only about the eminent; how frightful for a man ever to believe that God is concerned about him, consequently that he is important to God." Kierkegaard calls this paganism, or a god defined in terms of "the superlative of what it is to be man." What is at stake then is to clarify the essence of Christianity: "The more wretched, the more abandoned, the more insignificant, the more unhappy you are—be assured, the more God is concerned about you" (Pap X 4 A 442 n.d., 1851) (JP, 3062).

Kierkegaard pointed out frequently how his generation reduced Christianity to the enjoyment and the happy life of the well-to-do and, simultaneously, to the callousness toward the poor and forsaken, whose social redemption ultimately will take place in the hereafter: "We have put them aside and comforted ourselves on their behalf with the thought that it will last only a few years—and then the poor, the suffering, and the like will become just as blessed as everybody else" (Pap XI 1 A 143, n.d., 1854) (JP, 3777). Material improvement and God's blessing then go hand in glove within this conception of the retribution doctrine: "The deceivers, on the other hand, make a brilliant career, so that everyone can see that God is with them, an opinion in which they themselves are more and more confirmed" (AUC, 256). Still more clearly Kierkegaard states: "millionaires are the only ones who have the means to please God perfectly"[29] (AUC, 289).[30]

Kierkegaard maintains that the ideologists of adaptation or the promoters of the retribution doctrine have manipulated the religious element

---

29. Hinkelammert has compellingly argued that the retribution theology articulated by St. Anselm, has practically closed heaven and earth for the poor. St. Anselm insisted that, it was God's very own Son the only one who was able to satisfy God's justice, in giving his life by paying for humanity's debt. From that follows, according to St. Anselm, that all kinds of debts are unforgivable, they have to be paid, since God did not forgive not even God's own Son. Consequently: "as the impossibility to pay a debt is a sin, the capacity to pay it is an act of God's grace. That is, people who can afford to pay their debts are chosen by God; poor people are not." Furthermore, from such doctrine follows the beatitude which Kierkegaard is actually denouncing: "Blessed are you the wealthy, because you can afford to pay your debts." See Hinkelammert, *Sacrificios humanos*, 75, 88.

30. The term *billionaire* was invented in 1861.

of guilt, having as a consequence a perverted version of Christianity.[31] The rich and the powerful have a monopoly on the gospel. Therefore, Kierkegaard argues, their wealth and might are the signs of God's providence, "and these are the ones the clergy would rather associate with, for here the pay is best, both in money and in dignity" (Pap.X4 A570 n.d., 1852) (JP, 4682). Suffering people, on the other hand, are burdened with guilt in a very cruel way (Pap. X4 A578 n.d., 1852) (JP, 4685).

Kierkegaard did not allow this ideology of adaptation to go unnoticed. He reversed this reading of the gospel and categorically asserted that God is on the side of the poor. The marks of piety (the God-relationship) and its counterpart of guilt (the God-misrelationship) are, in effect, ways in which we defend ourselves: "we shield ourselves against him by making out that it is his own fault or that it is because of his sins"; or furthermore, "we shield ourselves against the unhappy and the wretched whose sufferings will disturb our zest for life and give us a different impression of God, that he is not the God of success, by saying: It is their own fault—and then we go on enjoying life and enjoying ourselves in the illusion that we have God on our side" (Pap. X4 A573 n.d., 1852) (JP, 4683).

Kierkegaard persuasively noticed that according to the clergy of the status quo, the lot of the poor is suffering and guilt, whereas the possessions of the rich are the mark of their piety. Examples are many of the way Kierkegaard imputed pastors for not only legitimizing wealth, but also for associating it with divine favor:

> The rich and the powerful not only get to keep everything, but their success becomes the mark of their piety, the sign of the relationship to God. "Look," they say, "because this man is pious and God-fearing, everything goes well for him, this is why he amasses one barrel of gold after another," and when he responds to the proclaimers of Christianity, with an appropriate contribution, they vouch for him that it is God's blessing, that it is because he is a true Christian, because this is more convenient both for him and for the preachers (Pap. X, 4 A 578 n.d., 1852) (JP, 4685)[32]

Merold Wesphal captures Kierkegaard's general ideas about the retribution doctrine or the relationship between God's grace, the poor,

31. Nordentoft, *Kiekegaard's Psychology*, 254.

32. See also Pap. X, 4 A 570 n.d., 1852; JP, 4682.

and the favored ones (the wealthy or the mighty).[33] According to this Kierkegaardian, both revelation and reason are socially functional by providing validation in the religious and secular realms.

In Kierkegaard's Golden Age Denmark, faith and reason, faith and civilization, faith and socialization, mingled: "We have made the finite and the infinite, the eternal and the temporal, the highest and the lowest, blend in such a way that it is impossible to say which is which, or the situation is an impenetrable ambiguity" (JFY, 123).

Søren Kierkegaard was very suspicious of ideology.[34] For him the state, to which Christianity is wedded, has deified society by putting socialization on par with salvation. Now in order not to make a fool of God, Kierkegaard elevates God's sovereignty above these relative, external, political forms. But in doing so, the New Testament historical and sociological setting is always present. What is at issue is God's resistance to being manipulated by kings, emperors, the pope, or whomever of all the authorities: "God is the one and only sovereign. In order to express this he chooses a very simple man as his envoy—that is the highest distinction. And then he requires that he, his ambassador and apostle, express that the great power whom he has the honor to represent is the one and only, which is the truth" (Pap. XI, 1 A 372 n.d., 1854) (JP 2976).

When Kierkegaard approaches the theme of "Christendom" he is actually addressing the Danish society and culture in which it takes place (Pap. XI 2 A 399 May 12) (JP, 6958). I have argued that as early as 1846 he had the suspicion that Christianity was a mere accommodation to bourgeois society.[35] Kierkegaard's attack upon the established church must be seen as an attack upon the established state, which was compromising the Christian message.[36]

33. Westphal, *Kierkegaard's Critique of Reason and Society*, 115.

34. Ibid.

35. Metz puts it bluntly: "If I am correct, Kierkegaard's critique of 'Christendom' may be understood already as an early form of criticism of bourgeois religion in Christianity. In fact, according to Kierkegaard, Christendom—without causing a sensation or even without noticing it itself—had more or less identified Christian existence with the 'natural' existence of the bourgeois; a covert transformation of the Christian praxis of discipleship into the bourgeois way of life took place" (Metz, *Emergent Church*, 5). See also JP, 6076.

36. Still following the same political theologian: "In the form of Christendom Christianity had once again successfully come to terms with the power of the prevail-

Kierkegaard is afraid of equating politics with the eternal truth: "[If] A policy which in the proper sense of 'eternal truth' were to make serious work of introducing 'eternal truth' into real life[, it] would show itself in that very same second to be in the most 'impolitic' thing that can be imagined" (PV, 118). Due to the disastrous consequences of this marriage, "this triumphant church, or established Christendom, does not resemble the church militant any more than a quadrangle resembles a circle. Imagine a Christian of those ages when the church was truly militant—it would be perfectly impossible for him to recognize the Church in its present perversion" (TC, 207).

In his attempt to separate the church from the state, Kierkegaard was not pursuing a kind of rejection of mundane politics. On the contrary, he was struggling in favor of the preservation of the Christian message as an instrument of social criticism. He was denouncing the manipulation of religious speech.[37] In Kierkegaard's opinion, what lies behind the doctrine of Christendom is an ideology that privileges the status quo of the aristocracy.[38]

Pastors legitimized the establishment. The important role that they played in reinforcing the status quo had strong direct political implications: "the 'priest' pronounced a blessing upon this Christian society, this Christian state, where they swindle just as in paganism, and do it also by paying the 'priest', who by this mark is the biggest swindler, they swindle themselves into the notion that this is Christianity" (AUC, 164).

Therefore, the ideology of adaptation or the retribution doctrine[39] finds its place: within *Christenheden* (Christendom), de Begunstigede (the favored ones), *de Rige* (the wealthy), and *de Mægtige* (the mighty) are the ones who possess *Guds Naade* (God's grace); in reciprocity they support Christendom (Pap. X, 4 A 570 n.d., 1852) (JP, 4682).

---

ing society, in this case with that of bourgeois society. Yet, at what price? No less a price, so claims Kierkegaard, than the abolition of Christianity itself, the Christianity of discipleship, as he never ceases to insist. I regard this primary and eminently prophetic critique of Christianity as bourgeois religion, one in no way obsolete today, but —for both Catholics and Protestants—more urgent than ever before" (ibid.).

37. See, e.g., Westphal, *Kierkegaard's Critique of Reason and Society*, 41.

38. Kirmmse, *Kierkegaard*, 514.

39. "It [the retribution doctrine] is very comfortable and has a tranquilizing effect for the people who own many possessions in this world; at the same time, it creates a sense of resignation with a guilty conscience in the people who lack possessions" (Gutiérrez, *Hablar de Dios*, 64; my translation).

Søren Kierkegaard was right in seeing how the government had undermined the content of the gospel through its economic assistance to the church: "There is one thing which Christ must unconditionally exclude: financial assistance. But Satan knows that there is only one way to annihilate Christianity—by means of financial assistance" (Pap. XI, 1 A 102) (JP, 4497). Kierkegaard's penetrating vision detected the transformation of the poor Jesus in the hands of the clergy and upper classes.

Kierkegaard faulted scholars and the interpretation of the New Testament by which they identified money and power as God's gifts. Kierkegaard repudiated intellectuality in the service of the mighty: "Christ preached with authority—so does the 'parson' nowadays, for he has the police and the prison in reserve."[40] The Dane also rejected the academic circle that favors the wealthy to the detriment of the "ordinary" person: "The professors are the very ones who have demoralized the race. Everything would be better if the true relationship could prevail: the few who are truly in the service of the idea, or still higher, in the service of God—and then the people" (Pap. XI 1 A 473 n.d., 1854) (JP, 3589).

The church had given her seal of approval to the retribution doctrine. Kierkegaard, on the contrary, fought for the poor and declared his solidarity with this cause: "Seldom, seldom had that been seen: a man who conscious of himself, and clear about what he is doing, works zealously and industriously—to make himself poor."[41] The retribution doctrine takes for granted that in the present order justice prevails; therefore, being poor or wealthy is a condition divinely wanted. Kierkegaard, on the contrary, proposes the theology of grace that repudiates the idea that "millionaires are the only ones who have the means to please God perfectly" (AUC, 289).

In Kierkegaard's view, under the theme of God's providence there are other interests lurking behind the scenes. In this case, our interpretation of the gospel has been tainted by economic interests: "But here as everywhere we treat Christianity as arbitrarily as possible. We men select what seems able to suit our self-indulgence and throw away what

---

40. Kierkegaard, *Kierkegaard's Journals*, (1274); (Pap., X 4 A 644).

41. Ibid., 1371; Pap., E.P. IX, 230.

does not please us—and thus we cook up a rascally religiosity which is supposed to be Christianity" (Pap. XI 1 A267 n.d., 1854) (JP, 3632).

Kierkegaard substantiates his point by interpreting the doctrine of providence (*Forsyn*) as a social and economic tranquilizer. He discovers a religious disposition in the people who belong to the middle and upper classes: "on behalf of the providence and governance they are champions of the beautiful, uplifting conception that the world we live in is the best, and so on." Kierkegaard's eye-opening method, however, takes a closer inspection. He detects cruelty and egotism in this reduction of the dogma of governance to the source of enjoyment and well being of the pious fortunate people: "such faith perhaps helps (strange as it may seem) fortify him against the impression of the suffering and the unfortunate, the perpetual reminders of the wretchedness of this life." This reading of what the retribution doctrine means has "a wonderful tranquilizing effect" on the fortunate. According to this, providence has distributed rewards to the good-fortunate people and punishment to the evil-unfortunate people. And moreover, God's governance has already set a place for each one in society: "in the existence of this providence he has a defense for not doing more for the sufferer than he is doing, because he fears to disturb the purposes of providence for every individual" (Pap. XI 1 A267 n.d., 1854) (JP, 3632).

This hermeneutical key used to explain God's governance perfectly suits the profit, prestige, and mighty agenda of the clergy: "In other words, when proclaiming Christianity is a livelihood, if possible even a lush livelihood, then, the gospel is preached best of all—for the rich—nothing is more obvious" (Pap. X4 A578 n.d., 1852) (JP, 4685). Within this framework, Kierkegaard compares Christendom in general and the retribution doctrine as a sedative, as a tranquilizer and can we say as opium?: "In the New Testament Christianity is the most intense unrest possible—God in heaven has not been able to find one more intense. And in Christendom Christianity is used —as a tranquilizer" (Pap XI 2 A 42 n.d., 1854) (JP, 4490).

Kierkegaard always seeks to dig beneath the surface. Consequently, he uncovers the economic agenda of the religious and political rulers. Robert Perkins has argued persuasively how the early egalitarianism of Kierkegaard's *The Concept of Irony* reaches a powerful political dimension when he addresses the reality of the "ordinary" person who has been ignored for centuries. The same Kierkegaard scholar also noticed how what lies behind the issues of hidden inwardness, establishment, ordination is nothing but a money question.[42]

Countless passages could be cited in the same vein. The one about Jensen, the butter-and-eggs man, is but an example. According to this businessman, it is so obvious that the clergy has an economic agenda: "the more I think of it the clearer it is—that neither wheat nor butter, meat, fish, salt, brandy—in short, no commodity, nor speculating in government bonds, pays so splendidly or yields as much as Christianity" (Pap XI 2 A 298 n.d., 1853-54) (JP, 3780). Along with the financial profit of the clergy come honor and prestige: "If I could manage to run my butter and egg business in the name of our Lord Jesus Christ in such a way—please note, in such a way—that I had the same financial profit I now have, perhaps a bit more—I would certainly relish the pleasure of no longer scraping and bowing, as I do now, before the dealers who buy my butter—"and the business man adds, "but having them come with their money and bowing deeply to me, embarrassed at having to mention money in my honored presence (—naturally we have to be sure that I get the money!)—scraping and bowing before a most eminent man of God" (Pap XI 2 A 298 n.d., 1853-54) (JP, 3780).

The vexing gadfly is trying, then, to make Christianity possible again by means of rejecting the reduction of the gospel to pecuniary interests and, above all, by repudiating the practice of absolutizing money in the name of the interest of Christianity (Pap XI 2 A 363 n.d., 1854) (JP, 2773). The princes of the church with their scientific illusions that hide reality are central to Kierkegaard's radical attack. Their whole project of spreading the doctrine with great zeal and fervor is motivated, according to Kierkegaard, by financial advantage and material power (AUC, 41).

To say that God's governance has ordered our station in life is another way of stating the retribution doctrine: "When proclaiming Christianity means acquiring rank and title, if possible a high rank and title, and medallions and ribbons—then, yes, then Christianity is proclaimed best of all for the mighty etc. (not only the preachers perceive this; I also perceive it)" (Pap. X 4 A 578) (JP, 4685).

Kierkegaard linked the uncritical acceptance of the status quo with the retribution doctrine and its oppressive consequences. This

42. Perkins, Review of *Kierkegaard in Golden Age Denmark*, 6.

ideology of adaptation appropriates the old adage of Epicurus: "*nihil beatum nisi quietum*"; i. e., nothing is happy unless it is in repose, or in Kierkegaard's translation: "'peace' is the first requisite for the enjoyment of life" (AUC, 18).

Golden Age Denmark was an ideal static order whose motto was "One Must Take the World as It Is." Kierkegaard took distance from this God-willed order and introduced the vitality of the reign of God, which was not built on the values of that society: "[the reign of God] is simply not a kingdom of this world because it will never respect the 'One must take the world as it is'" (Pap XI 2 A 46 n.d., 1854) (JP, 3561).

Kierkegaard wondered what is covered by a fixed concept of the world where everything is already given: ideas, thoughts, custom and usage, fortune, prestige, and where "—the specimen-man [*Exemplar-Mennesket.*]" cannot do anything to change it: "In their relation to life these specimen-men are like little fish in a net set for bigger fish"; the molesting mosquito, Kierkegaard, thus wants to make people aware, and instead of the behavior of "passing through freely like little fish," he questions this attitude of taking the world as it is. Therefore, in disagreement with the scholars who labeled Kierkegaard as an acosmic individualist, he declared: "This is what the apostle is talking about when he says that the Christian is not struggling with flesh and blood but with principalities and powers. This means that a Christian's existence radically affects life and thereby acquires the infinite ideality to set both heaven and earth in motion."[43]

Mynster, the symbol of peace (read: of the status quo), endorsed Epicurus's saying quoted above. The ideal order for him was to leave things as they were. In that context, he underestimated Kierkegaard's attempts to change reality, because the primate of Denmark realized his financial power was far superior to Kierkegaard's. In effect, the bishop used to affirm before Kierkegaard: "it is not a question of who has most strength, but who can last longest."[44] The clergy, as a consequence, will also work "to keep everything in good order," which, translated in theological and sociological terms, means the endorsement of the retribution doctrine, and means to perpetuate a bourgeois marriage model, cozy security, and the emasculation or castration of those who once

43. Ibid.
44. Kierkegaard, *Kierkegaard's Journals* (March 1, 1854), 1296; Pap., XI 1 A 1.

wanted to follow a higher ideal (Pap. X 3 A 502 n.d., 1850) (JP, 3156). This kind of pastor is, in Kierkegaard's view, but a charade due to the fact that he has mixed everything, i.e., to enjoy economic bonanza and simultaneously to enjoy a spiritual reputation, the pastor is "a nice man, *neutrius generis* (neither ecclesiastical not secular) or *generis utriusque*, an ecclesiastical-secular hermaphrodite" (Pap. X 3 A 514 n.d., 1850) (JP, 3157).

Kierkegaard also unmasks the economic and social agenda of the academicians who pretend to leave everything as it is through the elaboration of objective and fixed doctrines. Kierkegaard then plays his last card: "with God's help I will succeed in shedding light upon your glory, you venerable figures—I will shed light upon it—to my own detriment! I shall never let it become a matter of indifference and say as it is said nowadays: The doctrine, the objective doctrine, that is of course the main thing." The Dane's digging beneath the surface sees beneath objective knowledge a way of making a living, of practicing a career, of pursuing status, of doing business, of "taking the world as it is" (JFY, 127–28).

Kierkegaard adduces a supplementary argument. The retribution doctrine of the ideal static world is a construct whose rulers aspire to make everyone uniform. As an antidote to that state of affairs, Kierkegaard proposes primitivity, namely, to go back to that state of human beings where it was possible to perceive reality without the interference of other voices. Instead of aping the other and being reduced to a copy, the alternative is to stand alone. Neither the former nor the latter is an authentic choice for Kierkegaard except primitivity: "But both teachers and followers feel best in aping and by aping—therefore they are *lovingly* unanimous about it and call it love" (Pap XI 1 A 62 n.d., 1854) (JP, 3560).

Fædrelandet Stage, December 18, 1854–May 1855

> this is the issue—and it will be evident that the new Bishop, by thus canonizing Bishop Mynster, makes the Established Church, from the Christian point of view, an impudent indecency. For if bishop Mynster is a witness to the truth, then, as even the blindest can see, every priest in the land is a witness to the truth. (AUC, 18)

The Assault on Christendom

Because of the neglect in the practice of the values Mynster trumpeted in theory, Kierkegaard openly attacked the amalgamation of church-state, using the weapon he called "human honesty." Bruce Kirmmse draws our attention to the historical events that forced Kierkegaard to lay all his cards on the table.[45] Kierkegaard's admiration and disdain for the bishop led him to remain silent, although very active, waiting until the end in order to see some changes in Mynster's policy. Denmark's primate passed away on January 30, 1854, without touching his static society. On February 5, 1854, Martensen preached his famous eulogy over the deceased dignitary: "A Witness to the Truth" [*Sandhedsvidne*]. Martensen's association of this key Kierkegaardian category with Mynster, with Hegel's philosophy, and with official Christendom marked the end of Kierkegaard's patience.[46] In spite of this, the prophetic writer had to wait a few more months. First, because Kierkegaard could have been sued by Martensen, who was in the middle of his campaign for the bishop of Zealand's vacant chair, who was in the middle of his campaign for the position of bishop in Zealand's ancient chair, which he finally got on April 15, 1854. Once he was invested, Martensen could not blame Kierkegaard for trying to block his path. Second, because the mighty and reactionary A. S. Ørsted, Martensen's protector, was still the prime minister. It was not until December 1854 that the liberal C. G. Andræ replaced him.

This is to suggest that although Kierkegaard stopped taking communion early in 1852, he waited for the "eleventh hour," the opportune instant, to launch his open and "secular" attack.

Kierkegaard himself embraced the church and attended Sunday services regularly. He sometimes visited more than one church, and in a time when worship lasted three hours. He endorsed the Church's theology and practice. However, by 1846 Kierkegaard's mind began moving in a different direction, and a couple years after the bloodless revolution of 1848–1849, the vexing gadfly radicalized his position. What was at stake then was the redefinition of the folk church in contradistinction to the state church: the church of the "ordinary" person, i.e., of that one-third of the population. Kierkegaard was expecting that the emerging

45. Kirmmse, *Kierkegaard*, 185, 189, 449ff.

46. Hansen, *Revolutionœr Samvittighed*, 132.

people's church would actually replace the state church, but by 1855 it was already apparent that the change had taken place exclusively at the level of language. In the meantime, this theologian accumulated a great amount of material in his *Journals* against a church that was still taken in tow by the state. Finally he declared a public boycott of Christendom. Consequently, he addressed people in masse, abandoned his precious indirect communication through his pseudonymity, left behind his philosophical and specialized language, and made use of newspapers like the liberal *Fatherland* and his own *Instant*.

On March 31, 1855, Kierkegaard adopted the honesty agenda that consisted of a popular call for a boycott of "official Christianity," putting aside religious speech. On May 31, 1855, he broke with Christendom in calling upon all to cease to take part in the public worship of God, where the only thing one receives is tranquilizers (AUC, 260).

Kierkegaard perceived how conscious and hidden agendas affected theological systems and ecclesiastical praxis as well. Not surprisingly, he encouraged people to double their pledges to the church budget and, simultaneously, urged them to stop going to the church. He proposed to have a tenfold increase in the clergy salary and at the same time to empty the churches. Kierkegaard recommended those measures in order to show that money—contrary to how it is for the clergy—is not an absolute for the believer: "Nothing weakens the impression made by moral pathos more than bringing money into the matter. If someone wanted to express indignation by refusing to pay his church contribution, the whole thing can be explained as his desire to save the money." Everything is a matter of money, more than the loss of state support. What the church fears the most, Kierkegaard continues, is financial chaos: "It is also entirely certain that the bankruptcy of the Rothschilds would not result in such a great upheaval as would occur if Christianity went out of business" (Pap XI 2 A 22 n.d., 1854) (JP, 2772).

Commitment was another key concept in Kierkegaard's epistemology. Let us recall that Kierkegaard's late change of focus consisted in a slow evolution of his thought. Take for instance his treatment of church and street (*på gade*), namely, his insistence in articulating belief with actuality. Early in 1847 he affirmed that the authentic ethical communication takes place in real existence. Therefore, the teacher must "live and teach on the street." Original Christianity thus has "to be present for the mass, to live and learn on the street." Kierkegaard praised Luther, who was of the opinion that the gospel is to be announced on the street and not in churches, as in Kierkegaard's lifetime (That is, in Kierkegaard's own lifetime, the gospel was proclaimed only in churches): "the existential situation is represented at most by an assurance 'that if it is demanded—then'" (Pap. VIII 2 B 85 n.d., 1847) (JP, 653).

The divorce between theory and practice reduced preaching in churches to theatricality, Kierkegaard adds. That is why Mynster was unable to preach in the public square. It is because real proclamation consists of "preaching on the street and by acting." No wonder by the end of his life Kierkegaard was moving from the loci of traditional theology: "there should not be preaching in the church but on the street, in the middle of life, in the actuality of the daily, week-day life"(VIII 2 B232 85:18; IX A39; X4 A287; XI 3 B120). To articulate the gospel with actuality necessarily brings a collision: "for all this talk about quiet places and quiet hours as the proper element for the essentially Christian is upside down." In summing up, the shift of preaching from the church to the street has to do with reaching the actuality of ordinary weekday life. It is related to reaching Kierkegaard's constant companions, the "ordinary" person. It is also connected with Kierkegaard's "honesty agenda" in the use of the *Fatherland* and his purpose of bringing essential Christianity: "and to that end I decided to use this newspaper. It is a political paper, has completely different interests, concerns itself with a great variety of subjects—but not with Christianity" (Pap XI 3 B 120 April 8, 1855) (JP, 6957).

The Honesty (Redelighed) Agenda

> I am neither leniency nor severity: I am … a human honesty …
> If then official Christianity in this country takes occasion from what is said here to employ power against me, I am ready; for I want honesty. (AUC 37, 40)

It was long said that Kierkegaard enclosed himself in a cocoon. Today we know that this is incorrect. Simultaneously with his assault on Christendom, he openly confessed his socially transforming agenda under the names of human *redelighed* ("honesty") and *oprigtighed* ("sincerity").[47]

---

47. Hansen, *Revolutionær Samvittighed*, 110.

Kierkegaard perceived the correlation that exists between the church's highly organized bureaucracies and the availability of money. This religious and economic hierarchy is internalized by the worshipers who derive their sense of dignity depending on the economic power they have. As Kierkegaard puts it: "But if the clergyman explains that it costs $100 and $10 to the priest, then Martin Frandsen says, 'Well, now, this makes sense. Sure, it's a lot of money, but when a man has paid out $100 he can be sure that he is involved with God'" (Pap. XI 2 A 148 n.d., 1854) (JP, 3185).

In his last year, Kierkegaard openly declared his campaign against the establishment now under his "secular," "human honesty" banner. Nevertheless this did not take place in a vacuum or all of a sudden.

Søren Kierkegaard's sympathy for the poor has been questioned in *Works of Love*.[48] One can argue that Kierkegaard's main focus was the Danish church, and within his critique of Christendom, Kierkegaard did denounce economic sins, including slavery. On the other hand, let us bear in mind that *Works of Love*, the book being questioned, was published in 1847, during those transitional years of Kierkegaard's thought. Nonetheless, let us keep in mind the very fact that he denounced in a timely way how, in preaching about Christ's association with tax collectors and the common man of the streets, the entire life of the preacher needs to be consistent. Knowing and doing should go hand in glove; preaching must reflect one's own existence; otherwise, this is really nonsense:

> One of two things: *either* one's life should express in some measure that one is ridiculed, mocked; that one lives in the company of the common man on the streets and avenues and eats with tax collectors and sinners; that one is poor and pinched; *or* one shall hold his tongue about such things and preach about the advantages of being a highly regarded, magnificent gentleman, along with the methods used in achieving "this good," about the advantages of being a person of status along with the pleasantness of moving in the best circles, about the advantages of hav-

48. See, for example, his supposedly incredible insensitivity and obliviousness toward slavery in Christian Europe and North America, stating that non-Christians are appreciative of Christians for "saving humankind from the evil" "inhuman" institutions such as slavery and the caste system (SV 12, 72, 77, WL 80, 84). Jegstrup advances this point of view ("Kierkegaard on Citizenship and Character," 252 n. 24).

ing a fat salary along with the benefits collected with a velvet
paunch. (Pap. X, 1 A 650 n.d., 1849) (JP 1056)

Kierkegaard was demanding the engagement of the gospel with
reality, and in doing so, he was aware of the cost it implies. For instance,
in addressing the passage of the rich man and Lazarus, he reminded
us of the imperative of giving money to the poor, and not merely being a sentimental blabber as with the wealthy who ignore the ordinary
people: "a man of such distinction would be able to weep on Sunday
as he preaches about compassion. He will rapturously declare that
Christianity does not establish a separation as if we should be holy
only on Sunday; no, Christianity should penetrate the whole of life, the
everyday as well" (Pap. IX, A 379 n.d., 1849) (JP 6270). Kierkegaard confronted the dichotomy that existed between Sundays and weekdays, as
well as between the living room and the sanctuary, in order to eradicate
the superstitious idea of the "Sunday-go-to-meeting atmosphere" seeking absolution, a kind of indulgence for the whole week that has already
finished (CUP, 415, 416, 424, 459). Earlier, Kierkegaard had criticized the
church for its practice of privileging the wealthy members over the "ordinary" person, the same people who, inconsistently, strive against each
other in daily life, but who worship together on Sundays (CUP, 420).

What counts for Kierkegaard is "the correspondence or non-cor-
respondence of my life or thine" with the teaching of the church, and
not the calculation of scholarly correspondence between the different
dogmatic declarations. What come first are the transformed lives that
reconcile weekends with weekdays (CD, 222). Within this train of ideas,
Kierkegaard articulates his concept of idolatry, which has to be addressed at the level of practice more than at the theoretical level: "If one
who lives in the midst of Christendom goes up to the house of God, the
house of the true God, with the true concept of God in his knowledge,
and prays, but prays in a false spirit ... prays in truth to God though he
worships an idol" (CUP, 179–80).

A great deal of ink has been spilled on the topic of *The Corsair*
[*Corsaren*] and Kierkegaard's quarrel with this satirical journal. It would
be pointless to repeat that. Nonetheless, very briefly I will mention what
is relevant for our purposes. The clergy remained indifferent in the face
of this kind of newspaper: "With the largest circulation in the city and in
the country, with talented anonymous writers and cartoonists of wit and

malice, with a series of straw men as 'responsible editor,' with disdain for public position and personal privacy, *The Corsair* gathered and cleverly exploited fact, rumor and gossip."[49] On the other hand, Kierkegaard's sense of probity moved him to address much of his thunder toward it. Not surprisingly, the intellectual and graphic caricatures of Kierkegaard that the editor made in turn are still the main source of the interpretations of him. He unmasked the connivance that existed between *The Corsair* and the corrupt civil and ecclesiastical authorities. Mynster's personal friendship with the editor set the bishop in a safe place (Pap XI 2 A 296 n.d., 1853–1854) (JP, 6846). That is understandable if we take into account the bishop's political position. Mynster's agenda of "taking the world as it is" (JFY, 127–28), or the bishop's quoting out of context I Corinthians 14:33, 40 ("For God is not a God of confusion, but of peace . . . all things should be done decently and in good order"[50]) points to Mynster's static world of the status quo.

Now the dominant note Kierkegaard hears regarding the priest's silence in face of *The Corsair* affair and in general is, not surprisingly, money and making a living. That fact completely changes his perspective of reality: "I maintain that his [Mynster's] possibly well-written, warm, eloquent, enthusiastic, persuasive defense for the Establishment is nevertheless to be understood somewhat differently, when it is also known that he is monetarily interested. Isn't it so?" (Pap XI 3 B 117 April 7, 1855) (my translation).[51]

Kierkegaard's sense of integrity and actual commitment to physical reality not only repulsed the *fuga mundi* ideology, but the *fuga Denmark* advice as well:

> Those who think well of me do not realize that the small bit that every single person contributes is certainly little, nevertheless, when they are added up, all these small bits are a large quantity for the one who has to carry the whole. And were there one, both able and willing to understand, then I could move him no further than to this: that I can travel or evade. This means he has

---

49. Jansen, "The Individual versus the Public," 10.

50. Mynster, *Blandede Skrivter,* 315–16; quoted in Kirmmse, *Kierkegaard,* 133.

51. ". . . jeg siger, at hans mulige veskrevne, varme, ||veltalende||, begeistrede, over-bevisende Forsvar for det Bestaaende dog forstaaes noget anderledes, naar dete vides med, at han er pecuniairt interesseret. Er dette ikke saaledes?"

most profoundly misunderstood me. (Pap XI 2 A 12 n.d., 1854) (my translation)[52]

Kierkegaard contrasts essential Christianity with official Christianity and in his attempt to be congruent with the former he courageously committed himself to the "ordinary" person without being a suicidal man: "I am as far as possible from being a muddle head or misanthrope, who plunges ahead and blindly attacks." He was conscious of his place in society: "But of course I am but one man, the others have the power." In spite of all this, he revealed the sort of economic and social agenda that the clergy preached in their selective reading of the gospel: "And right here is the basic guilt, that men arrogantly want to decide for themselves and according to their own convenience what Christianity is to be" (Pap X 3 A 483 n.d., 1850) (JP, 6683).

Kierkegaard fought against *Christenhed* or (in German) *Christenheit*, i.e., the *orbis christianus* or *corpus christianum*, better known in English as Christendom, where people want to live in error. He was at odds with the pastors who abandoned the longing for truth of their early years and ended up capitulating to the establishment: "a man has to—as we say—keep up a bold front; he is forced farther and farther into untruth, becomes less and less a Christian, while all the time he obstinately boasts that of course he is a Christian, since he is a teacher of Christianity" (Pap. XI 3 B 43 n.d., 1854) (JP, 3068).

Kierkegaard insisted that his agenda was neither leniency nor severity but honesty. The interpretation of him as "a supporter of asceticism" can of course be balanced by other Kierkegaardian dicta where he discards suffering as an end in itself: "suffering itself must never be the *télos*, you must not dare in order to suffer, for that is presumptuous, and is to tempt God. To expose yourself to suffering for the sake of suffering is a presumptuous personal impertinence and forwardness towards God, as though you were challenging God to a contest." A higher commitment is the source of such painful experience: "But when it is for the cause—even though you see that the suffering is humanly speaking

---

52. "… De som mene mig det vel, ere ikke opmærksomme paa, at den lilleBrøksdeel, som hver contribuerer vistnok er lille, men alle disse Brøksdele forenede dog er et stort Qvantum for Den, der skal bære det hele. Og var der saa En, der baade kunde og vilde forstaae, ham faaer jeg saa ikke længere end til dette: at heg kan reise eller unddrage mig. Dette vil sige, han misforstaaer mig allerdybest."

unavoidable, just go on and dare. You do not dare for the sake of suffering, but you dare in order not to betray the cause."[53]

By 1853, Kierkegaard categorically declared that his task was not to reintroduce asceticism but to question the concept of Christian culture and civilization as a whole entity: "this culture and civilization has at the same time produced a development of rational understanding which is in the process of identifying being a Christian with culture, and with intelligence, desirous of a conceptual understanding of Christianity." And he adds: "This is where the struggle must come, and will be fought in the future."[54]

Kierkegaard's prophetic speech led him, by April 1855, close to ecclesiastical excommunication (AUC, 56), although he himself had already broken with Christendom. However, the annoying gadfly was conscious of the high price prophets have to pay when they touch political and economic interests: "If the official Christianity in this country wants to take the occasion to use force against me because of what is said here, I am prepared [rede], because I want honesty [Redelighed]" (AUC, 49). For the meantime, Kierkegaard was articulating his ideas for the next stage.

Øieblikket Phase, May 26, 1855–October 1855

> At one time there must have lived a few rogues, as Holberg says, who duped the state into thinking that the suffering and death of Jesus Christ and eternal salvation were something which could be used to raise money. (Pap. XI, 1 A 63 n.d., 1854) (JP, 4495)[55]

The period of the *Fatherland* constitutes Kierkegaard's last attempt to separate the church from the structures that deny essential Christianity. Now in the *Instant*, he emerges with more vitality.

The provoking gadfly's ultimatum of the *Fatherland* remained unanswered. Consequently, Kierkegaard made use of his entire arsenal against the self-deification of the established order through the founding of his own newspaper, In the *Instant* Kierkegaard's dialectics is more obvious. While he is working on the deception within himself,

53. Kierkegaard, *Kierkegaard's Journals*, 1270; Pap., X 4 A 630.

54. Ibid., 1288; Pap., X 5 A 89.

55. See e.g., Mynster and his connections with the elitist social circles (Pap. X, 1, A 228 n.d., 1849) (JP, 6378).

he continues working to fight against the social and political order that bewitches us.[56]

It is not for nothing that Kierkegaard named his newspaper the *Instant*. Kierkegaard loaded the word *Øieblikket* ("instant") with the meaning of the infinite qualitative difference between time and eternity. Some scholars have interpreted this concept in terms of Tillich's "Protestant Principle"; i.e., it is related to the break with immediacy. From the *Instant* follows a constant vigilance against ideology, either secular or sacred.[57] Or briefly put, "there is a radical element to [Kierkegaard's] social and political thought, an element that is tied to transcendence. Without a transcendent God in time, we humans will manufacture God in our own image, and we will do so to buttress the status quo."[58]

By mid-1855, Kierkegaard had abandoned the *Fatherland* and had given up the last attempt to challenge the establishment, i.e., the state-church. Now whereas in Jørgen Bukdahl's view, Kierkegaard is focusing his attack exclusively on the church for the cause of the "ordinary" person,[59] we can argue that within Kierkegaard's assault on Christendom there is a significant economic agenda that has not been fully appreciated.

The Instant meant a public call, especially to the "ordinary" person, to reject Christendom. Kierkegaard's honesty agenda led him to welcome in a warm way the ordinary person's growing awareness.[60] In a dialectical way, Kierkegaard raised a powerful denunciation against the elitist and money-centered policies of the clergy:

> from generation to generation there lives—how equivocal! a highly respected class in the community, the priests. Their métier is to invert the whole situation, so that what man likes becomes religion, on the condition, however, of invoking God's name and paying something definite to the priests. (AUC, 221)

That is, according to Kierkegaard, to want to be deceived: "The rest of the community, when one examines the case more closely, are seen

56. Kirmmse, *Kierkegaard*, 467.

57. Khan, "Opposition within Affinity," 199.

58. Evans, *Passionate Reason*, 154.

59. Bukdahl, *Søren Kierkegaard og den menige Mand* (*Søren Kierkegaard and the Common Man*), 114ff.

60. Kirmmse, *Kierkegaard*, 462.

to be egoistically interested in upholding the estimation in which the priests are held—for otherwise the falsification cannot succeed" (AUC, 221).

Fresh Air: The Cure of the Sickness of the Age

> What Christianity needs is not the suffocating protection of the State; no, it needs fresh air, it needs persecution, and it needs . . . God's protection. (AUC, 140)

I do not endorse the fatally one-sided reading of Kierkegaard as a theologian whose entire authorship promoted the person-to-person relationship. In this section I am going to argue that his thought and writings did address structural dimensions, e.g.: the age, the pyramid, the building, the external revolution, "the Fire Chief," and a diagnosis of society.

Kierkegaard was a sharp observer of the social and political events of his present age of the 1840s, which were crowned by the elaboration of the new democratic constitution of 1848–1849. From then until his last year, he was expecting substantial structural changes within Christendom. As time went by, instead of a new reality's materializing, things remained the same. The religiously, philosophically, and politically conservative Martensen was in charge of perpetuating Mynster's petrified Christendom tradition. The liberal party continued the elitist policy of the conservatives. With the removal of the finance minister, A. S. Ørsted, then, Kierkegaard restarted his fight against the entire established order. The vexing gadfly began by questioning the use of police power in the name of Christianity and by dethroning the state.

The molesting gadfly's task was to bring "fresh air" into a world that wanted to be deceived (*Mundus vult decipi*)—a world whose equivocal language was not noticeable:

> When a man has a toothache the world says: "Poor man";
> when a man's wife is unfaithful to him the world says: "Poor man;
> when a man is short of money the world says: "Poor man";
> when it pleases God to wish to suffer in this world in
> the form of a humble servant, the world says: "Poor man";

when an apostle acting on a divine mission has the honor of
suffering for the Truth, the world says: "Poor man": "Poor world."
(Øieblikket, no. 6, my translation)[61]

Kierkegaard's awareness detected that what was at stake was something that transcended the linguistic level, i.e., the human being's "deep need to be fooled," and the rapid answer of the clergy to satisfy it.

The cure for the age, according to Kierkegaard's prescription, is the introduction of Christianity into Christendom or, put in commercial terms, the resistance to the way the state is profiting with the gospel. Kierkegaard compared the state with a coachman who decides not to buy an incredible five-year-old horse because it is not suitable for his purposes. But after a dozen years, he goes ahead and buys it: "now I can make enough profit from it, from what is left in it, so that I can properly see my way of spending a little for its board." The state is not interested in buying "the eternally young Christianity," which would be the state's ruin, but the domesticated Christianity: It is better to buy the spavined and decrepit, spoiled and muddle-headed Christendom: "See, now I can bid on it; and smart as I am I can see very well that I can use it and profit from it enough so that I can properly see my way to spending a little to polish it up" (Pap XI 1 A 366 n.d., 1854) (JP, 4232).

Fresh air or the eternally young Christianity is contrary to the cheap gospel, the clearance sale, or the brilliant business of buying and selling eternity. Kierkegaard describes pastors as the ones who have the commercial monopoly on the gospel. The gospel, on the other hand, is described as a commodity of indescribable and costly commercial value. Kierkegaard's suspicion of ideology finally warned his age not to be fooled by the cheap grace, the clearance sale of this product of the clergy's exclusive private ownership: "But what makes me suspicious is whether 'the pastor' has such a relationship to eternal salvation that he is able to sell it" (Pap XI 2 A 75 n.d., 1854) (JP, 6926).

Kierkegaard was engaged with the eradication of the sickness of his age. The manipulation of Christianity, the exploitation of prestige, the commercialization of the holy followed from the Dane's addressing

---

61. *3. Naar en Mand har Tandpine, siger Verden «stakkels Mand»; naar en Mands Kone bliver ham utro, sige Verden «stakkels Mand»; naar en Mand er i Pengeforlegenhed, siger Verden «stakkels Mand». Naar det behager Gud i en ringe Tjeners skikkelse at ville lide i denne Verden, siger Verden «stakkels Menneske»; naar en Apostel i guddommeligt Ærinde har lide for Sandhed, sige Verden «stakkels Menneske»: «stakkels Verden»!*

of reality at the sociological and political levels. In this context, he again faulted professors, assistant professors, and in general the scientific and scholarly circles, who promoted the sickness of the age (Pap XI 1 A 56 n.d., 1854) (JP, 6859). He maintained his nonconformity with the status quo. He wanted to be heterogeneous with his present order of affairs. In short, he broke with his age in order to heal it: "Keep on our own side the profit and the decorations and the velvet etc.—I have to watch out so that there is not the least profit in lining up with me" (Pap XI 1 A 56 n.d., 1854) (JP, 6859). In summing up, Kierkegaard's "fresh air" contains not only elements of social liberation,[62] but a prophetic economic critique as well.

The Pyramidal View of Society

> God is infinite love and his paternal eye readily sees how cruel this human pyramid-idea can easily become toward the unfortunate, the ignored, and the like in the human race (which is the very reason why the God of love looks after them). (Pap XI 1 A 330 n.d., 1854) (JP, 4231)

The opening quotation of this subsection shows Kierkegaard's denouncing of the devastating effects of that abhorrent business of the pyramid. In effect, he resorts to this metaphor in order to home in on his political and economic critique. Let us note in passing the affinity that exists between the view of society as a pyramid and as an organism: "The State is an organism . . . in an organism only what is organic has

---

62. "Kierkegaard's work is the last great attempt to restore religion as the ultimate organon for liberating humanity from the destructive impact of an oppressive social order. His philosophy implies throughout a strong critique of his society, denouncing it as one that distorts and shatters human faculties. The remedy was to be found in Christianity, and the fulfillment in the Christian way of life. Kierkegaard knew that in this society such a way of life involved incessant struggle and ultimate humiliation and defeat, and that a Christian existence within current social forms was ever an impossibility. The church had to be separated from the state, for, any dependence on the state would betray Christianity. The true role of the church, freed of any restrictive force, was to denounce prevailing injustice and bondage and to point up the individual's ultimate interest, his salvation" (Marcuse, *Reason and Revolution*, 264–65).

Of course, we need to bear in mind that, when Marcuse wrote this appraisal the liberation theologies of the Third World as well as of other ethnic groups had not yet emerged. It was not until 1970 and 1971 when the issue about the fatherhood of liberation theology was raised by Rubem Alves, James Cone, and Gustavo Gutiérrez. Cf. Pérez-Álvarez, "Richard Shaull," 27–33.

validity and rights.... [In] the organism of the State nothing has political rights except the things that are themselves organized, thus estates and corporations."[63]

We must not fail to remember Kierkegaard's epoch and geographical context. The capacity of churches in Copenhagen at that time was only 5 percent of the city's population (i.e., the elite). This explains the fact that they were oriented towards the upper classes. In the entry, "Beware of Those Who Go Around in Long Garments," Kierkegaard affirms the legitimate right of the clergy to a salary as long as it is subordinated to the proclamation of Christianity. Nonetheless, he protests against the inversion that Christendom has done: "First of all a living is assured for a man and his family, with the possibility of advancement—then, then comes the matter of preaching Christianity," and he throws in some irony: "No, one must first have a clerical gown tailored, the vestments, the costume" (Pap. XI 1 A 68 n.d., 1854) (JP, 3172).

The prophetic gadfly detected in an early stage the depersonalization of human beings through the connivance between technology and social institutions. From the fact of measuring the power of a person in terms of horsepower follow the substitution of the person for the horse. If the power of fifty people is the same as the strength of one horse, then Kierkegaard highlights the danger of humans being subsumed by the machine: "Yesterday a meeting of one thousand people took place ...A meeting of twenty horses took place, and the chairman was ..." Or again:

> And eventually human speech will become just like the public: pure abstraction—there will no longer be someone who speaks, but an objective reflection gradually will deposit a kind of atmosphere, an abstract noise that will render human speech superfluous, just as machines make workers superfluous. (TA, 104)

Kierkegaard also anticipated cybernetic dating: "In Germany there are even handbooks for lovers; so it probably will end with lovers being able to sit and speak anonymously to each other" (TA, 104).

The industrialization of Denmark started in the second half of the nineteenth century. Nevertheless, Kierkegaard foresaw how the new economic system continued in the conservative line of this pyramidal view of society. The state had adopted an economic system based on

---

63. *Heibergs Prosaiske Skrifter*, 6, 270; quoted in Kirmmse, *Kierkegaard*, 161.

assembly-line production, and this system had also been transferred to the religious realm. Therefore, Kierkegaard denounced how Christians are but mere copies of others, or in other words, they particularly had been subsumed by the hierarchical principle of association:

> Just as production by machine is on a much larger scale and more accurate than by hand, so also generation after generation the State delivered an assortment of Christians, all with the factory stamp of the State, each Christian an accurate copy of the others, so accurate that the heart of every manager of a factory must leap to see what matchless heights of accuracy the art has attained.

Within this train of ideas then, to affirm the category of human being as spirit, as diverse per se, namely, the pluralism that each one of us manifests in being a Christian in a different way, is a socially and religiously disruptive element for Kierkegaard: "So the State took over Christianity, and the main point in being Christian came to be the greatest possible factory-made uniformity." And again, "The State, which is not completely secure, desires as much uniformity as possible—for the sake of supervision" (Pap XI 2 a 112 n.d.) (JP, 4502). From Kierkegaard's category of the human being as spirit, which includes diversity per se, does not follow an asocial individualism. Quite the contrary, it has social, religious, and economic implications.

Kierkegaard opposed the pyramidal view of society where the clergy played a crucial role. In response to the adage "In business every man's a thief," he expressed the same eloquently: "the 'priest' pronounced a blessing upon this Christian society, this Christian state, where they swindle just as in paganism, and do it also by paying the 'priest,' who by this mark is the biggest swindler, they swindle themselves into the notion that this is Christianity" (AUC, 164). And again, "the priest is not a thief but a liar in his business" (AUC, 214). Kierkegaard's honesty and economic agendas repudiated the reduction of the audience of Christianity to the charming bourgeoisie. That consists of making a fool of God, as he shows by having a closer look at church rites, such as confirmation:

> —a splendid invention, if one makes a double assumption: that divine worship is in the direction of making a fool of God; and that its principal aim is to provide an occasion for family festivities, parties, a jolly evening, and a banquet which differs in this

respect from other banquets that this banquet (what a refine-ment!) has 'also' a religious significance. (AUC, 217)

Kierkegaard's last *Journal* entry summarizes his ideas with pre-cision. To the question "what specifically, does God want?" the Dane answers: "He wants souls able to praise, adore, worship, and thank him—the business of angels. Therefore God is surrounded by angels. The sort of beings found in legions in 'Christendom,' who for a few dollars are able to shout and trumpet to God's honor and praise, this sort does not please him" (Pap. XI 2 A 439 September 25, 1855) (JP, 6969).

When Kierkegaard commented about the concept of human be-ings as "social animals," this thinker detected the power of association as one of its ramifications: "Let us all unite—if it were possible, all the kingdoms and countries of the earth—" but Kierkegaard saw the abso-lutization of this principle as well: "and this pyramid-union, rising ever higher and higher, carries at its peak a super-king—he must be regarded as being closest to God, so close in fact that he approaches so near to God that God is worried about him and pays attention to him." At this point Kierkegaard introduces the Christian "great reversal," which con-trasts with the "whole business of the pyramid." Whereas this society privileges the super-king who competes with God; the God of Scripture chose in the first place "the despised, the cast-offs of the race, one single sorry abandoned wretch, a dreg of humanity." Kierkegaard resisted a pyramidal idea of society where the raising of the pyramid is such that it would be ready "to shove God off the throne" (Pap XI 1 A 330 n.d., 1854) (JP, 4231).

There is thus interplay between the conception of a static world and the successful people: "Christianity has become nonsense, and now it goes in one ear and out the other; now we get millions of Christians and the preacher industry is flourishing" (Pap XI 2 A 426 July 10, 1855) (JP, 2455). Or even more clearly: "And this religion has become a national religion, on which 1000 oath-bound Falstaffs or veterinarians and their families are living, etc." (Pap XI 2 A 421 July 2, 1855) (JP, 2454).

Kierkegaard compared the principle of association as it was un-derstood by his pyramidal state with the Greek sophists' position: "that injustice on a vast scale is justice, that in a very peculiar manner the concepts turn around or flop over, that what counts is to practice it on a vast scale ... that quantity or the numerical defines the concept, that the greatest number is equivalent to the truth" (Pap XI 2 A 108 n.d., 1854) (JP, 4238). For Kierkegaard, however, what passes for virtue is merely the state-authorized egotism, and the immediate, the unrefined, the imprudent people are not as corrupt as the shrewdly prudent: "A swindler who knows precisely how far he dares to go with his swindling and still preserve the reputation and esteem of being a highly respectable man" (Pap XI 2 A 108 n.d., 1854) (JP, 4238).

The Building and the Reformists

> Think of a hospital. The patients are dying like flies. The methods are altered in one way and another. It's no use. What does it come from? It comes from the building; the whole building is full of poison. (AUC, 139)

On the occasion of the 1853 cholera epidemic, which spread rapidly in Copenhagen because of the poor housing conditions, Kierkegaard expressed his social, religious, and political views. For him, prior to nursing the sick one by one; the entire infected building of the hospital had to be sanitized.

I opened the section on economic issues at the structural level by citing Kierkegaard's medical diagnosis of his age and society. He conceived his Christian world as a monstrous illusion, a sick structural entity where the introduction of a new hymnal, another altar book, a renewal of musical service, etc., were solely analgesics, or reformists attempting to deal with the matter. Likewise, the cure had to be understood in structural terms due to the fact that it was the whole Christendom building that was full of poison (AUC, 139).

Since for Kierkegaard our interpretation of the gospel has been tainted by social and economic interests, the topic of taxes is central to his thought. In his *Journal* entry: "Has Not the Whole Business of Christendom Been Caused by a Confusion?" he stated that the main source of confusion consisted of the fact that from the outset Christendom mixed Christianity with the contemporary event of Caesar Augustus's levying taxes on everybody (Pap. XI 1 A 534 n.d., 1854) (JP, 4500). This partnership between church and state, in Kierkegaard's judgment, had psychological effects on the entire population. In a similar way in which the state wants to stamp its seal on every point of social life: "The common man, the people, always consider anything that is governmental (stamped by the State) as being better; it is better to be a royal hat maker than to be a pure and simple hat maker, etc., etc." The state also wanted to penetrate and domesticate Christianity. Kierkegaard did not fraternize with the clergy who derived their power from the crown: "The fact that he is authorized by the crown gives him status in the eyes of the people; they believe that to be the maximum—the higher the rank, the more status, the more badges—how utterly nonsensical this kind of Christian proclamation is" (Pap. XI 2 A 400 May 16, 1855) (JP, 3186). In order to deal with the sickness of the building (and not merely on a rugged, individualistic level), Kierkegaard broke with Christendom, and at the same time set his distance from atheism. He wanted to get rid of the clergy so that Christianity could emerge: "In his blind hatred of Christianity the atheist is sufficiently courteous to assume that from a Christian point of view the priest is justified. I see that the 'priest' and the atheist are allies, except that the priest is the more dangerous enemy" (Pap. XI 3 B 197 n.d., 1855) (JP, 3188).

The clergy, Kierkegaard argues, are also practical pagans because they have eliminated the disruptive elements of Christianity: "This is the 'priest's' importance to society, which from generation to generation consumes a 'necessary' number of perjurers, in order, under the name of Christianity, to be fully assured of being able to live a life of paganism, a paganism which is tranquillized and refined by the notion that it is Christianity" (AUC, 227).

Having diagnosed the problem on a systemic basis, the molesting gadfly goes on to emphasize how the opposite of his category of heterogeneity to the world is not the gnostic denial of the physical reality. Quite the contrary. The reverse of heterogeneity is homogeneity or being swallowed by the establishment.

"When the individual [*Individet*] has become entirely homogeneous with his world of time present, assimilated, as we say of the digestive process, the age has eaten him, he is as though lost, wasted. Time, the world of time present, tends to change everything into waste or waste gas" (Pap XI 1 A 320 n.d.) (JP, 2062).

A selective reading of the tradition portrays Kierkegaard as the champion of the "everyone-for-oneself" cause, as an apologist of anticlericalism, as the sponsor of the crucifixion of the intellect, as the proclaimer of the purely otherworldly hope, and the like. Kresten Nordentoft, however, has already shown the underside of that tradition.

According to Nordentoft, Kierkegaard together with Marx conceived of ideology in connection with social conflict and not as a Feuerbachian product of the sensuous yearning of the human mind. Furthermore, Kierkegaard's essential Christianity "made explicit the close connection that exists between ideology and the economic and social reality." Finally Kierkegaard articulated neither a purely theoretical assault on the church nor solely a critique of the clergy. Rather his work consisted of "an earlier critique of his society in which ideology guarantees the proclamation of the church."[64]

The Internal and External Revolution

> While we work on the problem "psychically," we must also work on it "physically."[65]

The overabundance of scholarship devoted specifically to the young Kierkegaard has overshadowed the economic, social, and political dimensions of the mature thinker. Furthermore, the overemphasis given to abstract aspects of his work—specifically in his philosophical books previous to 1846—has resulted in a one-dimensional characterization of his life and thought. Kierkegaard's last theological paradigm, however, shows that those readings have missed a large point emphasized in this dissertation.

I should mention at the outset the manner in which Kierkegaard's dialectics, in his task of dealing with reality, considers the individual and, simultaneously, the structural level. Putting it in medical terms, he recommended that for the fundamental recovery of the mentally ill, "One must work on psychic lines, says the physician; but it does not follow from this that there may be nothing to do physically" (AUC, 97). In confronting the extremely pervasive "retribution doctrine," or the "ideology of adaptation," Kierkegaard moves in two directions (1) to help dispel the "sensory illusion" within the individual as to what Christianity is, and (2) to attack the governmental and social apparatus that perpetuates these illusions. Or to put it in Nordentoft's translation:

---

64. Nordentoft, *Hvad Siger Brand-Majoren?* 276.

65. *Søren Kierkegaards Samlede Værker,* 119–20 quoted in Kirmmse, "Call Me Ishmael," 174.

"the inner revolution can be supported by an outer one."[66] Or to say the same thing another way, the internal revolution has to be followed by the commitment to work with the external revolution.[67]

This same framework houses Kierkegaard's economic criticism. He eyed with suspicion the socially located theology of his time, which was held in tow by the state and was pecuniarily motivated as well:

> There have been introduced by the State 1,000 officials who have such difficulty about seeing impartially because the question of Christianity is stated for them at the same time in pecuniary terms, and naturally *they do not want to have their eyes opened* to what has hitherto been regarded as the surest way to bread, the surest of all, though it is a questionable way of livelihood, perhaps, in a Christian sense even a 'prohibited way'; the reason is that hundreds of men are introduced who instead of following Christ are snugly and comfortably settled, with family and steady promotion, under the guise that their activity is the Christianity of the New Testament, and who live off the fact that others have had to suffer for the truth. (AUC, 42 [italics mine])

Kierkegaard believed that the introduction of the financial element into Christianity had "fostered hypocrites or troubled consciences." He observed how the church sided with the rich. For example: Kierkegaard compared the state with a millionaire who hired thousands of teachers of Christianity and paid them out of its own pocket. By doing so, the state committed a crime against the essential Christianity: "for one can give all his money to the poor in order to serve Christianity in poverty, but one cannot serve Christianity with contributions of money—this confuses Christianity with precisely that which it is not, an ordinary human enterprise." (Pap XI 3 B 115 n.d., 1855) (JP, 2774). From this economic perspective, Kierkegaard reached the conclusion that everything is a matter of money:

> now we see from a new angle how infinitely confusing and corrupting this whole thing is, since the state itself acquires the money by falsifying Christianity in one way or another; the falsifying of what Christianity is brings in the money, and this money again buys the falsification of what Christianity is. (Pap XI 3 B 115 n.d., 1855) (JP, 2774)

---

66. Nordentoft, *Kierkegaard's Psychology,* 331.

67. Nordentoft, *Hvad Siger Brand-Majoren?* "Profit is Truth," 184ff.

The state goes further and, Kierkegaard noticed, has in fact "turned the suffering and death of Christ into money." In this order of affairs, then, the state was in charge of getting us into the recreational park of Tivoli no less than in providing us with eternal salvation: "But if it is assumed that the value of Christ's suffering and death is measurable (commensurable) in money, then it is really simply and solely Christ's prerogative to say: It costs so and so much." Kierkegaard closed this *Journal* entry by faulting the state as a manipulator of the gospel, as a robber or a swindler, and on a structural level, on "so grand a scale":

> You have a fixed idea, most Honorable State, if you think it needs your help, or is it one of your tricks that in the name of serving Christianity you have wanted to utilize Christianity, perhaps in order to dominate men all the better, as if the state controlled or had the slightest influence on the decision: an eternal salvation. No, let Christianity shift for itself. And if there are some who want to use Christianity to swindle people, blackmail them, then let us just turn to the state, the police, to get protection against swindlers. (Pap XI 3 B 115 n.d., 1855) (JP, 2774)

Thus the Danish state, to which religion was wedded, was in charge of public security, water, illumination, roads, bridge-building, and (not surprisingly) eternal blessedness in the hereafter. And in every case, the economic aspect was crucial: "Of course it will cost money, for without money one gets nothing in this world, not even a certificate of eternal blessedness in the other world; no, without money one gets nothing in this world." And in all that, the ideological aspect was also central: "Yet all the same, what the State does, to the great advantage of the individual, is that one gets it from the State at a cheaper price than if the individual were to make some private arrangement; moreover it is more secure, and finally it is comfortable in a degree that only can be provided on a big scale" (AUC, 99).

According to Kierkegaard, the State agenda is "to make Christianity if possible, impossible," by reducing the gospel to a money issue: "The 'priest' is pecuniarily interested in having people call themselves Christians, for every such person is in fact (through the State as intermediary) a contributing member, and at the same time contributes to the power of the clerical order" (AUC, 84). The state agenda is "to leave the divine out of account," Kierkegaard argued: "So to be royally authorized may be more easy, comfortable, convenient . . . for the priest; but

Christianly it is a discommendation, precisely in the degree that, according to the State's order of precedence, one is in a higher station, has more orders, a bigger income" (AUC, 133). Within this structural perspective, this prophetic author calls the clergy traders who have exchanged the strength of the spirit for a money-centered civil religion: "this gigantic corpus of 1000 tradesmen-priests, who decline with thanks the offer of spirit, but heartily thank the Government for salary, titles, decorations, and the congregation for ... their sacrifice, the offering" (AUC, 186).

It is not easy to turn against the tide of the dominant ideas of an era, but Kierkegaard faced that monolithic entity called Christendom. In fact, I must mention in passing how this theologian vindicated human and religious freedom in front of the repressive state-church amalgamation. He conceived as radically wrong and very unchristian the official policy of making Christianity compulsory. In this connection, Kierkegaard made use of his skills in sarcasm: "What! You feel no need of Christianity? Perhaps you need to go to the Reformatory!' 'What! You feel no need of Christianity? Then perhaps you feel a need of becoming nothing; for unless you become a Christian all paths in society are closed to you!'" (AUC, 134–35).

The distressing gadfly, in addressing his economic critique to the clergy, called them cannibals (AUC, 269). Kierkegaard's philological sensitivity also led him to establish substantial nomenclature differences in his attack on the church. He established different levels of communication. At certain times he wanted to be sure his readers placed their judgments on the monetary level: "the question about the Established Church is not a religious but a financial question." At this point Kierkegaard was well aware of his lack of economic and political power; nevertheless, other sorts of power were on his side: "what keeps up the Establishment is the 1000 royally authorized teachers, who standing to the Establishment in the relation to shareholders, quite rightly are silent about what I talk of, for I have no power to take from them their incomes" (AUC, 72, 135).

Kierkegaard also widens his economic analysis by focusing his attention on the members of society. He repudiated commercial relations that associate themselves with an appearance of holiness. In a short narrative, he mentions a town that houses a stranger. This person possesses a bank note for a huge amount, which nobody in town is eager to redeem. Finally a man who recognizes the value of the note very well, tells him: "'I am your friend, as is becoming in a friend I will help you out of your embarrassment, I offer you'—and then he offers him the half of its value. This, you see, is refined!" Kierkegaard, then, dug deeper and rejected calculated cheating, which appears under the guise of friendship and devotion: "But that is not seen; the inhabitants of that town could in fact not see it; they see on the contrary the very unusual magnanimity, etc." (AUC, 291). Or take the case of the man who knows that his friend's wife is cheating him and decides to tell him the truth. The faithful husband replies: "But that I should therefore, now that I know it is so, divorce her—no, that I cannot decide to do. After all, I am accustomed to this domestic routine; I cannot do without it. Moreover, she has money; I cannot do without that either" (MLW, 260).

A detailed treatment of Kierkegaard's dialectics is beyond the scope of the present investigation. What is relevant, however, for the present discussion is the dialectical way in which Kierkegaard approached economic, social, and political matters. Under the theme of the monastery, Kierkegaard continues in the same line of interpretation that deals with the particular alongside the structural; or, to say the same, with the inner revolution supported by the external one.

The frequent depiction of Kierkegaard as affirming the *fuga mundi* is incorrect. Here a word must be said about monasticism that he understood exclusively in terms of a stratagem or a ploy to be applied to Christendom. Kierkegaard's dialectical mind never promoted a kind of transcendental meditation; on the contrary, he affirmed the world by taking a critical distance from it: "If one is to bring the pendulum of Christianity from an extreme of worldliness, it is necessary to exaggerate its swing just as violently in the opposite direction of unworldliness."[68]

Kierkegaard did not promote the collapse of the immanence; he faces the challenges of his historical context: "we, Protestants, we do not flee like cowards from life, and neither did Christ—no, we remain, as did Christ, in the world—lost in unmitigated profane secularism, worse than paganism." And, at the same moment, he did not foster the collapse of the transcendence. In effect, in his view, the monastery constituted a permanent reminder of the heterogeneity of Christianity: "We remain— just as Christ did—in the world! What a superb big lie for hypocritical, lying orators! If great achievements are the theme for speakers gener-

---

68. Seidel, "Monasticism as a Ploy in Kierkegaard's Theology," 301.

ally, this duplicity and falsification is for hypocritical orators" (Pap XI 1 A 263 n.d., 1854) (JP, 2764).

Another piece worthwhile of citing is Kierkegaard's *Open Letter* of 1851. It was written on the occasion of the publication of *Om det borgerlige Ægteskab* (*On Civil Marriage*), whose author, Andreas Gottlob Rudelbach (1792–1862) was a frequent guest in the home of Kierkegaard's father. With respect to this piece, Kirmmse has convincingly pointed out that when Kierkegaard elaborates on his concept of inwardness, he is in fact assuming his earlier position. Nonetheless when the Dane cites civil disobedience in the book of Acts and in veneration of Luther's *true* reformation, Kirmmse sees that the *Open Letter* "points forward toward the radical intervention Kierkegaard was to make approximately four years later."[69] Kierkegaard's dialectics also allowed us to elucidate the matter by putting in tension the internal and the external: "Christianity is inwardness, inward deepening. If at a given time the forms under which one has to live are not the most perfect, if they can be improved, in God's name do so" (*Armed Neutrality; and, An Open Letter*, 49–50).

In closing, let us keep in mind that Kierkegaard's radical suspicion of ideology must be understood in structural terms. The provoking gadfly worked with structural categories; he was not entrapped in a cocoon. He did believe in the reality of the world, he was concerned about and got involved with his society. Now, his dynamic concept of reality (as opposed to a static one) saved him from setting universal or absolute judgments. We have to deal with the internal and external revolution within our historically different contexts: "All development is always dialectical; the 'next generation' will always need the 'opposite' as corrective" (Pap. X 5 A 106 n.d., 1853) (JP, 710).

The Fire Chief and the Political Dimension of Love

> Rid me of these damn people with their pitchers and squirts; and if they won't yield to fair words, smear them a few over the back, so that we may be free of them and get down to work. (AUC, 193)

---

69. Kirmmse, "'This Disastrous Confounding of Politics and Christianity,'" 184.

Kierkegaard's paradigm shift was so dramatic that the entry of the *Instant* No. 6 demands an entire reinterpretation of his work. In their approach to Kierkegaard, scholars such as Kersten Nordentoft[70] have taken seriously the Kierkegaardian dictum quoted above in a whole different perspective, contrasting with the conservative and liberal views.

In his social diagnosis, Kierkegaard resorts to the fire-chief parable. The actions of the Dane's contemporaries in applying the remedies at hand as an attempt to save their society were similar to people reacting to a fire. They are eager to help, and in a cordial and polite manner they start putting together their pitchers, basins, squirt bottles, and the like for the sake of extinguishing the fire.

The fire chief's forceful language exhibits an entirely different way of looking at things. The right person, Kierkegaard continues, "sees with half an eye" (*han seer med et halvt Øie*) that the remedy is worst than the illness; that these well-meaning people must get out; that he "must not have the least thing to do with this company." For Kierkegaard it is not enough to remain at the innocuous level of the do-gooder. From the promise of social amelioration follows the search for the real causes of social evils: "But everything depends on getting rid of that company; for the effect of this is, in the form of hearty sympathy, to eradicate the real seriousness from the cause" (AUC, 195).

In effect, the inevitable result of implementing superficial remedies is the validation of the whole order of Danish Christendom, including its unjust social and economic systems, which widen the gap between the rich and the poor. Needless to say, the vexing gadfly was not a "bleeding-heart liberal": Kierkegaard was not a reformer but rather a revolutionary:[71] (*Brandmajoren er ikke reformist, han er revolutionær*).[72]

---

70. Nordentoft, *Hvad Siger Brand-Majoren?* 217.

71. In Westphal's opinion, Kierkegaard's theology in fact conceives that "all theology should be a liberation theology, a guide to the practice of overcoming oppression in all its forms." Cf. Westphal, "Levinas, Kierkegaard, and the Theological Task," 246. It is not for nothing that Christian-Marxist philosophers and social activists like Simone Weil found in Kierkegaard inspiration for their journey: "The truth of the matter was that Simone Weil could not read Kierkegaard without feeling moved. Although her rationalistic upbringing still shut her off from Kierkegaard's teaching, she was close to him in spirit—so close, in fact, that she did not need to refer to him in her writings" (Cabaud, *Simone Weil: A Fellowship in Love*, 117; quoted in Andic, "Simone Weil and Kierkegaard," 20).

72. Nordentoft, *Hvad Siger Brand-Majoren?* 217.

At the beginning of the second period and especially during his last two years, it became apparent that Kierkegaard directly approached the simple person in structural terms *(en masse)* and no longer as the single individual. By returning to the political newspaper of the *Fatherland*[73] and by editing his own the *Instant*, he could directly address his new subjects: the people on the street, the "ordinary" person whom he esteemed.[74]

Bruce Kirmmse has pointed out how the Liberal Party, which supposedly was on the side of the "ordinary" person, contradicted itself: In the late 1840s they established the Society of Friends of the Peasant, and in general lionized their cause. Nonetheless, in the 1850s the same liberals, through the national liberal press in Copenhagen "waged a war of mockery and insult, ridiculing the simplicity, rude dress, boorish habits, narrow-mindedness, and lack of culture of the very peasantry."[75]

Kierkegaard, in contradistinction to the Liberal Party, remained committed to the cause of the poor. He also charged the clergy with having hidden class or economic presuppositions, of constituting a social class whose real task was the enjoyment of riches to the detriment of the poor. In dealing with loving the poor at the structural level, the following Kierkegaardian entry needs no comment:

> "It is so moving," one says, "to hear this one or that one movingly expound, for example, on poverty"—but let him beware that he is not himself impoverished by this discourse. No, if by means of this moving discourse about poverty he could even succeed in becoming a rich man, possessing, if possible, all earthly goods: Sir, you have made a hit; you have hit the taste of the newspapers, of the public, of humanity. "With him one is so safe, the enjoyment of feelings of assuring; we understand each other"—that it is riches that matter! (Pap. X 6 B 29:3 n.d., 1851–52) (JFY, 248)

Kierkegaard's political love for the poor unmasked the ulterior motives in the preaching Christianity as an accompaniment to the enjoyment of life. He criticized the "teachers of Christianity," i.e., the ones who had made preaching their career, for having transformed the glad news for the poor into the opposite. In Kierkegaard's view, the arbiters of truth had "really reached the point that the sufferers are not benefited

---

73. Ibid., 196.

74. Malantschuck, in Kierkegaard, *Armed Neutrality, and An Open Letter*, 24.

75. Kirmmse, *Kierkegaard*, 73.

at all, but rather that one ingratiates himself with the fortunate and the powerful by preaching to them a cozy Christianity. This is what the 'teachers' are doing since preaching Christianity is their career" (Pap. X 5 A 28, October 7, 1852) (JP, 4697).

In an early entry Kierkegaard had qualified his concept of neighbor: "What Socrates says about loving the ugly[76] is really the Christian doctrine of love to the neighbor. The ugly is the reflected, consequently the ethical object; whereas the beautiful is the immediate object which all of us therefore most willingly love. In this sense 'the neighbor' is the 'ugly'"[77] (Pap VIII 1 A 189 n.d., 1847) (JP, 942).

In his major ethical work, *Works of Love*, Kierkegaard goes on to promote loving the unlovable object—not only the beautiful and the good—as the mark of true love, of the love of self-renunciation: "Consequently, in order to be able to praise love, there is need for *inward* self-denial and *outward* sacrificial disinterestedness" (WL 343). In a late *Journal* entry Kierkegaard observes how the love of the ugly has been abandoned: "Lectures are delivered in Christendom, in the name of Christianity, on the subject that to love God is to fill one's life, one's time, one's thoughts with the pursuit of the earthly, to thank God when one succeeds and pray to him for success. In other words, loving God is loving the beautiful." And he states: "Therefore there also flourishes in Christendom—something it is very proud of and calls Christianity's newest development and most beautiful flower—Christian family life. Splendid!" (Pap XI 2 A 426 July 10, 1854) (JP, 2455).

---

76. Plato *Symposium* 210 b–c.

77. "The ugly" can very well be a Kierkegaardian weapon against the retribution principle, which asserts that justice reigns in this world, and against Adam Smith's "invisible hand," which believes that the world is spontaneously ordered through the observation of the contracts and the protection of private property. In contradistinction to Kierkegaard's category of "the ugly" or the excluded, John D. Rockefeller took the side of Adam Smith in his option for "the beautiful": "The *American Beauty* rose, can only be cultivated in order to reach the maximum of its splendor and fragrance, which provides so much joy to the people who are able to appreciate that the first blossoms that grow around her had been sacrificed." Transferred into the business field, this means that Rockefeller's financial empire did not stop him from continuing to be a faithful Sunday school teacher, as he himself recognized: "That [the sacrifices of the *American Beauty*'s blossoms] is not an evil tendency in the business. It is only the execution of a law of nature and of a law of God." Cf. Hofstadter, *Social Darwinism in American Thought 1860–1915*, 45, 31. Cited in Galbraith, *A Era da Incerteza*, 40–41.

In Kierkegaard's opinion, the social position of the clergy influenced the abandonment of the suffering people. If, on the one hand, the clergy was called to live a life of renunciation and service, on the other hand, "Satan slips into the clergy and in spiritual arrogance it occurs to them to want to be something other than the medium, to be the intermediary authority between God and man and thus be repaid for what they temporarily renounced" (Pap. XI 1 A 532 n.d., 1854) (JP, 3182). Taking the side of the ugly ones, evidently, is far from the people-eaters who count on advancing in salary: "And not only that. The cannibal, of course, does not claim to be the best and truest friend of those he slays and eats. But the minister, the professor, also enjoys the honor and esteem of being the true friend and follower of the noble ones" (Pap. XI 1 A 100 n.d., 1854) (JP, 3583).

Kierkegaard converted to the perspective of the "ordinary" person (*Det menige folk*) in order to experience and understand from within the situation and events in which those people were caught up. This is one of the most substantial Kierkegaardian contributions in having a new interlocutor, i.e., the simple people (*Det menige folk*).

It has been my claim that in 1852 another significant turning point took place in the Dane's mind. In that year there is no doubt that he left behind his conservative political position. He refused Communion. He radicalized his speech and entered into a period of voluntary silence. As a result, by 1855, very apparent was the way that Kierkegaard lifted up his new subject (the "ordinary" person) in the theological enterprise. My point is that in placing the "ordinary" person as the locus in his task of doing theology, our prophetic theologian became an organic intellectual, that is, a thinker who was very much concerned with the problems of his society in general and with the poor people in particular: "I cannot stop being fond of the common man, even though journalistic scurrility has done everything to confuse him in his relationship to me and spoils for me what I loved so unspeakably, what to me was the most salutary respire from my intellectual endeavors—living together with the common man" (Pap. XI 1 A 234 n.d., 1854) (JP, 2971).

Kierkegaard's political love for the ugly, his conversion to the cause of the poor, can be very well appreciated in his last essay, published a month before he collapsed in the street. Then he was hospitalized until his death. I quote Kierkegaard at some length:

Thou plain man! The Christianity of the New Testament is infinitely high; but observe that it is not high in such a sense that
it has to do with the difference between man and man with respect to intellectual capacity, etc. No, it is for all . . . .

Thou plain man! I have not separated my life from thine;
thou knowest it, I have lived in the street, am known to all;
moreover I have not attained to any importance, do not belong
to any class egoism, so if I belong anywhere, I must belong to
thee, thou plain man . . . [in respect to the superior people] I
have never definitely united with them but merely maintained
a looser relationship.

Thou plain man! . . . shun the priests . . . a paid member
of the State Church, or the National Church, or whatever they
prefer to call it. Shun them. But take heed to pay them willingly
and promptly what money they should have. With those whom
one despises, one on no account should have money differences,
lest it might perhaps be said that it was to get out of paying them
one avoided them. No, pay them double, in order that thy disagreement with them may be thoroughly clear: that what concerns them does not concern thee at all, namely, money; and on
the contrary, that what does not concern them concerns thee
infinitely, namely, Christianity. (AUC, 287–88)[78]

---

78. Cf. Bukdahl, *Søren Kierkegaard og den menige Mand*, 126ff.

Conclusion

Without religion, how could we have order in the State? Society cannot continue to exist without inequalities in personal fortunes; for inequality to continue we must have religion. When someone is dying of hunger and some else nearly has everything, it would be impossible for the starving man to acquiesce to such disparity if there were no authority to tell him: God wills it so; in this world there must be rich and poor but in the hereafter for all eternity, fortunes will be reversed.[1]

—Napoleon Bonaparte

Since proclamation of the gospel to the rich, the powerful, etc., has been discovered to be advantageous, we are right back again to the very things Christianity wanted to oppose. The rich and the powerful not only get to keep everything, but their success becomes the mark of their piety, the sign of the relationship to God. (Pap. X 4 A 578) (JP, 4685)

—Søren Kierkegaard

THE LINCHPIN OF MY ENTIRE READING OF KIERKEGAARD HAS BEEN my claim that—with his attack upon Christendom as a backdrop—Kierkegaard did address economic matters, which have barely been taken into account by Kierkegaardian circles, and (most important), which can illuminate our current socioeconomic and political situation.

My interpretative tools included the study of Kierkegaard's development of his economic ideas conjointly with his entire historical setting, namely, Golden Age Denmark and its 1848–1849 political transition from an absolutist to a democratic monarchy. I have limited my investigation to Kierkegaard's "second authorship," i. e., his writing from after *Concluding Unscientific Postscript* up to his death. Throughout my

---

1. Letter of Napoleon Bonaparte to Roederer, in 1801. Bonaparte, Napoleón, Pensées politiques et sociales. ed. Dansette, 146, cited by Casalis, Las buenas ideas no caen del cielo; elementos de "teología inductiva," 47. See also Liégé, Présence mutuelle de l'Église et de la Pauvreté.

developmental approach, I included the vexing gadfly's published and
unpublished writings, his *Journals*, for instance. True, I have analyzed
a good deal of data from Kierkegaard's *Journals*; yet a great amount of
work in exploring these diaries remains to be done. It is precisely in
his intimate diary that we have access to the Kierkegaard who lived in
solidarity with the rural and urban "ordinary" folks, with the working
class, with women, with children, etc.[2]

It has been my contention that the radicalization of Kierkegaard's
thought during the years 1852 to 1855 can very well be appreciated
within the linguistic domain.[3] In his last four years, one can observe
how Kierkegaard's abandonment of his indirect, pious, and scholarly
language is very significant. The molesting gadfly was not only replac-
ing his academic jargon with a most readable style; in fact, he began
addressing "the simple people" and changing his language to suit his
new audience.

Contrary to what is believed, even during his lifetime Kierkegaard
exercised a strong influence on his society.[4] Yet, more important, my
claim has consisted of affirming that his thought is particularly applica-
ble for our current theological milieu, and to our specific sociohistorical
context. Kierkegaard himself recognized that he was a contextual thinker. Kierkegaard's addressing concreteness in a dynamic way prevented
him from being a dogmatic thinker who would dictate universal laws:
"It is an unhappy mistake if the person who is used to introduce the
corrective becomes impatient and wants to make the corrective norma-
tive for the others, an attempt that will confuse everything" (Pap. X 4 A
596, n.d., 1852) (JP, 709).

2. Cf. Pérez-Álvarez, "Kierkegaard," 204–5.

3. Bjerg, "Kierkegaard's Story-Telling," 122, goes further back. He has substantiated
the fact that from the literary perspective, the Dane suffered a conversion by 1850 when
he stopped using narrative as an antinarrative narrativity or as a coitus interruptus. In
Bjerg's opinion, Kierkegaard started utilizing it without leaving anything to the personal interpretation of his audience: therefore, the young Kierkegaard is a destroyer
but the late Kierkegaard an upbuilder of narrative. Even more, Kierkegaard turns the
Christian story into living practice.

4. At his death, Fædrelandet [The Fatherland] called Kierkegaard "Denmark's greatest religious author" (Fædrelandet, 16th year, no. 270 [Monday, November 19, 1855]),
and the Stockholm newspaper Aftonbladet [The Evening Newspaper] called him
"Scandinavia's greatest religious author" (reprinted in Fædrelandet, 16th year, no. 272
[Thursday, November 21, 1855]); cited by Kirmmse, "A Rose with Thorns," 72 n. 3.

Søren Kierkegaard opposed emphasizing abstract thought cut off from passion and commitment.[5] Kierkegaard claimed that Hegelianism, in the Danish version of Martensen and Heiberg, consisted of a bourgeois conformity of the self-satisfied, finer portion [*den finere Portion*], the people who have the leisure time to think. Kierkegaard became suspicious of the equation of reasonableness with the fundamental presupposition of the elitist people who defined it, and with the reduction of Christianity to a mere act of cognition as it was established by the *haute bourgeoisie*. The theoretical enterprise or the building of doctrinal systems was fine; what Kierkegaard rejected was the supremacy given to thought and its consequent prevention from actualizing theoretical knowledge. From this follows his insistence on correlating doctrine with existence:

> The rule in the original Christianity was: your life should guarantee what you say. The modern rule is: by expressing just the opposite of what you depict beautifully and picture fascinatingly, your life should guarantee that the whole thing is a game, a theatrical treat—then the congregation declares: "By God, that was a lovely sermon." (Pap. X, 3 A 720 n.d., 1851) (JP 4559)

"Having someone to tell me about God while I am shaving" (CUP, 391–92) was compared by Kierkegaard to the speculative thinker who has been trapped into the category of intellectual interestingness.

The epistemological place to know God is, in Kierkegaard's view, the following of Jesus Christ. The Dane embraced the real truth principle of knowing, acting, and feeling. The Christian has to take the leap of faith that conciliates the intellect with the will: "The true is not higher than the good and the beautiful, but the true and the good and the beautiful belong essentially to every human existence, and are united for an existing individual not in thinking this, but in existing" (CUP, 311).

Whereas speculative people adopt the contemplative ethos by their choice not to choose, Kierkegaard's hermeneutic of commitment fosters obeying as the only appropriate way to know Jesus Christ. The Dane's coming to terms with the Hegelian reason or the popular solafideism, then, introduces faith as the dynamic category that enables human be-

---

5. Fromm dedicated one section to Kierkegaard's upbuilding discourses *To Will One Thing*, regarding decision and commitment: "The first condition to reach something more than a middling position in any field, including the art of living, is to will one thing." (Cf. Fromme, *Del tener al ser*, 47).

ings to practice Christianity. To be a contemporary [*Samtidighed*] or an imitation [*Efterfølgelse*] of Christ points to a historically and politically located Christ. This is not the Christ in silk but the degraded Christ of the outcasts and have-nots. Kierkegaard's Christology takes into consideration the social and economic setting of Jesus as a poor person. However, Kierkegaard did not address Jesus Christ ascetically, doloristically, or deterministically; he set his conception of Jesus Christ in tension with the establishment.

The distressing gadfly's critique of the fetishisation of Christianity (CD, 85–86) is another way of stating Kierkegaard's suspicion of ideology in relation to Christendom. Kierkegaard resisted the myths of reason, science, and progress without bounds, together with the idea of the superiority of Christianity, as the evolutionary paradigm of the nineteenth century. If, on the one hand, speculative philosophy sustained a necessary link between Christianity and state,[6] on the other hand, Kierkegaard warned his contemporaries about royalism,[7] and the conception of religion as an affair of the state. The Dane perceived how, from the ideological sources of the royal theater, royal church, and royal university followed important economic consequences.

The doctrine of temporal retribution or the ideology of adaptation—which proclaims that wealth is God's reward to the hard-working and honest person, and that poverty is God's punishment to the idle and sinful person—was hair-raisingly articulated by Napoleon Bonaparte. He detected very well that the religious-political monism, i.e., Christendom, was not economically disinterested: "In my case, I don't see in religion the incarnation mystery, but the social order mystery: it relates with heaven an idea of equality which prevents the wealthy from being massacred by the poor."[8] As honored members of state bureaucracy, the clergy exchanged ideology for money. The church

6. Cf. Hegel's *Phil. Der. Rel. I*, C, III, in vol. 16, 236. "Religion and the basis of the State are one and the same thing, identical in themselves and for themselves."

7. I am following Gutiérrez's conception of royalism in *Las Casas: In Search of the Poor of Jesus Christ*: "With Constantine it will give rise to a veritable political pendulum: depending on the circumstances and personalities at hand, the accent will fall now on 'service to the church,' now on 'religion as an affair of state.' And the seed is sown for what will later be called theocratism and royalism" (146).

8. Napoleon Bonaparte, the same emperor who inspired the Civil Code, the Concordat of 1801 and the "organic articles" which still are in used in Alsatia. Cited by Casalis, *Las buenas ideas*, 47.

canonized the whole set of values of the fortunate classes; in turn, the state supported the church.[9] The doctrine of temporal retribution[10] utterly legitimized the ideal static world of decency and order as they were defined by the bourgeois philistine.

The transcendent God of the molesting gadfly did not encourage *fuga mundi*.[11] This God stressed instead the dangers of manipulating the gospel or the idolatrous connivance between Christianity and bourgeois culture.[12] Kierkegaard faced the sorry version of Christianity as a tranquilizer (read: "the people's opiate") with his ideal type of the prophetic church that judges social structures: "Religion, deriving its beginning from above seeks to explain and transfigure the world" (PV, 107). Kierkegaard was not a reformist who sought to introduce some changes within the system. On the contrary, he was a radical Christian who saw structural connections between poverty and the whole system based on comparison and competition of the mimetic desired.

Within the general framework of the assault upon Christendom, the vexing gadfly did consider economic realities. Crucial to my conviction is the claim that he developed a dialectical treatment of economic matters. He was sensitive to real, material poverty, and he simultaneously worked for the desacralization of real wealth. He affirmed and argued for the deromanticization of material poverty, the mimetic desire for

9. See Plekon. "Introducing Christianity into Christendom," 329ff.

10. "The doctrine of temporal retribution gives no account of its own experience nor of the experience of many others. Consequently, in its search for a correct talk about God, it takes as a point of departure the most tense and the thorniest human condition: the suffering of the innocent" (Gutiérrez, *Hablar de Dios*, 169).

11. Kierkegaard's conception of transcendence was similar to the one Ellacuría holds: "transcendence is something that transcends in and not something that transcends of, is something that physically pushes to more but without taking it out of; is something that speeds along, but at the same time grabs. In this conception, when you historically reach God—and the same is true for reaching God personally—the human is not abandoned, real history is not abandoned, but you deepen into its roots, what was already present is now more present and effective. God can be separated from history, history can not be separated from God" (Ellacuría and Sobrino, *Mysterium Liberationis: Conceptos fundamentales de la teología de la liberación*, 329).

12. "Any limited being—and humankind is limited—that considers itself as the ultimate, the highest and the unique, converts itself into an idol which hungers for blood sacrifices, besides having the demonic capacity of changing its identity and assigning different meaning to things" (Horkheimer, "La añoranza de lo completamente otro." In Marcuse, Popper, and Horkheimer, *A la búsqueda del sentido*; quoted in Sung, *Desire, Market and Religion*, 96).

appropriation, culture as a market commodity, Christianity's preference for the poor; the sickness-poverty correlation, the doctrine of temporal retribution, Jesus's economic and social location,[13] the heresy of prosperity, economic sins, and so forth.

Kierkegaard recalled Aesop's fable of the fly and the stag: "the fly settled upon one of the antlers and said to the stag, 'I hope I am not a burden to you.' 'I was not aware of your existence,' was the reply" (AUC, 255). In the same way that the deer did not even notice the fly's presence, the Dane observed, God is "in one sense" so infinitely easy to ignore. Golden Age Denmark had mingled God's name with all sorts of injustices. They had falsified the gospel by reducing it to economic success and brilliant careers. They had protected the state and church developing the doctrine of temporal retribution. Therefore, the gadfly's prophetic task concentrated on eradicating that bourgeoisified, cheap version of the gospel: "The gospel no longer benefits the poor essentially; no, it has even become a downright injustice to those who suffer (although one is not always conscious of this)" (X 4 A 578 n.d., 1852) (JP, 4685).

Consistent with the prime concern of this study, I have used economic matters as the paradigm for my reading of Kierkegaard. Now, within this interpretative universe, Kierkegaard's preference for the "ordinary" person in his advocacy of cottagers, peasant farmers, and the urban proletariat is already apparent. This is correct; Kierkegaard did not build on the loaded categories of freedom and equality. Nonetheless, he did use the sociological concept of leveling in his approach to reality.[14] In fact, it was during that age of leveling that he articulated his "thorough" (SD, 86) study of human envy with the Roman institution of private property, always in a dialectical fashion: "All earthly and worldly property is, strictly speaking, selfish, envious; its possession, envious or envied, is bound either way to impoverish others. What I have, no one else can have; the more I have, the less can anyone else have."[15]

---

13. Or putting in contemporary terms, "In Mary's womb God became human being, and in Joseph's workshop God became class as well" (Vigil ¿Qué es optar para los pobres? 126; my translation).

14. Nordentoft, *Kierkegaard's Psychology*, 249.

15. *Kristelige Taler* (*Christian Discourses*), vol. 10:120–21. Quoted in Schoeck, *Envy*, 175.

Allow me to conclude with the beginning of Kierkegaard's appraisal of his life:

> My life achievement amounts to nothing at all, a mood, a single color. My achievement resembles the painting by that artist who was supposed to paint the Israelites' crossing the Red Sea and to that end painted the entire wall red and explained that the Israelites had walked across and that the Egyptians were drowned. (EO/I, 28)

Nothing could be further from the truth than the presumably flat life of the vexing gadfly. As has been noted previously, the relevance of Kierkegaard's thought lies in the fact that he integrated word with deed in his life,[16] he did theology *ex-homine*, namely, out of his own life, as we can observe in his understudied *Journals*. Precisely these autobiographical materials, together with the Dane's writings of his late period, are the place where he privileges economic matters, within the attack upon Christendom as a backdrop. From these sources we are confronted with the definitive Kierkegaard of the mature last years who sided with the "dregs of society" and attacked the bourgeoisie who reflected the *imago Mammonis*.

The twenty-first century lies before us, a fascinating and cruel century: fascinating for the fewer and fewer winners; and cruel for the expanding vast majority of "ordinary" people.[17] The twenty-first century will confront theology with burning economic issues in a more dramatic way, and in doing that, Søren Kierkegaard's insights on this topic are extremely enlightening. Kierkegaard's pushing people into corners won't allow us to remain indifferent; from his suspicion of ideology follows his epistemology of commitment. The vexing gadfly's economic, religious, and social criticism can very well be antidotes against the current societal paradigm based on the insatiability of acquisitiveness and on "an uninterrupted fabrication of pseudo-needs."[18]

16. "[Kierkegaard] is not concerned in some detached way with a theoretical 'introduction' to, but with practical 'training' in, Christianity," Küng and Jens, *Literature & Religion*, 194.

17. See Gutiérrez, "Una teología de la liberación en el contexto del Tercer Milenio," 117.

18. Lasch, *Culture of Narcissism*, 72ff. See also Baudrillard, *System of Objects*.

Kierkegaard collapsed[19] in the street and entered Frederiks Hospital on October 2, 1855. He passed away on November 11 and was buried on November 18. From that date an ironic process of Kierkegaard's appropriateness began: he died in Mynster's Hall of Frederiks Hospital; his eulogy took place at the most important church of the country, the Church of Our Lady in Copenhagen; his burial at Assistens Cemetery was with full pomp; and by 1971 his statue joined the select club of Mynster, Martensen, Grundtvig, and others as they surround the wealthy Marble Church (*Marmorkirken*), two blocks away from what used to be Frederiks Hospital.[20]

In spite of this, the Gadfly's sting was already at work. To quote just one example, Kierkegaard's nephew (and his physician during his stay at Frederiks Hospital), Henrik Lund, was prohibited from speaking at Assistens Cemetery. The archdeacon Eggert C. Tryde of the Church of Our Lady, who was responsible for the ceremony, argued that Lund was not an ordained minister,[21] but the "large number of obscure personages"[22] empowered him to speak:

> He then continued and said that he had waited until now in order to see how far the clergy would go in their lip service. They thought they could earn a good fee, because they thought Søren was rich. Had he been poor, on the other hand, then we would have seen what would have become of him. Jews are not buried by official Christendom, nor are Mohammedans, Catholics, Mormons, etc. But here could be seen the clearest proof of the lukewarm state of affairs. Then he read a section of Revelations 3, which he applied to the clergy (the Established Church was equated with the great whore, Babylon). Then he read something from *The Moment* (no. 2, "To Bury with Full Honors") and declared that he and Søren had placed themselves outside the

19. In late September 1855 the theological student Christian Henrik de Thurah wrote a coarse poem against Kierkegaard, which according to some people led to Kierkegaard's fainting on the street. Emil Boesen, Kierkegaard's lifelong friend, reported that on October 15, 1855, both friends discussed "Thurah and Martensen" right there at the hospital. Cf. Kirmmse, *Encounters with Kierkegaard*, 302 n. 4.

20. Cf. Cain, *An Evocation of Kierkegaard*, 121.

21. Kierkegaard himself considered that he was a man without authority, in the sense that he never was ordained. That is why he called many of his literary pieces "discourses" (*taler*) rather than "sermons" (*prædikener*). Cf. Plekon, "Kierkegaard's Last Sermon," 2.

22. Reported by Martensen (Kirmmse, *Encounters with Kierkegaard*, 135).

Church. The crowd yelled "Bravo!" and voices were heard to call, "Down with the clergy."[23]

Henryk Lund had to pay one hundred rix dollars plus court costs for violating the law, which forbade unauthorized persons to speak at such events.[24] But his uncle's cause was vindicated.

Søren Kierkegaard's prophetic religious and economic agenda was still boldly affirmed a few days before his passing:

> When hunters go after the wild boar it will be trapped, but the dog who gets him will pay for it. I will gladly die. Then I will be certain that I accomplished the task. Often people would rather hear v   dead person has to say than someone who is alive.[25]

23. Kirmmse, *Encounters with Kierkegaard*, 133, as F. Soderman reported it on November 18, 1855.

24. Martensen's immediate impulse was to punish the offense of such scandal with firmness: "as far as I can see must be met with serious steps." However, by June 5, 1856, when the court reached a decision, the bishop realized that it would be more profitable for the established order not to make a big case out of it. Ibid, 135, 307 n. 21.

25. Ibid., 125. According to Emil Boesen's account of his hospital conversations with Kierkegaard.

Appendix A

Denmark's Geopolitics

PETER CHRISTIAN KIERKEGAARD OBTAINED HIS DOCTORATE FROM Göttingen. Søren Kierkegaard acquired his from the University of Copenhagen. Niels Andreas Kierkegaard, on the other hand, wanted to study at the university, but he was destined by his father to steer the family business. He rebelled and in 1832 came to New Jersey and took Spanish lessons in order to trade with Spaniards; however, soon he realized that "the country that was supposed to be flowing with milk and honey was populated with restlessly busy fortune hunters who did not keep their word but cheerfully bluffed their way through as best they could."[1]

On September 21, 1833, he died and was buried in Paterson, New Jersey. J. Christian Lund, his merchant brother-in-law, took care of the burial expenses.[2] Two of Søren's sisters married the Lund brothers, who had a third brother: the renowned Peter Wilhelm (1801–1880), a botanist and naturalist who settled in Brazil. Now, we need to situate these facts within the broader geopolitical context.

Søren Kierkegaard saw his ex-fiancée, Regine, for the last time right before she went to the Danish West Indies as his "little Governess." She married the General-Governor J. F. Schlegel, who, as shown below, represented an obstacle for Danish West Indies democracy and industrialization. It was from the same Danish Caribbean Islands that Søren

---

1. Garff, *Søren Kierkegaard: A Biography*, 42.

2. Niels Andreas Kierkegaard, contrary to Peter and Søren, showed a lot of concern for his mother to whom he gave all the credit for his religious education. His father was not even mentioned during his last days, as reported by an Episcopal priest. Cf. Weltzer, *Peter og Søren Kierkegaard.*

Kierkegaard's father increased his fortune by trading in sugar, coffee, and syrup.[3]

In 1848, Santa Ana sold more than half the Mexican territory to the United States, and shortly after that he retired to one of the Danish West Indies. He took with him his millions in Mexican silver,[4] which had long been the most widely used coinage[5] in the Caribbean.[6] There, in St. Thomas, William Seward, the USA's secretary of state, met with the ex-president of Mexico in 1866.[7]

Facts such as those quoted above tell us about the importance of not neglecting them from the official historical report; of not divorcing what is happening in the center from the events of the periphery.[8] One has to approach Danish history from a geopolitical point of view, considering the colonies and slaves of the periphery as subjects and as part and parcel of the larger history, rather than as mere anecdotes of the metropolitan community.[9]

Denmark as a Colonial Power

Kierkegaard's Denmark was of some significance as a colonial power. From 1665 (with the codification of the Lex Regia) until 1848–49, this

---

3. Lowrie, *Kierkegaard*, 25.

4. Lewisohn, *St. Croix under Seven Flags*, 289, 340–41.

5. The token chained the workers to their employer, assuring him their availability, their unconditionality and of the profitability of the business. The token served also as a system of self-financing by creating fluid capital. The token also postponed payments for a month while the employers took advantage of interest. During the shift from slavery to the salary regime, the system of mixed shops was established. When slaves got their "freedom," they started earning tokens and usually they got a sum in advance in order for them to be indebted on a permanent basis. Copper, nickel, and bronze were the most common metals for coinage. Gold and silver were used only as a symbolic and commemorative value. As trade instruments, tokens did not have any economic value. They were a vehicle of exploitation. Cf. Moreno Fraginals, *La historia como arma*, 145–59.

6 Lewisohn, *St. Croix under Seven Flags*, 335, 340.

7 Ibid., 289.

8 Mintz has already warned us in the sense that the concept of periphery is very slippery. Minorities have been marginalized from the benefits of full citizenship, but on the other hand, they are at the very core of society by making their direct contribution to the economic order. Cf. Mintz, "África en América Latina," 394.

9. Hall, *Slave Society*, xix.

monarchy was legally "the most unlimited absolutism in Europe."[10] However, the revolution set the stage for the transition to a democratic and popular regime.

As far back as 1493, the Danish king (who was the sovereign over Sweden, Norway, Iceland, Greenland, the Faeroes, and the duchies of Holstein and Schleswig) protested against the papal bulls that granted Portugal a monopoly over the East Indies trade. Greenland [Grønland] had been under Norwegian rule since 1261, and its coast remained closed to foreign countries from 1721 to 1950. Between 1262 and 1264, Iceland was annexed by the Norwegians and did not recover its independence as a republic until 1944. Norway, together with its possessions, became part of Denmark in 1380. In the sixteenth century, Denmark participated in the Livonian War (1558–1583) together with Poland-Lithuania, Sweden, and Russia. The greater Livonia (Livland) included Estonia, Livonia, Courland, and Oesel. As a result of the war, Denmark got the island of Oesel, and Sweden took Estonia, but by the end of the eighteenth century, Russia had imposed its dominion over all the Baltic states. In the seventeenth century, Denmark lost Skåne, but in the same century and in the next one the Danes added new territory possessions in privileged locations. The Portuguese had held a monopoly on slave trade from 1450, but by the seventeenth century, the slave trade became an international free-for-all. In 1620 Denmark acquired Tranquebar, on the Coromandel Coast of India. From 1658 the Danes owned some settlements on the Gold Coast [Guldkysten], until 1850 when Danish settlements were handed over to the British. At the beginning of the seventeenth century, Danish King Christian IV (1588–1648) opened trade with the West Indies. In 1671 Christian V granted a charter to his subjects for the colonization of the West Indies, and he ratified the Royal Danish West Indies Company. During the following years, the influence of Denmark as a minor colonial power expanded through the buying of St. Thomas, St. Croix, and St. John in the Caribbean Sea. The Danes held those islands until 1917 when USA purchased them. These West Indies, later rebaptized as the USA Virgin Islands, changed flags seven times, depending on the colonial power: Spain, Denmark, England, Holland, France, the Knights of Malta, or the USA.

---

10. Feldbaek, "Organization and Structure," 136.

The Triangular Slave Trade

The Danes not only participated in the triangular slave trade, but they themselves had their own triangle between Tranquebar (India), some settlements on the Gold Coast of West Africa, and three Caribbean islands. Denmark had small but strategically located and interconnected colonial possessions.[11] With the "discovery of the New World," the trade center moved from the Mediterranean to the Caribbean, "The American Mediterranean," and this continued to be so until the late nineteenth century. The same papal bull of 1493 quoted earlier granted Spain the possessions of the West Indies, but the Spaniards could not manage their vast territory. When Denmark purchased its third island in 1733, in fact it closed the first century of non-Hispanic Caribbean colonization. The Danes arrived late to the conquering of the Caribbean; the Spanish, the British, the French, and the Dutch were far ahead. Nonetheless, Denmark learned from the new European empires about the new colonization strategy. Instead of an "effective occupation" through viable economic activity in the colonies and the obvious deterrent of a military presence, the Danes opted for "colonization by invitation," which included a significant foreign European population. Now, in the case of Denmark, that enterprise was led by companies, because of the narrow resources bases and its inadequate public means.[12] The Danish Trade Companies and the East Indian Company (1616–1650) as well played an important role in the modernization and in the starting period of industrialization of the country.[13] The Danish companies were not as powerful as the ones from England, Holland, and France. In spite of that, they were large and pivotal.[14] They were a source of employment for a large number of Danes in the metropolis, on board ships, and in the colonies. They exported cargoes of goods, some of them manufactured by the crown. Denmark exported merchandise such as Danish guns, iron, textiles, and spirits:

> The State had received considerable sums in customs and duties on the companies' own trade . . . The State on a number of occasions had been able to make use of the companies to

11. Hernæs, "Danish Slave Trade," 35ff.

12. Hall, *Slave Society*, 5ff.

13. Feldbæk, "Organization and Structure," 157–58.

14. Ibid., 157.

raise loans abroad . . . In this period a money economy began to play a prominent part; the ties to the European trade and capital markets were tightened; a bank and an adequate insurance system were established; and the eighteenth century finally saw the establishment of a regular stock market and a familiarization—also in the larger groups of society—with other forms of investment than those that the traditional agrarian economy could offer.[15]

The Danes imported guns, gunpowder, liquor, pewter, copper, lead, brass, iron, hoes, knives, padlocks, mirrors, tobacco pipes, caps, hats, fallow, corals, cowries, and European and Indian textiles. They shipped raw materials to Denmark in order to process them there, but the Danes also produced salted herring, meat, cereals, bread and butter, and the like.[16] Danes traded with Africa and the Americas. They even shipped rum as far as Alaska.[17]

An episode of the Danish slave-trade triangle is worth narrating. On July 18, 1778, the *Royal Danish American Gazette* of St. Croix announced that the "prime condition" of the slaves that had just arrived would allow the Danish slave ship *Christiansborg* to depart for Denmark by the end of July. Governor Schimmelman had already advertised that the vessel would be departing no later than July 24. However, since the slaves were not really in good shape, and the majority still remained in the ship, Schimmelman did not dare risk a costly delay: "To resolve the dilemma, the 150 'Refuse Slaves' were made to disappear."[18]

Slavery and the Slave Trade

Denmark traded for a wide range of goods, but the most profitable was "black ivory," i.e., slaves. Danish economic historian Per O. Hernæs reports the following global estimates in round figures, regarding the Atlantic slave trade: Ten million, eight hundred seventy thousand slaves were imported to the Old and New Worlds from 1451 to 1870. Within the period of 1660 to 1806, Danish sailors and Danish ships such as

---

15. Ibid., 158.

16. Hernæs, "Danish Slave Trade," 40, 92.

17. Lewisohn, *St. Croix under Seven Flags*, 215, 221.

18. Donoghue, "Refuse Slaves," 9.

the famous *Patriarch Jacob*[19] traded with 97,850 "heads" (slaves).[20] The Lesser Antilles and particularly St. Thomas (the "Middle Passage") were the ports for voyages of slave-laden vessels that came from Africa and left for the American slave markets.

In April 1764 Frederik V in an ordinance declared St. Thomas a free port for European or American goods. What this king really did was to increase Danish commercial transactions through Denmark's neutrality during the American Revolution. On March 12, 1787, Paul Erdmann Isert, the medical officer on Danish slave ships, reported how a ship built to carry two hundred slaves was crammed with 452, and only thirty-six whites were in charge of keeping them in line. He also reported how shortly after disembarking at St. Croix the slaves were better fed, their limbs and bodies washed and oiled. And Isert counts the amount of 364,000 kroner as the sum for selling them, at an average of 750 Kr.[21] According to one scholar, the average age of the slaves in the ships was between fifteen and twenty years until the beginning of the nineteenth century, and from nine to twelve when the slave-trade abolition was imminent.[22]

Denmark is proud of being the first European colonial power to abolish African slave trade. On March 16, 1792, a royal edict issued by Christian VII declared that by 1803 the trading should stop. However, the truth is that the trade continued in a clandestine way within Denmark itself and in other countries until the second half of the nineteenth century, resulting in approximately three hundred fifty years of slave trade.[23]

Ernst Schimmelmann, the Danish finance minister (later governor) and the owner of a large sugar plantation and a slave trader[24] established a Slave-Trading Commission in 1791. The main motivation of that measure was the impression the Danes had that Britain was about

19. Other nations used disgusting names for slave-trade ships, such as the *Liberty*, the *Jean Jacques Rousseau*, and the *Social Contract*. See Éla, "The Memory of the African People and the Cross of Christ," 33.

20. Hernæs, "The Volume of the Danish Transatlantic Slave Trade 1660–1806," 56, 29.

21. Paiewonsky, *Eyewitness Accounts of Slavery*, 20, 28ff.

22. Fraginals, *La historia como arma*, 29.

23. Ibid., 24ff.

24. Green-Pedersen, "Economic Considerations," 409, n.4.

to abolish slave trading.[25] The Danes wanted the credit of being the first abolitionists, even though they continued the business after abolishing slavery. Meanwhile in Denmark, Frederick VI, the largest landholder of the nation, was trying to improve production by means of allowing the peasants to own a portion of land in the Danish West Indies. The reform-minded king adopted an ameliorative policy in order to buy time and delay the end of slavery. Schimmelmann was also experimenting in order to increase the slaves' fertility by providing a better diet and better living conditions because he foresaw the end of slave trading. There is also the possibility that Schimmelmann followed Isert's recommendations of providing better treatment to slaves.[26]

Denmark, as a European maritime state, also had to justify slavery. On August 14, 1838, a prestigious newspaper declared: "Africans had made no advance in the last 3,000 years of history; they have no capacity for memory and even less for reason."[27] The *Fædrelandet*, the same newspaper Kierkegaard used in his attack upon the church, opposed on December 15 and 22, 1840, the construction of an "enormous prison" of "sinister significance" in St. Croix and commented: "blood ought not to be shed to compensate for an inability to reconcile the slaves to their existence."[28] Nevertheless, the same political newspaper published an article on January 15, 1841, that stated: "They [Africans] are humans but the animal characteristics in Africans predominate."[29] The *Dansk Tidskrift* in 1848 transmitted this racial pessimism in the sense of the Africans' need of white tutelage.[30]

Eurocentrism did not emerge out of the attempt to monopolize reason and science. The Danes did not add something new. That mentality existed since the fourteenth century. Hegel himself, in writing about Africans, is included in such a paradigm: "The weakness of their psyche was one of the main reasons why the Negroes were brought to America as a labor force."[31] On the other hand, with respect to Europeans, he

---

25. Ibid., 418.

26. Paiewonsky, *Eyewitness Accounts of Slavery*, 34.

27. *Kjøbenhavn posten*, cited in Hall, *Slave Society*, 49.

28. *Fædrelandet*, cited in Ibid., 135.

29. Quoted in Ibid., 49.

30. (1848) 390–95 published by Prosch's *"Om Slave emancipation paa de dansk-vest indiske Øer"*; quoted in Hall, *Slave Society*, 50.

31. Hegel, *Lectures on the Philosophy of World History*, 165.

affirmed: "The emigrants have brought with them the assets of European culture, so that they began life in America with advantages which, in Europe, were the fruit of thousands of years of development."[32] The German thinker moved from the romanticization of African slavery to the justification of the quest for wealth and dominion:

> The Negroes have no sentiments of regret at this condition of slavery. When the Negro slaves have labored all day, they are perfectly contented and will dance with the most violent convulsions throughout the night.[33]

> Those who sail the seas will and can profit and earn in the process ... they thereby place their lives and property at risk. This invests their employment of such means with a courageous quality, and gives the individual a consciousness of greater freedom and independence. It is this which elevated acquisition and trade above their usual level and transforms them into a courageous and noble undertaking ... The quest for riches, as already remarked, is elevated into a courageous and noble activity in so far as it is directed towards the sea.[34]

Slavery was twisted into a racial issue first against the *homo africanis* and later against the *homo caribensis*. However, slavery was not the result of racism; quite the opposite, racism was derived from slavery, which existed as an economic fact.[35] Furthermore, African slavery was an essential element of European capitalism.[36] The Danish West Indies as trade posts were an economic advantage to Denmark: "[In the Danish colonies,] the slave trade and slavery played an important role in the economic development of the 'mother country.'"[37] That is why Denmark, together with other countries, had not only African labor but also white "slavery," though for short periods of working (indentures); and later, coolie labor as well. It is not an accident that shortly after the

32. Ibid., 215.
33. Ibid., 219.
34. Ibid., 160–61.
35. Williams, *Capitalism and Slavery*, 7.
36. Mintz, "África en América Latina," 381.
37. Mintz, *Caribbean Transformations*, 64.

declaration of freedom, the first shipload of coolies from India arrived at St. Croix in 1855.[38]

St. Thomas

In 1801 England bombarded Copenhagen, and from April of the same year to February of 1802, they seized the Danish West Indies. In 1807 the British again bombarded the capital of Denmark, and once more they seized the islands up until October 1814. With the Treaty of Paris and the defeat of Napoleon, Denmark regained its possessions.

St. Thomas possessed a large, deep, and commodious natural harbor. From 1821 to 1830, the harbor had an average annual visitation of 2,890 vessels, with a total tonnage of 177,441.[39] From 1841 to 1867, this island profited very much as a transit center. Ships from Europe and from North and South America were always waiting their turn for repairs or waiting to take passengers, mail, and Danish manufactured commodities to other parts of the world.[40] Instead of getting a supply of coal in Santa Lucía or getting tanks of water in San Juan, sailors preferred to obtain both supplies from St. Thomas. After 1867 its importance declined, and St. Thomas became a dry dock for repairing vessels; and finally in 1885 the packet station was moved to Barbados.

St. Thomas was the West Indian center for steamships in the 1850s. Johan Frederik Schelegel (1817–1896), Kierkegaard's ex-fiancée's husband, as the West Indies governor, did not expand the harbor. On the contrary, he focused all his energy on large public buildings and lawns, on the luxurious uniforms of the bureaucratic apparatus, on immaculate barracks for the soldiers and so on.[41] In 1848 Danish absolute monarchy was replaced by parliamentary monarchy. In the same year the St. Croix slave uprising achieved freedom for the Danish West Indies. Consequently, on August 30, 1852, both events contributed to the issuing of a new colonial law by the Parliament. Such a law granted the islanders for the first time in 120 years a real voice in government. However, in practice the measure did not work, because Schelegel, from 1855 to 1859, "arbitrarily failed to call the Colonial Council into Session

38. Lewisohn, *St. Croix under Seven Flags*, 277.

39. Westergaard, *Danish West Indies*, 252.

40. Dookhan, *History of the Virgin Islands of the United States*, 101.

41. Ibid., 208.

at all, although it was supposed to meet for four weekly sessions yearly."[42] Schelegel reduced that governmental body to a mere advisory committee that seconded the grandeur of his position.

In St. Thomas, even the Prussians made inroads into the slave trade and commerce. From 1685 to 1715, the German state of Brandenburg-Prussia, through the Great Elector Frederick William I, established a company to trade with Guinea and the West Indies and owned a plantation as well.[43] The State of Brandenburg did successful business for thrity years, usurping the profits from the Danes.[44] In the nineteenth century, Prussian slaveholders were welcomed in Denmark by the very A. S. Ørsted who said slavery should not be tolerated among the Danes, but who allowed residents from other countries to take their slaves with them and exercise their rights over them.[45]

St. Croix, the "Sugar King," and Freedom

This island had famous U.S. traders such as Sarah Roosevelt, John Hancock, and Abram Markoe, who gave his home in Pennsylvania for the new U.S. site of the first White House.[46] Also on this island Alexander Hamilton was reared, himself partly of African ancestry, the first secretary of the treasury of U.S.A.[47] St. Croix is a small island, but it was a flourishing sugar plantation. As sugar was very profitable, Denmark paid homage to "king sugar." In 1812 alone Denmark exported 20,535 tons.[48]

Sugar originated in the South Pacific. From there eventually it was taken to China, India, the Canary Islands, and Santo Domingo. Nevertheless it had been taken to Hawaii since 800 AD most probably by a wave of Polynesians from the South Pacific.[49] "Sugar money" had a great economic importance for Denmark: in the Copenhagen refiner-

42. Lewisohn, *St. Croix under Seven Flags*, 285.

43. Williams, *From Columbus to Castro*, 81–82.

44. Baa, "The Brandenburges at St. Thomas."

45. Ørsted, *Beholdes Herredømmet over en vestindisk Slave, naar han betræder dansk-europæisk Grund, Arkiv for Retsvindenskaben of den Anvendelse*, 459–85, quoted in Hall, *Slave Society*, 35ff.

46 Lewisohn, *St. Croix under Seven Flags*, 185–87.

47. Lewisohn, *"What So Proudly We Hail."*

48. Williams, *From Columbus to Castro*, 115, 134, 366.

49. Deerr, *History of Sugar*, 2:13.

ies, it was processed and exported to Sweden, England, and other parts. A large number of merchants of the city had to do with sugar or slaves.[50] Sugar played a central role in European economies. To mention one example: In 1845 Thomas Babington Macaulay, later Lord Macaulay, with horrifying and cynical lucidity criticized those who consumed sugar. But he himself supported slavery and the marketing of the imports of Brazilian sugar:

> We import the accursed thing; we bond it; we employ our skill and machinery to render it more alluring to the eye and to the palate; we export it to Leghorn and Hamburg; we send it to all the coffee houses of Italy and Germany; we pocket a profit on all this; and then we put a Pharisaical air, and thank God that we are not like those sinful Italians and Germans who have not scruple about swallowing slave-grown sugar.[51]

But St. Croix is also well known for having witnessed the second successful Caribbean slave revolt, after Haiti's revolt between 1791 and 1804. In 1848 Danish parliamentary monarchy emerged. That same year, on July 2 and 3, 1848, Buddoe led a slave uprising and forced the Governor-General Peter Carl Frederick von Scholten (1784–1854) to grant their freedom. Scholten had to stand trial in Denmark for negligence, and by September 22, 1848, the Danish government officially declared emancipation. The truth is that the slaves achieved their freedom, but only in the narrow sense of the legal abolition of servitude: "Victory achieved through the mediation of state approval also left intact, with the exception of legal slavery, the institutional structures of the colonial polity, including the mechanism for the administration of law and order."[52]

Runaway slaves were a constant threat against the institution of slavery. It is not by chance that those who deserted their masters were called maroons, i.e., *marrano* in Spanish ("wild pig"), or *cimarron* (i.e., "monkey," "simian").[53]

---

50. Green-Pedersen, "Economic Considerations," 402–3.

51. Hansard, *Three Series* LXXVII, 1290,1292, 1300, 1302, Feb. 26, 1845. Quoted in Williams, *From Columbus to Castro*, 194.

52. Hall, *Slave Society*, 211.

53. Deerr, *History of Sugar*, 2:318.

The Moravians

At the beginning of the eighteenth century, Lutheran missionaries failed to face the challenge of evangelizing the West Indies. The Bohemian or the Moravian Brethren filled the gap and started working in 1732; later on, some of them arrived in Greenland as well. From the outset they demonstrated that the slaves behaved much better with their religion.[54] The Moravians also were known as *Herrnhuters* for being protected in the village of Herrnhut, in Saxony. In that place they had organized the "shelter of the Lord."

The Herrnhuters arrived in Denmark in the late 1720s and reached Copenhagen by 1739. They influenced Danish society up until 1840. Michael Pedersen Kierkegaard (Søren Kierkegaard's father) was their supporter, and the elder Kierkegaard attended their services on Sunday afternoons. Emil Boesen, his lifelong friend, belonged to a pietist Moravian congregation in Copenhagen.[55] This "congregation of brothers" (*Brødremenighed*) always worked in parallel with the state church. In Jutland there even existed the "Herrnhut Belt" which particularly appealed to the "ordinary" person.

Count Nikolaus Ludwig von Zinzendorf (1700–1760) was the leader and head of the movement. He studied at the University of Halle. He followed two premises: the primacy of moral life over theological formulations, and the contemplation of Christ and his suffering in the cross. He personally landed in the Danish West Indies in 1739 in order to oversee the religious work. The slaves worked from 5:00 am to 6:30 pm,[56] and in general their situation was wretched, but the Moravian faith "was a powerful influence urging their converts to accept their lot in this world and to pray for redemption in the next."[57] In the 1740s the Moravians established the first missionary station on St. John. The

54. Green-Pedersen, "Economic Considerations," 407.

55. Kirmmse, *Encounters with Kierkegaard*, 269 n. 2; 279.

56. Paiewonsky, *Eyewitness Accounts of Slavery*, 324.

57. Ibid., 111. In the British West Indies the Methodist missionaries played a similar role: "it was missionary influence that moderated their passions, kept them in steady course of duty, and prevented them from sinning against God by offending the laws of men. Whatever outbreaks or insurrections at any time occurred, no Methodist slave was ever proved guilty of incendiarism of rebellion for more than seventy years, namely from 1760 to 1833" (Woodson, *History of the Negro Church*, 27; cited in Niebuhr, *Social Sources of Denominationalism*, 251).

Moravians, Lutherans, Roman Catholics, Dutch Reformed, Anglicans, and Methodists owned personal slaves. The clergy were an instrument of social control, preaching duty, the importance of maintaining geographic bonds, servitude, resignation and humility.[58]

The prophetic critique of Christendom was a qualified critique. Søren Kierkegaard was cautious enough to limit his examination to Danish Lutheranism and to Roman Catholicism.[59] In passing, one may add that the Danish West Indies illustrates very well the truth that the connection between Protestantism and capitalism is unfair. In this period of history, we can also see how the Roman Catholic economic ideas were very similar to Protestantism.[60] It follows from the foregoing that scholars must locate the Protestant and Roman Catholic economic ethics on the different levels of capitalistic empire development, and not on doctrinal divergences.[61]

58. Oldendorp, *History of the Mission of the Evangelical Brethren.*

59. Cf. the parallel Don Quixote played as a gadfly, ending up aborting his prophetic role, in Ziolkowski, "Don Quixote and Kierkegaard's Understanding," 130–45.

60. Cf. Hobsbawn, *Industry and Empire,* 37–38: "The Reformation occurred more than two centuries before the Industrial Revolution, and—to take an obvious example—the parts of the Netherlands which remained Catholic (Belgium) industrialized before the part which became Protestant (Holland)."

61. We can observe this based on the fact that the division of Latin America and Anglo-Saxon America was based on economic and political criteria and not on cultural, religious, or social ones. Cf. Mintz, "África en América Latina," 391.

Appendix B

Journals and Papers

Some Untranslated Kierkegaardian Material		
PENGE (money)	1847	VIII 1 A: 162, 457
	1848	VIII 1 A: 513
	1849	X 1 A: 79, 99, 117 X 5 B: 35
	1850	X 2 A: 511 X 3 A: 177, 291, 345
	1849–1851	X 6 B: 246
FATTIGE (the poor)	1850	X 3 A: 123, 135
	1852	X 4 A: 453, 578, 649
ARMOD (poverty)	1850	X 3 A: 215, 249
	1851	X 4 A: 116, 417 X 6 B: 3
	1851–1852	X 6 B: 29
OECONOMIE (finances)	1847	VIII 1 A: 495
	1849	X 1 A: 442, 280, 302, 413, 421
	1850	X 2 A: 511, 538 X 3 A: 50, 70, 92, 300, 345
	1849–1851	X 6 A: 249
	1852	X 4 A: 116, 560, 631 X 5 A: 16
	1854	XI 2 A: 34

	1847	VIII 1 A: 282
	1848	IX A: 212, 370, 386, 388
	1849	X 1 A: 117, 145, 315, 431 X 2 A: 98, 511 X 5 B: 18
UDKOMME (livelihood)	1850	X 3 A: 345
	1852	X 4 A: 600
	1853	X 5 A: 89
	1854	XI 2 A: 12
	1848	IX B: 64
FORMUE (fortune)	1849	X 2 A: 82, 172, 511 X 5 B: 201
	1850	X 2 A: 528 X 3 A: 343, 345, 539
	1855	XI 3 B: 105

Appendix C

Papirer X 3 A 135 n.d., 1850

#

DEN PRÆDIKEN AF MYNSTER "BETRAGTNING AF DERES SKJEBNE HVEM de sædvanlige Evner ere negtede" er egentlig ikke holdt til Trøst for saadenne Lidende, men til behagelig Beroligelse for de Lykkelige, at de fra Kirken maae gaae hjem væbnede mod Indtrykket af saadanne Lidende.

Der er noget Underfundigt heri. Ganske ignorere saadanne Lidende, om hvilke Evangeliet saa ofte taler, mener M. ikke at kunne. Saa gives da Sagen den Vending, at man dog til syvende og sidst benegter saadanne Lidelser egentlig Smerte; han taler ikke Trøst til de Lidende, men til de Lykkelige siger han: trøster Eder, Sagen er da ikke saa forfærdelig, den har ogsaa sin mildere Side: man har Exempler paa, at Blinde have haft ‹et› desto klarere Aands—Øie (f. E. Homer kan jeg tænke), at Tunghøre have været dybsindige Tænkere.

See det er at prædike! Det er egentlig at spotte de Lidende. Men de Lykkelige, ja de ere glade for saadanne Prædikener, der saa aldeles berolige dem i uforstyrret Lyst til at nyde Livet efter den størst mulige Maalestok, uforstyrrede af Livets Elendighed—"det er ikke saa farligt; der har ogsa sin mildere Side."

I det Hele er her et heelt Gebee for psychologist Iagttagelse: den Underfundighed, med hvilken den menneskelige Egoisme under Skin af Medlidenhed søger a værge sig mod Indtrykket af Livets Elendighed, at det ikke skal forstyrre Livslystens Graadighed.

Det er a la Goethe. Og Mynster har jo ogsaa dannet sig efter ham.

Men er det ogsaa Christendom! Er det ogsaa en Prædiken om Ham, Medlidenheden, der søgte saadanne Lidende, satte sig ganske i deres Sted.

Hvor ofte prækes og tales der ikke ogsaa om: at den Fattige er langt
lykkeligere en den Rige—og det gjøres under Skin af Medlidenhed; man
fremstiller det saa rørende, hvor lykkeligt den Fattige kan leve, fri for
alle Rigdommens Byrder. Er det nu en Tale for at trøste den Fattige? Nei,
det er en Rigmændene yderst velkommen Vending; thi saa behøve de
da ikke at give de Fattige Noget eller noget Synderligt—Den Fattige er i
Grunden lykkeligere; Fattigdom har sin smukke Side. Fre Kirken gaader
den Rige hjem til sine Skatte, som han nu holder ‹end› fastere paa, op-
bygget ved det skjønne Foredrag, der talte Medlidenhedens Sprog.

Men er det ogsaa Christendom! Er det ogsaa en Prædiken om
Ham, Medlidenheden, der, for at trøste Armoden, selv blev lige Vilkaar
undergivet.

Men som "den Christelige Stat" egentlig kun kjender een Art
Forbrydelse: Tyverie—frygtelige indirect Beviis mod «den Christelige
Stat": saaledes har ogsaa de begunstigede Stænder deres Præster, der ere
som Medsammensvorne. De vide nu at tale saaledes, at Livsnydelsen
paa ingen Maade forstyrres.

Saadanne Præster øvne saa den Kunst at komme Evangeliet
saa nær som muligt, dog saaledes, at det ikke kommer til a forstyrre
Besiddelsen og Nidelsen af alle de jordisk Goder, eller Livet, som sysler
med disses Erhvervelse og Bevarelse. Dersom En vilde forkynde dem
Evangeliet gratis: den vilde de ikke finde dem i. Det er af Vigtighed,
at „deres Præst" er i Besiddelsen omtrent af de samme Goder, som de
selv. Hans Indtægter maa være svarende omtrent til deres, hans Rang og
Stilling i Samfundet svarende til deres, han maa være Ridder omtrent
af de samme Ordener: saa mener man heri at have en Garantie for, at
det er en Mand, der vilde at tage de behørige Hensyn, en Garantie for,
at han i at forkynde Evangeliet ar behørig generet, saa Evangeliet bliver
ugenerende.

Dette gjælder nu forresten om alle Samfunds-Classerne i Selskabet:
enhver ønsker sin Præst i udvortes Stilling o: s: v: saa omtrent svarende
til dens ydreVilkaar. Saa er man da sikkret, at han ikke gaaer forvidt.
Borgerskabets Præst kan saa gjerne ivre mod de Fornemmes Luxus o: s:
v:, det er endogsaa Borgerskabet ret kjert, som mangler Betingelserne;
men han maa canonisere det Livs-Vilkaar, som ‹er› hans respektive
Samfunds-Classes.

Jeg har hørt en Præst ivre mod de store geistlige Embeder; han var
af den Mening, at en Præst skulde være lønnet, saa han kunde leve an-

stændigt, men heller ikke mere. Og hvor meget fordredes dertil? Ja det var paa Mark og Skilling omtrent hans Gage; og han sad i et Embede, fra hvilket han ikke ventede at blive forflyttet.

Jeg har hørt en Præst ivre mod at Geistligheden udpyntedes med Stjerner og Baand—men Ridder af Dannebroge meente han nok han kunde være uden at det var forargeligt—naturgliviis han var selv Ridder.

Bibliography

Primary Sources

Kierkegaard, Søren. *Kierkegaard's Attack upon "Christendom," 1854–1855*. Translated with an introduction by Walter Lowrie. Princeton: Princeton University Press, 1991.

———. *Armed Neutrality; and, An Open Letter: With Relevant Selections from His Journals and Papers*. Introduced and translation by Howard and Edna Hong. Bloomington: Indiana University Press, 1968.

———. *Christian Discourses; and The Lilies of the Field and the Birds of the Air; and Three Discourses at the Communion on Fridays*. Translated by Walter Lowrie. 2nd ed. London: Oxford University Press, 1952.

———. *A Crisis in the Life of an Actress, and Other Essays on Drama*. Translated with an introduction and notes by Stephen Crites. London: Collins, 1967.

———. *Edifying Discourses*. Translated by David F. Swenson and Lillian Marvin Swenson. 4 vols. Minneapolis: Augsburg, 1943–1946.

———. *Eighteen Upbuilding Discourses*. Introduction, notes, and translation by Howard and Edna Hong. Kierkegaard's Writings 5. Princeton: Princeton University Press, 1990.

———. *Either/Or*. Introduction, notes, and translation by Howard V. Hong and Edna H. Hong. 2 vols. Kierkegaard's Writings 3–4. Princeton: Princeton University Press, 1987.

———. *Fear and Trembling (with Repetition)*. Introduction, notes, and translation by Howard and Edna Hong. Kierkegaard's Writings 6. Princeton: Princeton University Press, 1983.

———. *For Self-Examination; and Judge for Yourself*. Introduction, notes and translation by Howard and Edna Hong. Kierkegaard's Writings 21. Princeton: Princeton University Press, 1990.

———. *The Journals of Søren Kierkegaard*. Selections translated by Alexander Dru. London: Oxford University Press, 1938.

———. *Kierkegaard's Concluding Unscientific Postscript*. Translated by David F. Swenson and Walter Lowrie. 3rd ed. Princeton: Princeton University Press, 1974.

———. *Letters and Documents*. Translated by Henrick Rosenmeier. Kierkegaard's Writings 25. Princeton: Princeton University Press, 1978.

———. *"The Moment" and Late Writings*. Introduction, notes, and translation by Howard V. Hong and Edna H. Hong. Kierkegaard's Writings 23. Princeton: Princeton University Press, 1998.

————. *The Point of View of my Work as an Author: A Report to History, and Related Writings*. Translated by Walter Lowrie. New York: Harper and Brothers, 1962.

————. *Practice in Christianity*. Introduction, notes and translation by Howard and Edna Hong. Kierkegaard's Writings 20. Princeton: Princeton University Press, 1991.

————. *The Present Age, and Of the Difference between a Genius and an Apostle*. Translated by Alexander Drew. Harper Torchbooks. Cloister Library 94. New York: Harper and Row, 1962.

————. *The Sickness unto Death*. Translated with an introduction and notes by Alastair Hannay. Penguin Classics. London: Penguin, 2004.

————. *The Sickness unto Death*. Translated by Howard V. Hong and Edna H. Hong. Kierkegaard's Writings 8. Princeton: Princeton University Press, 1980.

————. *Søren Kierkegaard's Journals and Papers*. Edited and translated with notes by Howard V. Hong and Edna H. Hong, assisted by Gregor Malantschuk. 7 vols. Bloomington: Indiana University Press, 1967–1978.

————. *Søren Kierkegaards Papirer. The Papers of Søren Kierkegaard*. Edited by P. A. Heiberg, V. Kuhr, and E. Torsting. 16 vols. in 25 tomes. 2nd augmented edition, ed. N. Thulstrup. Index by N. J. Cappelørn. Copenhagen: Gyldendal, 1968–78.

————. *Søren Kierkegaards Samlede Værker. The Collected Works of Søren Kierkegaard*, edited by A. B. Drachmann, J. L. Heiberg and H. O. Lange. 20 vols. 3rd ed. Copenhagen: Gyldendal, 1962–1964.

————. *Training in Christianity; and the Edifying Discourse which Accompanied It*. Introduction, notes, and translation by Walter Lowrie. 3rd ed. Princeton: Princeton University Press, 1972.

————. *Two Ages: The Age of Revolution and the Present Age, A Literary Review*. Introduction, notes, and translation by Howard and Edna Hong. Princeton: Princeton University Press, 1978.

————. *Upbuilding Discourses in Various Spirits*. Introduction, notes, and translation by Howard and Edna Hong. Princeton: Princeton University Press, 1993.

————. *Works of Love: Some Christian Reflections in the Form of Discourses*. Translated by Howard and Edna Hong, preface by R. Gregor Smith. New York: Harper & Row, 1962.

Mynster, J. P. *Prædikarne paa Alle Søn-og Hellig-dage i Aaret. af Dr. J. P. Mynster, Biskop over Siellands Stift, kongelig Confessionarius, Storkors af Dannebrogen en og Dannebrogsmand*. København: Gyldendalske Boghandlings, 1845.

Secondary Sources

Adorno, T. W. "On Kierkegaard's Doctrine of Love." *Studies in Philosophy and Social Sciences* 8 (1940) 413–29.

Aguirre Batres, Francisco Javier. *Ser o tener. ¡He ahí el dilema!* Guatemala: Impresores Unidos, 1984.

Alves, Rubem. *Protestantism and Repression: A Brazilian Case Study*. Translated by John Drury; revised by Jaime Wright. Maryknoll, NY: Orbis, 1985.

Andic, Martin, "Simone Weil and Kierkegaard." *Modern Theology* 2 (1985) 20–41.

Assmann, Hugo. *René Girard com teólogos da libertação: um diálogo sobre ídolos e sacrifícios*. San José, Costa Rica: DEI, 1991.

Baa, Enid M. "The Brandenburges at St. Thomas." A paper presented at the 10th Annual Conference of the Association of Caribbean Historians. St. Thomas, 1978.

Barzun, Jacques. *Race: A Study in Superstition*. New York: Harper & Row, 1965.

Baudrillard, Jean. *The System of Objects*. London: Verso, 1996.

Bauer, Bruno. *Kritik der evangelischen Geschichte der Synoptiker*. Vol. 1. Leipzig: Wigand, 1846.

Bellinger, Charles. "Toward a Kierkegaardian Understanding of Stalin, Hitler, and the Cold War." In *Foundations of Kierkegaard's Vision of Community: Religion, Ethics, and Politics in Kierkegaard*, edited by George B. Connell and C. Stephen Evans, 218–30. Atlantic Highlands, NJ: Humanities, 1992.

Best, Steven, and Douglas Kellner. "Modernity, Mass Society and the Media." In *The Corsair Affair*, edited by Robert L. Perkins, 23–61. International Kierkegaard Commentary 13. Macon GA: Mercer University Press, 1990.

Bjerg, Svend. "Kierkegaard's Story-Telling." *Studia Theologica* 45 (1991) 111–25.

Brazill, William J. *The Young Hegelians*. Yale Historical Publications. Miscellany 91. New Haven: Yale University Press, 1970.

Bonhoeffer, Dietrich. *Ethics*. Edited by Eberhard Bethge. Translated by Neville Horton Smith. New York: Macmillan, 1967.

Brandt, Frithiof, and Else Rammel. *Søren Kierkegaard og Pengene* [*Søren Kierkegaard and Money*]. Copenhagen: Levin & Munksgaard, 1935.

Bukdahl, Jørgen. *Søren Kierkegaard og den menige Mand*. [*Søren Kierkegaard and the "Ordinary" Person.*] Copenhagen: Gyldendal Uglebøger, 1970.

Busto, Rudy B. *King Tiger: The Religious Vision of Reies López Tijerina*. Albuquerque: University of New Mexico Press, 2005.

Bykhovskii, Bernard. *Kierkegaard*. Amsterdam: Grüner, 1976.

Cain, David. *An Evocation of Kierkegaard*. Copenhagen: Reitzel, 1997.

Casalis, Georges. *Las buenas ideas no caen del cielo: elementos de "teología inductiva."* San José, Costa Rica: Editorial Universitaria Centroamericana, 1979.

Cavanaugh, William T. *Torture and Eucharist: Theology, Politics, and the Body of Christ*. Challenges in Contemporary Theology. Oxford: Blackwell, 1998.

Cela, Jorge. "Cuerpo y solidaridad." *Revista de Interpretación Latinoamericana* 19 (1994) 63–73.

Comblin, Joseph. "The French Revolution: A Bourgeois Revolution." *Concilium* 201 (1989) 61–70.

Connell, George B. "Introduction." In *Foundations of Kierkegaard's Vision of Community: Religion, Ethics, and Politics in Kierkegaard*, edited by George B. Connell, and C. Steven Evans, i–xxii. Atlantic Highlands, NJ: Humanities, 1992.

Connell, George B., and C. Stephen Evans. *Foundations of Kierkegaard's Vision of Community: Religion, Ethics, and Politics in Kierkegaard*. Atlantic Highlands, NJ: Humanities, 1992.

Curtin, Philip D. *The Atlantic Slave Trade: A Census*. Madison: University of Wisconsin Press, 1969.

Davis, David Brion. *The Problem of Slavery in Western Culture*. Ithaca, NY: Cornell University Press, 1966.

Deerr, Noël. *The History of Sugar*. 2 vols. London: Chapman & Hall, 1949.

Donoghue, Eddie. "Refuse Slaves: Slaves Nobody Wanted." *St. Croix Avis*, January 16–17, 2000, 9.

Dookhan, Isaac. *A History of the Virgin Islands of the United States*. Epping Essex, UK: Caribbean University Press, 1974.

Duchrow, Ulrich. *Alternatives to Global Capitalism: Drawn from Biblical History, Designed for Political Action*. Translated by Elizabeth Hicks et al. Utrecht: International Books, 1995.

Duchrow, Ulrich, and Gerhard Liedke. *Shalom: Biblical Perspectives on Creation, Justice & Peace*. Geneva: WCC Publications, 1987.

Dussel, Enrique D. *El dualismo en la antropología de la Cristiandad: Desde el origen del cristianismo hasta antes de la conquista de América*. Buenos Aires: Guadalupe, 1974.

———. *Las metáforas teologicas de Marx*. Estella, Navarra: Verbo Divino, 1993.

———. *Método para una filosofía de la liberación: Superación analéctica de la dialéctica hegeliana*. 2nd edition. Salamanca: Sígueme, 1974.

Eicher, Peter. "Revolution and Church Reform: Ecclesiastical Power after the French Revolution." *Concilium* 201 (1989) 89–106.

Éla, Jean-Marc. "The Memory of the African People and the Cross of Christ." In *The Scandal of a Crucified World: Perspectives on the Cross and Suffering*, edited by Yacob Tesfai, 17–35. Maryknoll, NY: Orbis, 1994.

Ellacuría, Ignacio, and Jon Sobrino. *Mysterium Liberationis: Conceptos fundamentales de la teología de la liberación*. Vol. 1. San Salvador: UCA Editores, 1993.

Elrod, John W. "Passion, Reflection and Particularity." In *Two Ages*, edited by Robert L. Perkins, 1–18. International Kierkegaard Commentary 14. Macon, GA: Mercer University Press, 1984.

Engels, Frederick. *Outlines of a Critique of the Political Economy*. Written in October and November 1843. First published in *Deutsch Französische Jahrbücher* in 1844. Online (translated by Martin Milligan for the *Collected Works*): http://www.marxists.org/archive/marx/works/1844/df-jahrbucher/outlines.htm/.

Engels, Frederick, and Karl Marx. "Contribution to the Critique of Hegel's Philosophy of Law" In *Karl Marx–Frederick Engels Collected Works*, Vol. 3. New York: International, 1975.

———. "Economic and Philosophic Manuscripts of 1844." In *Karl Marx–Frederick Engels Collected Works*. Vol. 3. New York: International, 1975.

Evans, C. Stephen. *Passionate Reason: Making Sense of Kierkegaard's Philosophical Fragments*. The Indiana Series in the Philosophy of Religion. Bloomington: Indiana University Press, 1992.

Evans, Richard I. *Dialogue with Erich Fromm*. Dialogues with Notable Contributors to Personality Theory. New York: Harper & Row, 1966.

Feldbaek, Ole. "The Organization and Structure of the Danish East India, West India and Guinea Companies in the 17th and 18th Centuries." In *Companies and Trade: Essays on Overseas Trading Companies during the Ancient Regime*, edited by Leonard Blussé and Femme Gasstra, 24–33. The Hague: Leiden University Press, 1981.

Fenger, Henning. *The Heibergs*. Translated and edited by Fredrick J. Marker. Twayne's World Authors Series 105. New York: Twayne, 1971.

Forrester, Duncan B. "The Attack on Christendom in Marx and Kierkegaard." *Scottish Journal of Theology* 25 (1972) 181–96.

Fraginals, Manuel Moreno. *La historia como arma: y otros estudios sobre esclavos, ingenios y plantaciones.* Crítica/Historia 25. Barcelona: Crítica, 1983.

Freire, Paulo. *Pedagogía de la autonomía: Saberes necesarios para la práctica educativa.* México, D. F.: Siglo XXI, 1998.

Fromm, Eric. *The Art of Listening.* New York: Continuum, 1994.

———. *Del tener al ser: caminos y extravíos de la conciencia.* México: Paidós, 1994.

Fuentes, Carlos. *El Naranjo.* Madrid: Alfaguara Hispánica, 1993.

Galbraith, John Kenneth. *A Era da Incerteza.* [*The Age of Uncertainty*]. Translated by F. R. Nickelsen Pellegrini. São Paulo: Pionera, 1982.

Garaudy, Roger. *Marxism in the Twentieth Century.* Translated by René Hague. London: Collins, 1970.

Garff, Joakim. *Søren Kierkegaard: A Biography.* Princeton: Princeton University Press, 2005.

Girard, René. *La violencia de lo sagrado* [*Violence and the Sacred*]. Barcelona: Anagrama, 1998.

González, Justo L. *From the Protestant Reformation to the Twentieth Century.* A History of Christian Thought 3. Nashville: Abingdon, 1990.

———. *Mañana: Christian Theology from a Hispanic Perspective.* Nashville: Abingdon, 1990.

Green-Pedersen, Svend E. "The Economic Considerations behind the Danish Abolition of the Negro Slave Trade." In *The Uncommon Market: Essays in the Economic History of the Atlantic Slave Trade,* edited by Henry A. Gemery and Jan S. Hogendorn, 399–418. New York: Academic, 1979.

Gutiérrez, Gustavo. *Hablar de Dios desde el sufrimiento del inocente; Una reflexión sobre el libro de Job.* Salamanca: Sígueme, 1995.

———. *Las Casas: In Search of the Poor of Jesus Christ.* Maryknoll, NY: Orbis, 1993.

———. *The Power of the Poor in History: Selected Writings.* Maryknoll, NY: Orbis, 1983.

———. "Theological Language: Fullness of Silence." In *The Density of the Present: Selected Writings,* 186–208. Maryknoll, NY: Orbis, 1999.

———. *A Theology of Liberation: History, Politics and Salvation.* 3rd ed. Maryknoll, NY: Orbis, 1990.

———. "Una teología de la liberación en el contexto del Tercer Milenio." In *El futuro de la reflexión teológica en América Latina,* edited by Luciano Mendes de Almeida et al., 97–165. Bogotá: Paulinas, 1996.

Haecker, Theodor. *Der Bückel Kierkegaards.* Zurich: Thomas, 1946.

Hall, Neville A. T. *Slave Society in the Danish West Indies, St. Thomas, St. John, and St. Croix.* Edited by B. W. Higman with a foreword by Kamau Brathwaite. Mona, Jamaica: University of the West Indies Press, 1992.

Hansen, Knud. *Revolutionær Samvittighed. Essays og Taler om Søren Kierkegaard og Karl Marx* (*Revolutionary Conscience: Essays and Addresses on Søren Kierkegaard and Karl Marx*). Copenhagen: Gyldendal Uglebøger, 1965.

Hegel, George Wilhelm Friedrich. *Determinate Religion.* Edited by Peter C. Hodgson. Lectures on the Philosophy of Religion 2. Berkeley: University of California Press, 1987.

———. *Introduction to the Philosophy of Right*. Translated by T. M. Knox. Oxford: Clarendon, 1952.

———. *Lectures on the Philosophy of World History*. Translated by H. B. Nisbet. Introduction by Duncan Forbes. Cambridge Studies in the History and Theory of Politics. Cambridge: Cambridge University Press, 1975.

Heiss, Robert. *Hegel, Kierkegaard, and Marx: Three Great Philosophers Whose Ideas Changed the Course of Civilization*. Translated by E. B. Garside. New York: Delacorte / S. Lawrence, 1975.

Hernæs, Per O. "The Danish Slave Trade from West Africa and Afro-Danish Relations on the 18th-Century Gold Coast." PhD diss., University of Trondheim, 1992.

Hinkelammert, Franz J. *Sacrificios humanos y sociedad occidental: Lucifer y la bestia*. Colección Teológica Latinoamericana. San José, Costa Rica: DEI, 1991.

———. *La fe de Abraham y el édipo occidental*. San José, Costa Rica: DEI, 1989.

Hobsbawn, Eric J. *The Age of Revolution, 1789–1848*. The World Histories of Civilization. Cleveland: World, 1962.

———. *Industry and Empire: From 1750 to the Present Day*. The Pelican Economic History of Britain 3. Hammondsworth, England: Penguin, 1969.

Hofstadter, Richard. *Social Darwinism in American Thought, 1860–1915*. Philadelphia: University of Pennsylvania Press, 1945.

Horkheimer, Max. "La añoranza de lo completamente otro." In *A la búsqueda del sentido*, by Herbert Marcuse, Karl Popper, and Max Horkheimer, 65–124. Salamanca: Sígueme, 1976.

Hunsinger, George. "A Marxist View of Kierkegaard: George Lukács on the Intellectual Origins of Fascism." *Union Seminary Quarterly Review* 30 (1974) 29–40.

Illich, Ivan. *Toward a History of Needs*. New York: Pantheon, 1978.

Jansen, Nerina. "The Individual versus the Public: A Key to Kierkegaard's Views of the Daily Press." In *The Corsair Affair*, edited by Robert L. Perkins, 1–22. International Kierkegaard Commentary 13. Macon GA: Mercer University Press, 1990.

Jegstrup, Elsebet. "Kierkegaard on Citizenship and Character: A Philosophy of Political Consciousness." PhD diss., Loyola University (Chicago), 1991.

Keynes, John Maynard. "Economic Possibilities for Our Grandchildren." In *Essays in Persuasion*, 358–74. Collected Writings of John Maynard Keynes 9. London: Macmillan, 1972.

Khan, Abrahim. "Opposition within Affinity between Religion and Politics with Reference to Golden Age Denmark and Brazil." In *Religious Transformations and Socio-Political Change in Eastern Europe and Latin America*, edited by Luther Martin, 189–203. Religion and Society 33. Berlin: De Gruyter, 1993.

King, Martin Luther Jr. *A Testament of Hope: The Essential Writings of Martin Luther King Jr.*, edited by James Melvin Washington. San Francisco: Harper & Row, 1986.

Kirmmse, Bruce H. "Call Me Ishmael—Call Everybody Ishmael: Kierkegaard on the Coming-of-Age Crisis of Modern Times." In *Foundations of Kierkegaard's Vision of Community: Religion, Ethics, and Politics in Kierkegaard*, edited by George B. Connell and C. Stephen Evans, 161–82. Atlantic Highlands, NJ: Humanities, 1992.

———. *Encounters with Kierkegaard: A Life as Seen by His Contemporaries*. Princeton, NJ: Princeton University Press, 1996.

————. *Kierkegaard in Golden Age Denmark*. The Indiana Series in the Philosophy of Religion. Bloomington: Indiana University Press, 1990.

————. "'Out with it!': The Modern Breakthrough, Kierkegaard and Denmark." In *The Cambridge Companion to Kierkegaard*, edited by Alastair Hannay and Gordon Marino, 15–47. Cambridge: Cambridge University Press, 1998.

————. "Psychology and Society: The Social Falsification of the Self in *The Sickness unto Death*." In *Kierkegaard's Truth: The Disclosure of the Self*, edited by Joseph Smith, 167–92. Psychiatry and the Humanities 5. New Haven: Yale University Press, 1981.

————. "A Rose with Thorns: Hans Christian Andersen's Relation to Kierkegaard." In *Early Polemical Writings*, edited by Robert E. Perkins, 69–85. International Kierkegaard Commentary 1. Macon, GA: Mercer University Press, 1999.

————. "'This Disastrous Confounding of Politics and Christianity': Kierkegaard's Open Letter of 1851." In *The Corsair Affair*, edited by Robert L. Perkins, 179–84. International Kierkegaard Commentary 13. Macon GA: Mercer University Press, 1990.

Küng, Hans, and Walter Jens. *Literature & Religion: Pascal, Gryphius, Lessing, Holderling, Novalis, Kierkegaard, Dostoyevsky, Kafka*. New York: Paragon, 1991.

Lasch, Christopher. *The Culture of Narcissism: American Life in An Age of Diminishing Expectations*. New York: Norton, 1991.

Lewisohn, Florence. *St. Croix under Seven Flags*. Hollywood, FL: Dukane, 1970.

————. *"What so Proudly we Hail": The Danish West Indies and the American Revolution*. St. Thomas: American Revolution Bicentennial Commission of the Virgin Islands, 1975.

Lichtheim, George. *Marxism: An Historical and Critical Study*. 2nd rev. ed. London: Routledge & Kegan Paul, 1964.

Liégé, A. *Présence mutuelle de l'Église et de la Pauvreté*. Paris: n.p., 1965.

Löwith, Karl. *From Hegel to Nietzche*. New York: Holt, Rinehart and Winston, 1964.

Lowrie, Walter. *Kierkegaard*. Gloucester, MA: Smith, 1970.

Malantschuk, Gregor. *The Controversial Kierkegaard*. Translated by Howard V. Hong and Edna H. Hong. Kierkegaard Monograph Series. Waterloo, Ontario: Wilfred Laurier University Press, 1978.

Marcuse, Herbert. *Reason and Revolution: Hegel and the Rise of Social Theory*. Beacon Paperbacks 110. Boston: Beacon, 1960.

Marker, Frederick J., editor and translator. *The Heibergs*. Twayne's World Authors Series 105. New York: Twayne 1971.

Martensen, Hans Lassen. *Af mit Levnet* [*From My Life*]. 3 vols. Copenhagen: Gyldendal, 1882–1883.

————. *Christian Dogmatics: A Compendium of the Doctrines of Christianity*. Translated by William Urwick. Clark's Foreign Theological Library, 4th series, 12. Edinburgh: T. & T. Clark, 1886.

Marx, Karl. *Early Writings*. Translated and edited by T. B. Bottomore. New York: McGraw-Hill, 1964.

————. *Economic and Philosophic Manuscripts of 1844*. Translated by Martin Milligan. Edited by Dirk J. Struik. New York: International, 1864.

Marx, Karl, and Frederick Engels. "*Theses on Feuerbach,*" "*The German Ideology*" *and Related Manuscripts.* Collected Works of Marx and Engels, 1845–1847 5. New York: International, 1976.

———. *The German Ideology,* 1846, 321, in, *Selected Works of Marx and Engels,* New York: Lawrence & Wishart, 1975–2005.

———. *Werke.* 42 vols. East Berlin: Dietz, 1956–1968.

McKinnon, Alastair. "Kierkegaard's Attack on Christendom: Its Lexical History." *Toronto Journal of Theology* 9 (1993) 95–106.

Meeks, M. Douglas. *God the Economist: The Doctrine of God and Political Economy.* Minneapolis: Fortress, 1989.

Metz, Johaness Baptist. *The Emergent Church: The Future of Christianity in a Postbourgeois World.* Translated by Peter Mann. New York: Crossroads, 1981.

———. "Facing the Jews: Christian Theology after Auschwitz." In *The Holocaust as Interruption,* edited by Elisabeth Schüssler Fiorenza and David Tracy. Special issue, *Concilium* 175 (1984–1985) 26–33.

Mintz, Sydney W. *Caribbean Transformations.* Chicago: Aldine, 1974.

———. "África en América Latina: una reflexión desprevenida." In *África en América Latina,* edited by Manuel Moreno Fraginals, 378–97. México: Siglo XXI, 1977.

Miranda, José Porfirio. *Being and the Messiah: The Message of St. John.* Translated by John Eagleson. Reprint, Eugene,OR: Wipf & Stock, 2006.

Moltmann, Jürgen, "Revolution, Religion and the Future: German Reactions." *Concilium* 201 (1989) 43–50.

Moore, Stanley R. "Religion as the True Humanism: Reflections on Kierkegaard's Social Philosophy." *Journal of the American Academy of Religion* 37 (1969) 15–25.

Moreno Fraginals, Manuel. *La historia como arma y otros estudios sobre esclavos, ingenios y plantaciones.* Barcelona: Crítica, 1983.

Mullen, John Douglas. *Kierkegaard's Philosophy: Self-Deception and Cowardice in the Present Age.* New York: New American Library, Mentor Paperback, 1981.

Mullin, Redmond. *The Wealth of Christians: A Study of How Christians Have Dealt with Questions of Riches through History.* Maryknoll, NY: Orbis, 1984.

Mustard, Helen M. "Søren Kierkegaard in German Literary Periodicals 1860–1930." *The Germanic Review* 26 (1951) 83–101.

Niebuhr, H. Richard. *Christ and Culture.* New York: Harper & Row, 1951.

———. *The Social Sources of Denominationalism.* New Haven: Yale University Press, 1954.

Niebuhr, Reinhold. *Christian Realism and Political Problems.* New York: Scribner, 1953.

Nordentoft, Kresten. *Søren Kierkegaard. Bidrag til kritikken af den borgerlige selvoptagethed. [Søren Kierkegaard: Contribution to the Critique of Bourgeois Self-Absorption.]* Copenhagen: Dansk Universitets Press, 1977.

———. "Hvad Siger Brand-Majoren?" Kierkegaard's Opgør med sin Samtid ["What Does the Fire Chief Say?": Kierkegaard's Settling-Up with His Times]. Copenhaguen: G. E. C. Gad, 1973.

———. *Kierkegaard's Psychology.* Duquesne Studies: Psychological Series 7. Translated by Bruce Kirmmse. Pittsburgh: Duquesne University Press, 1978.

Oldendorp, C. G. A. *History of the Mission of the Evangelical Brethren on the Caribbean Islands on St. Thomas, St. Croix, and St. John.* Edited and translated by Arnold R. Highfield and Vladimir Barac. Ann Arbor: Korma, 1987.

Paiewonsky, Isidor. *Eyewitness Accounts of Slavery in the Danish West Indies: Also Graphic Tales of Other Slave Happenings on Ships and Plantations.* New York: Fordham University Press, 1989.

Pelikan, Jaroslav. *Fools for Christ: Essays on the True, the Good, and the Beautiful. Impressions of Kierkegaard, Paul, Dostoyevsky, Luther, Nietzsche, Bach.* Philadelphia: Muhlenberg, 1955.

Pérez-Álvarez, Eliseo. "Kierkegaard." In *The Westminster Dictionary of Theologians,* edited by Justo L. Gonzalez, 204–5. Louisville: Westminster John Knox, 2004.

————. "Richard Shaull: sobre la marcha." *CENCOS,* May 1997, 27–33.

————. "Walter Lowrie." In *Westminster Dictionary of Theologians,* 204–5. Louisville: Westminster John Knox Press, 2006.

Perkins, Robert L. "Review of *Kierkegaard in Golden Age Denmark,* by Bruce Kirmmse." *Søren Kierkegaard Newsletter* 23 (1991) 4–7.

Plekon, Michael Paul. "Blessing and the Cross: The Late Kierkegaard's Christological Dialectic." *Academy Lutheran in Professions* 39 (1983) 25–50.

————. "Introducing Christianity into Christendom: Reinterpreting the Late Kierkegaard." *Anglican Theological Review* 64 (1982) 327–52.

————. "Kierkegaard: Diagnosis and Disease. An Excavation in Modern Consciousness." PhD diss., Rutgers University, 1977.

————. "Kierkegaard and the Eucharist." *Studia Liturgica* 22 (1992) 214–36.

————. "Kierkegaard's Last Sermon." Typewritten manuscript not signed (photocopy), 20.

————. "Kierkegaard's Theological Fullness in *For Self-Examination* and *Judge for Yourself!*" In *"For Self-Examination" and "Judge for Yourself!"* edited by Robert L. Perkins, 1–11. International Kierkegaard Commentary 21. Macon, GA: Mercer University Press, 2002.

————. "Prophetic Criticism, Incarnational Optimism: On Recovering the Late Kierkegaard." *Religion* 13 (1983) 137–53.

————. "Protest and Affirmation: The Late Kierkegaard on Christ, the Church, and Society." *Quarterly Review* 2 (1982) 43–62.

————. "Towards Apocalypse: Kierkegaard's Two Ages in Golden Age Denmark." In *Two Ages,* edited by Robert L. Perkins, 19–52. International Kierkegaard Commentary 14. Macon, GA: Mercer University Press, 1984.

Schoeck, Helmut. *Envy: A Theory of Social Behaviour.* Translated by Michael Glenny and Betty Ross. New York: Harcourt, Brace & World, 1969.

Seidel, George J. "Monasticism as a Ploy in Kierkegaard's Theology." *The American Benedictine Review* 20 (1969) 281–305.

Silva, Carmen. "Del empirismo inglés a la ilustración francesa." In *La Revolución Francesa; doscientos años después,* edited by Griselda Gutiérrez Castañeda, 35–45. Mexico, DF: UNAM, 1991.

Sløk, Johannes. *Kierkegaard-Humanismens Tænker [Kierkegaard: Humanism's Thinker].* Copenhagen: Reitzel, 1978.

————. *Da Kierkegaard Tav: Fra Forfatterskabet til kirkestorm. [When Kierkegaard Remained Silent: From the Authorship to the Attack on the Church.]* Copenhagen: Reitzel, 1980.

Smith, Adam. *An Inquiry into the Nature and Causes of the Wealth of Nations*, edited by R. H. Campbell and A. S. Skinner. 2 vols. Glasgow Edition of the Works and Correspondence of Adam Smith 2. Oxford: Clarendon, 1976.

Sobrino, Jon. *Christology at the Crossroads: A Latin American Approach.* Reprint, Eugene, OR: Wipf & Stock, 2002.

————. *Resurrección de la verdadera iglesia: Los pobres, lugar teológico de la eclesiología.* Santander, Spain: Sal Terrae, 1981.

Stepelevich, Lawrence S., editor. *The Young Hegelians: An Anthology.* Texts in German Philosophy. Cambridge: Cambridge University Press, 1983.

Stroupe, Nibs, and Inez Fleming. *While We Run This Race: Confronting the Power of Racism in a Southern Church.* Maryknoll, NY: Orbis, 1995.

Sung, Jung Mo. *Desire, Market, and Religion.* London: SCM, 2007.

Toews, John Edward. *Hegelianism: The Path towards Dialectical Humanism 1805–1841.* Cambridge: Cambridge University Press, 1980.

Townsend, Joseph. *A Dissertation on the Poor Laws by a Well-Wisher to Mankind.* Berkeley: University of California Press, 1971.

Thulstrup, Niels. *Kierkegaard's Relation to Hegel.* Translated by George L. Stengren. Princeton: Princeton University Press, 1980.

Valls, Álvaro L. M. "Amar o Belo—Amar o Feio—Amar o Pobre." *Estudos Teológicos* 34 (1994) 159–75.

Vibæk, Jens. *Dansk Vestinden. 1755–1848*, Vol. 2, *Vore Gamle Tropekolonier.* Edited by Johaness Brøndsted, (1966). Quoted in Neville A. T. Hall, *Slave Society in the Danish West Indies, St. Thomas, St. John, and St. Croix*, edited by B. W. Higman with a foreword by Kamau Brathwaite. Mona, Jamaica: University of the West Indies Press, 1992, 17.

Vigil, José María. *¿Qué es optar por los pobres?* Bogotá: Paulinas, 1994.

Weiss, Robert O. "The Leveling Process as a Function of the Masses in the View of Kierkegaard and Ortega y Gasset." *Kentucky Romance Quarterly* 7 (1973) 22–36.

Weltzer, Carl. *Peter og Søren Kierkegaard.* Copenhagen: Gads, 1936.

Westergaard, Waldemar. *The Danish West Indies: Under Company Rule (1671-1754).* New York: McMillan, 1917.

Westphal, Merold. "Kierkegaard as a Prophetic Philosopher." Paper presented to the Twenty-third Annual Wheaton College Philosophy Conference, Wheaton, IL, October 23, 1976.

————. *Kierkegaard's Critique of Reason and Society.* Macon, GA: Mercer University Press, 1987.

————. "Levinas, Kierkegaard, and the Theological Task." *Modern Theology* 8 (1992) 241–61.

Williams, Erick Eustace. *Capitalism and Slavery.* London: Deutsch, 1964.

————. *From Columbus to Castro: The History of the Caribbean 1492–1969.* New York: Vintage, 1984.

Willis, Jean Louise. "The Trade between North America and the Danish West Indies, 1756–1807 with Reference to St. Croix." PhD diss., Columbia University, 1963.

Ziolkowski, Eric J. "Don Quixote and Kierkegaard's Understanding of the Single Individual in Society." In *Foundations of Kierkegaard's Vision of Community: Religion, Ethics, and Politics in Kierkegaard*, edited by George B. Connell and C. Stephen Evans, 130–45. Atlantic Highlands, NJ: Humanities, 1992.